THE
SCRABBLE WORD GUIDE

THE

Reg'd Trade Mark

WORD GUIDE

By

JACOB ORLEANS

and

EDMUND JACOBSON

HODDER AND STOUGHTON
LONDON · AUCKLAND · SYDNEY · TORONTO

*First printed 1955. Tenth impression 1974. ISBN 0 340 01755 4.
All rights reserved. No part of this publication may be repro-
duced or transmitted in any form or by any means, electronic
or mechanical, including photocopy, recording, or any informa-
tion storage and retrieval system, without the permission in
writing from the publisher. Printed in Great Britain for
Hodder and Stoughton Limited, St. Paul's House, Warwick
Lane, London EC4P 4AH by Compton Printing Limited,
Aylesbury.*

FOREWORD

JUDGING from the correspondence we have received, more and more SCRABBLE players have found their pleasure with the game increasing as they devoted more serious attention to it. An interesting result of this trend has been a widespread concern with learning more words, especially those recondite words that may make possible an especially high-scoring play.

It was inevitable that out of this interest should come a word guide such as this. No less inevitable was the happy choice of Dr. Orleans and Mr. Jacobson as compilers. They have devoted the same care and enthusiasm to preparing this book as to its companion volume, *How to Win at SCRABBLE*.

This book is not essential to playing SCRABBLE, but those who play intently and play to win will welcome this guide with enthusiasm. Those who take their SCRABBLE more casually will find this a handy reference to settle many questions about words.

JAMES BRUNOT

Newtown, Connecticut

Publishers' Note

Hodder & Stoughton are glad to acknowledge the ready and full co-operation of Messrs. J. W. Spear & Sons Ltd. in the preparation of this work for the British market.

INTRODUCTION

New York Edition

The principal purpose of this guide is to help you play winning SCRABBLE by making better use of the letters you place on your rack. It may also be used as a convenient source for checking words that have been played.

The major part of the book is devoted to a list of approximately 30,000 words, selected especially for use in SCRABBLE. The scope of this list is roughly equivalent to a college-level dictionary, since words of no value in the game are eliminated. By use of regular prefixes and suffixes you can add thousands more words to those listed.

In addition to the master list, you will find shorter lists of special value for making high-score plays and recovering from difficult situations in the game. Glance over these lists just before you play; you may pick up the one word that will make the difference between a high-score play and being unable to take your turn. You do not have to know the meanings of these unusual words, but it will help you remember them if you do. When in doubt about a weird-looking word, *we* always guess that it means: 1. a three-toed sloth; 2. an exotic plant; or 3. a foreign coin. But if you really want to know a meaning, most of these words may be found in any of the "college" dictionaries. The authors wish to point out, however, that their selection was made from the Funk & Wagnalls' *New College Standard Dictionary* with permission of the publishers. The meaning of any word in this book is sure to be found in that comprehensive work.

It has been our plan to make the master list compact; therefore, you will not, in general, find in it regular plurals of words; parts of verbs formed by adding such regular endings as -ed or -ing; or words formed by adding -ly, -ness, -ment, -able, -er. We have included unusual plural endings and other words that are formed irregularly.

Remember always that it is worth your while to consider adding -un, mis-, inter-, or re- at the beginning of words, just as you will add at the end the suffixes mentioned above.

Because you play with only seven letters on your rack, you will be interested mainly in the shorter words; we have not included any words in the general list that are longer than nine letters. We hope that you will find yourself making words that long by adding to existing words, but you will not very often make words of more than seven letters. You will find that most words of more than nine letters may be divided into smaller words. Take, for example, the word IMPONDERABLE. You will find that the elements from which it is built up are all in the list as shorter words: IMP, POND, PONDER, ERA, and ABLE.

You will find some words in the list that make use of a letter more times than there are tiles for it in the game. In such cases, the blank tiles may be used.

Every word in these lists may be used in playing SCRABBLE. There are, of course, many other words that may legally be used; no book short of an unabridged dictionary could list them all.

INTRODUCTION

In the English spoken and written on either side of the Atlantic there are greater differences than in the pronunciation of TOMATO and the spelling of COLOUR. London's DRAUGHT is New York's DRAFT and *vice versa;* Birmingham's DRAWING-PIN is Boston's THUMBTACK; Idaho's SOMERSET is Somerset's SOMERSAULT.

During the editing of this guide to suit the needs of the English-speaking player of SCRABBLE outside the country of its origin, a number of such difficulties were encountered—and not entirely overcome without, for instance, parenthetical additions to such nine-letter words as HEMATINIC, MACIN-TOSH and MYXODEMIA.

The rules of the game allow no hyphenated words, a restriction more irksome to ourselves than to our American cousins, who have no hesitation in writing COOPERATE and DRYCLEAN. It has not been thought quite fair to prune the original list of all such words, and players are recommended to decide among themselves that if a word appears without a hyphen in this list, its use in the game is permissible. Accents have been added to French words not so endowed in the original list.

Scientific progress and the incidence of World War II have led to the birth of a great host of new words. It has even been found necessary to invent PROTO-GRAM, which describes such contractions as ANZAC, NAAFI and UNESCO, while QUISLING now takes its ignoble place in the company of BURKE and MARTINET.

It is doubtful whether all the words in this edition, which is not so far removed from the original as to be more than an Anglo-American compromise, are to be found in any single dictionary, whether it be published in the United States, Great Britain or the Commonwealth, yet users of it can rest assured that these are, or have been, living words in a vocabulary so rich and universal that even Shakespeare only skimmed it.

SWITCH WORDS

Frequently the same group of letters can spell two or more different words. This fact may be very important to you in playing SCRABBLE. You have the letters that enable you to make the word NIGHT. But if you form instead the word THING with the same letters you may be able to place the H on a triple-letter-score square, thus increasing your scope by 9 points. Whenever you try to form a word from some or all the tiles you have, see what other words you can make with the same letters.

This list illustrates groups of word where all the words in the group are formed from the same letters.

abed bade bead
abets bates baste beats beast
ache each
acres cares races scare
aids dais said
ales sale seal
amen mane mean name
amend maned named
angel angle glean
arid raid
aril lair liar rail
arise raise
ascot coast
aside ideas
aster rates stare tares tears
astir stair

bales blasé sable
bared beard bread
below bowel elbow
bleating tangible
bleats stable tables
braid rabid
brief fibre
browse bowers

capers crapes pacers scrape recaps spacer
capes paces space scape
caret cater crate trace
cartel claret
cause sauce
chaste cheats scathe
cheater teacher
cited edict
cleat éclat
coil loci
coins icons scion sonic
corset sector
credit direct
crisp scrip

dale deal lade lead
dare dear read
danger gander garden ranged
dealer leader redeal
denied indeed
design signed singed
detail dilate tailed
diet edit tide tied
draws sward wards
drapes parsed spader spared spread

earth hater heart
east eats etas sate seat seta
elapse please
emit mite time item
emits smite times items
entrap parent
erring ringer
ester steer trees
ether there three

fares fears safer
faster strafe
field filed
file life lief
filer flier rifle lifer
finger fringe

garnets strange
girth right
glare lager large regal
gnat tang
granite tearing
groan organ orang

hares hears share shear
hewn when
hinge neigh
hoes hose shoe
horse hoser shore

1

inert inter nitre trine
inks kins sink skin
inset nites stein tines
itself stifle filets

laces scale
lame male meal
laves salve slave vales
leap pale peal plea
least slate stale steal tales
license silence
lilts still
limes miles slime smile
lose loes sloe sole
lustre result

mate meat tame team
mason moans
master remats stream
meteor remote

nets tens sent
night thing
notes onset seton stone tones

orts rots sort tors
ought tough

pares pears rapes reaps spare
pastel plates pleats staple
parts sprat strap traps
paws swap wasp
pest pets step
pines snipe spine
paste pates spate tapes
pointer protein tropine
pores poser prose ropes spore
priest ripest spiter sprite stripe tripes

quote toque

rats star tars
relating triangle
respect spectre
reserve severer reverse
riot tiro trio
rites tires tries
rivets strive

saint satin stain
serve sever veers verse
sheet these
skate stake steak takes teaks

throw worth wroth

wider weird

THE BIG FOUR

The letters J, Q, X, and Z are the "Big Four" among the SCRABBLE tiles. Their values are eight and ten times that of the vowels. Since they occur rarely by comparison with most of the other letters, it is important to know as many as possible of the words listed below in which they are used. The words are arranged by the number of letters. Word containing two of the high-value letters are in heavier type.

Words Containing the Letter J

3 Letters	jive	jetty	canjar	jostle	jaggery
	joad	jewel	deject	jounce	jalapin
haj	join	jihad	donjon	jovial	jambeau
jab	joke	jimmy	enjoin	joyful	janitor
jag	jole	jinni	frijol	joyous	jargoon
jam	jolt	jinny	hadjee	jubate	jasmine
jar	jowl	jocko	hejira	juggle	javelin
jaw	juba	joint	inject	jugate	jealous
jay	jube	joist	injure	jumble	jejunum
jee	jump	jolly	injury	jujube	jeofail
jet	juju	joram	jabber	jungle	jessant
jib	jura	jorum	jaboty	jungly	jewelry
job	jury	jougs	jacana	junior	jewfish
jog	just	joule	jackal	junket	jingall
jot	jute	joust	jacket	jurant	jinglet
joy	raja	judge	jackey	jurist	jobbery
jug	soja	jugal	jackie	moujik	jocular
jus		juice	jadish	**muzjik**	jollity
raj		juicy	jaeger	object	joinder
		julep	jaguar	reject	joinery
	5 Letters	jumbo	jangle	rejoin	**jonquil**
4 Letters		jumpy	jarabe	swaraj	journal
	banjo	junco	jarfly	unjust	journey
ajar	bijou	junta	jargon	wejack	joyless
hadj	eject	jupon	jarina		jubilee
haje	ejido	jural	jasper		jugular
haji	enjoy	jurat	jaunty		jujitsu
hajj	fjord	juror	jejune	*7 Letters*	juniper
jack	hadji	jutty	jennet		junkman
jade	hajji	major	jerboa	abjurer	juridic
jady	jabot	mujik	jereed	adjourn	juryman
jail	jacal	rajah	jerkin	adjudge	jussive
jamb	jacko	sajou	jersey	adjunct	justice
jape	jacky	slojd	jetsam	adjurer	justify
jarl	jaggy	thuja	jetton	basenji	majesty
jazz	jalap		jigget	cajeput	mojarra
jean	jambe	*6 Letters*	jiggle	canjiar	perjure
jeep	japan		jigsaw	conjoin	perjury
jeer	jaspé	abject	jingal	conjure	project
jerk	jaunt	abjure	jingle	disject	pyjamas
jess	jazzy	acajou	jingko	disjoin	rejoice
jest	jebel	adjoin	jinnee	ejector	sapajou
jibe	jehad	adjure	jitter	frijole	sejeant
jill	jemmy	adjust	jockey	jacinth	sjambok
jilt	jenny	**bijoux**	jocose	jackdaw	sojourn
jinn	jerky	cajole	jocund	jackpot	subject
jinx	jerry		joggle	jaconet	subjoin
			joseph	jadeite	traject

3

Words Containing the Letter Q

3-4 Letters	quire	liquid	squawk	**jonquil**	quinary
	quirk	liquor	squeak	lacquer	quinate
qua	quirl	maquis	squeal	liquefy	quinine
quad	quirt	masque	squill	marquee	quinnat
quag	quish	mosque	squint	marquis	quinoid
quay	quite	opaque	squire	masquer	quinone
quid	quoin	piquet	squirm	oblique	quintal
quip	quoit	pulque	squirt	obloquy	quintan
quit	quota	quaere	toquet	obsequy	quintet
quiz	quote	quagga	torque	oquassa	quitter
quod	quoth	quaggy	unique	parquet	quittor
	roque	quahog		pasquil	quondam
	squab	quaint		pasquin	racquet
5 Letters	squad	qualmy	*7 Letters*	picquet	relique
equal	squat	quanta		piquant	request
equip	squaw	quarry	acquire	quadrat	requiem
fique	squib	quarte	aliquot	quadric	require
pique	squid	quarto	aquaria	quaffer	requite
quack	toque	**quartz**	aquatic	qualify	ronquil
quaff	tuque	quaver	aqueous	quality	rorqual
quail	usque	queasy	bequest	quamash	sequela
quake		quench	bouquet	quantic	sequent
qualm		**quezal**	briquet	quantum	sequoia
quart	*6 Letters*	quince	brusque	quarrel	siliqua
quash		quinic	cacique	quartan	silique
quean	acquit	quinin	cliquey	quarter	squabby
queen	aequum	quinsy	coequal	quartet	squalid
queer	aquose	quirky	conquer	quassia	squally
quell	barque	quiver	coquina	quassin	squalor
querl	basque	quohog	cumquat	quavery	squalus
quern	bisque	quorum	enquire	quayage	squamae
query	caique	risqué	enquiry	querist	squashy
quest	cinque	roquet	equable	quester	squatty
queue	cirque	sacque	equator	**quetzal**	squeaky
quick	claque	sequel	equerry	quibble	**squeeze**
quiet	clique	squail	esquire	quicken	squelch
quill	clinquy	squall	flanque	quiddle	squilla
quilt	coquet	squama	inquest	quietus	squinch
quint	equate	square	inquire	quillai	squirmy
quipu	equity	squash	inquiry	quilter	unequal

Words Containing the Letter X

2-3 Letters	oxen	kylix	calxes	oxalic	boxhaul	maxwell
	oxid	latex	caudex	oxalis	boxwood	mixable
ax	oxim	laxly	climax	oxygen	bureaux	mixible
axe	pixy	malax	coaxal	oxygon	cachexy	noxious
box	sext	maxim	coccyx	oxymel	carapax	overtax
fix	taxi	mixer	commix	paxwax	chevaux	oxazine
fox	taxy	murex	convex	phenix	coaxial	oxidase
kex	text	nixie	cortex	pickax	coexist	oxidate
lax	xyst	noxal	cruxes	plexes	complex	oxidize
lex		oxbow	dexter	plexor	conflux	oxyacid
lux		oxeye	dioxid	plexus	context	oxymora
mix		oxide	diplex	pollex	coxcomb	oxyntic
nix		oxime	duplex	praxis	dextral	oxysalt
ox	5 Letters	oxlip	efflux	prefix	dioxide	oxytone
pax		phlox	elixir	prolix	exactly	paradox
pox	addax	proxy	exceed	reflex	examine	pemphix
pyx	admix	pulex	except	reflux	example	peroxid
sax	affix	pyxie	excess	scolex	exclaim	perplex
sex	annex	pyxis	excite	sexfid	exclude	phalanx
six	ataxy	radix	excuse	sextan	execute	phoenix
tax	axial	relax	exempt	sextet	exhaust	pickaxe
vex	axile	remex	exhale	sexton	exhibit	pretext
vox	axiom	silex	exhort	sexual	expanse	pyrexia
wax	axled	sixth	exhume	spadix	expiate	pyrexic
zax	axman	sixty	exodus	sphinx	explain	radixes
	axone	toxic	exotic	storax	explode	salpinx
	beaux	toxin	expand	suffix	exploit	sandbox
	borax	unfix	expect	surtax	explore	saxhorn
	boxen	unsex	expend	syntax	expound	saxtuba
4 Letters	boxer	varix	expert	syrinx	express	sexless
	braxy	vixen	expire	taxine	expunge	sextant
apex	buxom	waxen	export	taxite	extract	sextile
axil	calyx	xebec	expose	thorax	extreme	simplex
axis	cimex	xenia	extant	toxine	fixture	simplex
axle	codex	xenon	extend	turnix	flexile	sixfold
axon	cylix	xerus	extent	tuxedo	flexion	sixteen
coax	exact	xylan	extort	vertex	flexure	soapbox
coxa	exalt	xylem	fixate	vortex	fluxion	synaxis
crux	excel	xylic	fixity	xylene	foxbane	taxable
eaux	exert	xylol	flaxen	xyloid	foxfire	taxicab
exit	exile	xylyl	flexor	xylose	foxfish	taxitic
flax	exist		galaxy	xyster	foxhole	tectrix
flex	expel		hallux		foxhunt	textile
flux	extol	6 Letters	hatbox		foxskin	textual
foxy	extra		hexane	7 Letters	foxtail	texture
hoax	exude	adieux	hexone		foxtrot	toxemia
ibex	exult	admixt	icebox	anthrax	foxwood	toxemic
ilex	flaxy	afflux	larynx	anxiety	hexadic	toxical
ixia	galax	ataxia	laxity	anxious	hexagon	trioxid
jinx	helix	ataxic	luxate	apyrexy	laxness	triplex
lynx	hexad	axilla	luxury	axillae	lexical	xanthic
minx	hexyl	axseed	matrix	axillar	lexicon	xanthin
moxa	hyrax	biaxal	maxima	axolotl	mailbox	xerosis
next	index	bijoux	maxixe	bandbox	maxilla	xerotic
onyx	infix	bombyx	meninx	bauxite	maximal	xiphoid
oryx	ixtle	boxcar	orexis	biaxial	maximum	xylidin

Words Containing the Letter Z

3-4 Letters

adz, adze, azo, azym, buzz, coz, cozy, czar, daze, doze, dozy, faze, fez, fizz, friz, fuze, fuzz, gaze, haze, hazy, **jazz**, laze, lazy, maze, mazy, ooze, oozy, oyez, **quiz**, raze, size, sizz, tzar, whiz, **zax**, zany, zeal, zebu, zein, zero, zest, zeta, zinc, zip, zoea, zoic, zone, zoom, zoon, zyme

5 Letters

amaze, azoic, azote, azure, azyme, bazar, bezel, blaze, bonze, booze, bortz, braza, braze, colza, cozen, craze, crazy, croze, dizen, dozen, enzym, fizzy, frizz, furze, furzy, fuzee, fuzil, fuzzy, gauze, gauzy, glaze, graze, hazel, huzza, **jazzy**, kazoo, lazar, maize, mazer, mezzo, mirza, mizen, nozle, ozena, ozone, ouzel, plaza, prize, razee, razor, seize, sezin, sizar, sized, sizer, sozin, spitz, topaz, vizir, vizor, waltz, winze, wizen, zamia, zayin, zebec, zebra, zibet, zincy, zinky, zloty, zombi, zonal, zooid, zoril, zymic

6 Letters

ablaze, amazon, assize, azalea, azonic, azotic, azymic, bazaar, benzin, benzol, benzyl, bezant, bezoar, blazer, blazon, blowzy, borzoi, brazen, brazil, breeze, breezy, bronze, bronzy, buzzer, chintz, coryza, cozily, crazed, crozer, dazzle, eczema, evzone, fizgig, fizzle, foozle, frazil, freeze, frenzy, frieze, frozen, frowzy, gazebo, guzzle, hazard, huzzah, huzzay, izzard, mazily, mizzen, mizzle, mizzly, muzhik, **muzjik**, nozzle, nyanza, ozaena, ozenic, ozonic, panzer, piazza, podzol, puzzle, **quartz**, **quezal**, razzia, rezone, seizor, sizzle, sleazy, sneeze, snooze, sozine, stanza, syzygy, teazel, touzle, tweeze, tzetze, vizard, vizier, wheeze, wizard, zaffar, zaffir, zaffre, zanana, zapote, zareba, zebeck, zealot, zebras, zechin, zenana, zendik, zenith, zephyr, zeugma, zinced, zincic, zincid, zincky, zinnia, zipper, zircon, zither, zodiac, zombie, zonary, zonate, zonula, zonule, zoonal, zounds, zygoma, zygote, zymase

7 Letters

agonize, alcazar, analyze, apprize, azimuth, azotite, azurite, azygous, azymous, bazooka, benzene, benzine, benzoic, benzoin, benzoyl, **bezique**, bizarre, blowzed, bonanza, brazier, britzka, bromize, buzzwig, canzone, canzoni, capsize, chintzy, citizen, coenzym, cognize, cozener, crazier, crazily, crozier, cruzado, cyanize, czardom, czarina, czarism, diazine, diazole, dozenth, drizzle, drizzly, ebonize, elegize, emblaze, frazzle, frizzle, frizzly, fuzzily, gazelle, gazette, gizzard, grizzle, grizzly, horizon, itemize, lazaret, lazarly, matzoon, matzoth, mazurka, mestiza, mezuzah, mitzvah, muezzin, obelize, outsize, **oxazine**, **oxidize**, ozaenic, ozonide, ozonize, ozonous, pectize, peptize, pretzel, **quetzal**, realize, rhizoid, rhizoma, rhizome, scherzo, scherzi, seizure, **squeeze**, stylize, swizzle, trapeze, tzarina, zacaton, zaptiah, zaptieh, zareeba, zealous, zebrass, zebrine, zebroid, zebrula, zebrule, zecchin, zedoary, zemstvo, zeolite, zestful, zincate, zincify, zincing, zincite, zincked, zincous, zingara, zittern, zoisite, zooidal, zoology, zoonomy, zootomy, zorilla, zygosis, zymogen, zymosis, zymotic, zymurgy

WORDS WITH MANY VOWELS

Few things are more frustrating in playing SCRABBLE than to find yourself with a rack full of vowels. The words listed here will help you use vowels to form words with consonants that may already be on the board.

One Consonant	inia	alive	cookie	initial	paleae
aalii	io	aloof	donee	inure	payee
adieu	iota	alulae	dulia	ionic	peace
aerie	ixia	ameer	eaten	iota	pease
agee	lea	anaemia	eerily	irate	peewee
agio	lee	anuria	elate	iris	piano
ague	miaou	aorta	elide	lease	piece
aim	moo	auodad	élite	leave	quaere
aloe	oaf	apogee	elope	mania	radii
amia	oii	aquose	emeute	mêlée	radio
area	ocean	arena	enate	ocean	ragee
aria	oleo	areola	enema	oleate	ramee
asea	olio	arete	epopee	olein	ramie
audio	out	aside	epopoeia	olive	ratio
aural	pea	ataxia	etwee	onion	reeve
beau	pie	audile	fiancée	oogone	riata
bee	queue	aureous	galeae	oolite	rodeo
boa	raia	aureus	giaor	oomiak	seine
boo	roué	aurora	guaiac	opera	seize
cooee	tie	avail	heaume	opiate	siege
eat	too	aviate	hoodoo	oribi	sieur
eau	unau	axial	hoopoe	oriel	sieve
eerie	wee	bureau	hoopoo	oriole	souari
emeu	woo	cause	house	ouabain	suede
etui		cease	idiom	ovaria	taboo
fee	*Many Vowels*	ceria	idiot	ovoli	taenia
fie	acacia	calorie	iguana	ovolo	taiga
gee	aculei	cilia	ileac	paean	unique
idea	aerial	cilium	ileitis	paeon	unite
ilia	alienee	cooer	imbue	palea	woodsia

Words Ending in "A"

aloha	cicada	donna	hula	lacuna	ova
alumna	cinema	drama	hurra	lama	pagoda
aorta	cobra	duenna	hydra	larva	papa
area	cocoa	edema	ilia	mama	parka
aroma	coda	enema	inia	mamma	pascha
asthma	cola	enigma	insula	manila	pasha
aurora	coma	era	iota	manna	patella
balboa	comma	fiesta	jerboa	media	patina
balsa	conga	fistula	juba	mica	pelota
banana	corona	flora	junta	moa	persona
camera	crania	folia	ka	mocha	phobia
canna	dicta	fuchsia	kabbala	olla	piazza
cantata	diorama	gala	kana	omega	pica
charta	diploma	gamma	kola	opera	pika
china	dogma	ganglia	la	ora	pinna

Words Ending in "A" (continued)

plasma	retina	sierra	stanza	ultra	vodka
platina	rhumba	siesta	strata	urea	volva
plaza	rostra	sigma	tea	uremia	vomica
pleura	rota	silica	tapioca	uria	whoa
pneuma	rotunda	soda	testa	uva	xenia
proa	rumba	sofa	tiara	uvea	yea
puma	saga	solaria	tibia	uvula	yoga
punka	saliva	soya	toga	vacua	yucca
pupa	salvia	spa	trauma	via	zanana
quanta	schema	spectra	tuba	visa	zebra
quota	sepia	stadia	tuna	vista	zeta
raia	shea	stamina	ulna	viva	zinnia
raja	sienna				

Words Ending in "B"

absorb	coulomb	gamb	lamb	rhubarb	stab
adsorb	coxcomb	garb	limb	rhumb	stilb
adverb	crib	gib	lob	rib	stob
alb	crumb	glib	mib	rob	stub
aplomb	cub	gob	mob	scab	succumb
ardeb	curb	grab	nab	scarab	superb
bib	daub	grub	nabob	scrub	swab
blab	drab	herb	neb	shrub	swob
blob	drib	hob	nib	sib	tab
bomb	drub	hub	nub	sibb	throb
cab	dub	iamb	numb	slab	thumb
carob	dumb	intomb	orb	slob	tomb
climb	entomb	jamb	pleb	slub	tub
club	enwomb	jib	plumb	snob	verb
cob	fib	kab	resorb	snub	web
cobweb	fob	kerb	reverb	sob	womb
comb	fub	knob	rhomb	squib	

Words Ending in "F"

Ending in one f	grief	massif	shaduf	cuff	quaff
	half	motif	sheaf	doff	raff
alef	hereof	naif	shelf	draff	rebuff
aloof	herself	oaf	sherif	duff	ruff
beef	himself	of	shereef	enfeoff	scoff
brief	hoof	pelf	surf	feoff	scruff
calf	if	proof	thereof	flu	sheriff
chef	ingulf	reef	thief	griff	skiff
chief	itself	relief	turf	gruff	sniff
clef	kalif	reproof	waif	guff	snuff
coif	keef	roof	wharf	huff	staff
corf	kef	scarf	woof	infeoff	stiff
deaf	kerf	scurf		luff	stuff
dwarf	khalif	self	*Ending in two f's*	muff	tariff
engulf	kief	serf		off	tiff
fief	leaf	serif	buff	pontiff	tuff
gonof	lief	shadoof	cliff	puff	whiff
gulf	loof				

Words Ending in "I"

aalii	cocci	kadi	octopi	saluki	thalli
abri	corgi	kaki	oii	scenari	ti
agni	cormi	kali	okapi	scherzi	timpani
agouti	crotali	kepi	onagri	scirrhi	tipi
ai	dromoi	khaki	oribi	scudi	titi
alibi	effendi	krupi	ourebi	serai	tori
alkali	emboli	litchi	palpi	soldi	torsi
alumni	epi	loci	pappi	soli	tragi
ani	etui	loculi	papyri	solidi	tripoli
asci	foci	lungi	peri	sori	tumuli
aurei	fungi	mallei	pili	souari	tutti
bonaci	genii	miladi	quillai	splenii	urari
borzoi	ghetti	mufti	rabbi	stelai	vagi
bronchi	gingeli	nimbi	rabboni	stimuli	virelai
cacti	glutei	nidi	radii	sulci	volvuli
calami	grigri	nielli	ragi	swami	wadi
calli	gyri	nilgai	rami	syllabi	wapiti
caroli	hamuli	nisi	ravioli	tali	woorali
carpi	houri	nuclei	reguli	tarsi	woorari
chili	iambi	nylghai	safari	taxi	yogi
cirri	indri	oboli	salmi	thalami	zombi
coati	jinni	ocelli			

Words Ending in "O"

(not over 5 letters)

also	curio	ho	loo	pro	tho
altho	dingo	hobo	loto	radio	thoro
alto	ditto	hollo	lotto	ratio	tiro
azo	duo	hoo	mango	recto	to
bilbo	echo	igloo	milo	rhino	too
bingo	ergo	inro	misdo	rodeo	torso
bolo	faro	into	motto	rondo	two
bongo	folio	jacko	oleo	sago	tyro
bubo	fordo	jocko	olio	salvo	umbo
burro	forgo	jumbo	outdo	shako	undo
cameo	fresco	junco	outgo	shoo	verso
canto	fro	kazoo	patio	silo	video
cello	go	keno	pedro	soldo	vireo
chico	gusto	kino	pengo	solo	wahoo
cisco	hallo	largo	pepo	taboo	whoso
coco	halo	limbo	piano	tango	woo
compo	hello	lingo	polo	taro	zero
congo	hero	loco	potto	tempo	

Words Ending in "U"

babu	coypu	kudu	miaou	rondeau	thru
baku	dhu	landau	nylghau	rouleau	tinamou
beau	fichu	leu	ormulu	sabicu	tolu
bureau	gnu	lieu	pareu	sajou	tonneau
caribou	habu	litu	parvenu	sapajou	turacou
catechu	iglu	manitou	perdu	sou	unau
congou	jujitsu	manitu	pilau	tabu	virtu
congu	juju	menu	quipu	thou	zebu
coypou					

UNUSUAL WORDS

You always thought that "peepul" was the local politician's poor pronunciation in addressing his constituents. But you may use it in playing SCRABBLE—it is the name of the sacred fig tree of India (also spelled "pipal"). If you place the word "tink" or the word "peag," your opponents may accuse you of not knowing how to spell. But you can show them that they are perfectly good English words—or at least that they are English words.

Here are only a very few of the very many unusual words in the English language. There are so many of them that some SCRABBLE enthusiasts who have peeked into an unabridged dictionary are under the impression that almost any combination of letters which can be pronounced (and some that can't) is very likely to be a word. Look through this list and you'll have good reason to wonder whether English is really English, sometimes. Remember many of them, and the strange combinations of tiles that you sometimes face in your rack will not look so discouraging.

aalii	cumin	fipple	jaboty	nixie	quern	soja
abb	cylix	fitch	jacana	nth	quetzal	soke
addax	dhoti	flanch	jacko	nub	quipu	sprag
ai	dhow	fletch	jarl	nurl	quirl	squama
alb	dhu	flitch	jocko	obol	quod	stilb
amock	dirndl	foh	joram	od	quoin	stob
amyl	diss	fub	juju	oii	raphe	sump
ankh	doit	fubsy	ka	orc	resh	swage
awn	dowle	fyke	kadi	oryx	ret	swart
azo	drachm	fylfot	kaiak	osar	rhaphe	swiple
babu	draffy	gamb	keef	oxeye	rhea	swot
basenji	drib	gar	kef	oxim	rhein	sybo
bel	drongo	gecko	kerf	pah	riley	tain
bice	duad	glume	kex	palpi	roc	targ
bilbo	dubh	graul	kibe	pawl	rotch	tenrec
bleb	dyad	greige	knop	peag	rotl	tink
bongo	ecad	grigri	krubi	peepul	ruth	titi
bortz	edh	haaf	kudu	phat	rynd	tolu
bot	eft	haak	lakh	phot	ryot	toph
bott	eikon	habu	leet	pili	samp	trasko
braxy	ejido	hadj	lehr	pipal	sapajou	umbo
brut	ekka	haj	lehua	placebo	scaup	unau
bubo	emyd	haje	leu	podzol	scend	ut
buhl	enfeoff	haji	lev	pome	schuit	valkyr
burke	ens	hajj	marl	potto	schwa	vomito
burl	ensky	hogan	marly	pugh	scurf	wejack
canjar	epi	hoicks	maw	puisne	sedum	winze
chico	epopee	hoopoo	mel	pulkha	shaduf	wych
cimex	epopoeia	ictus	mho	punka	shawm	xylyl
cisco	epopt	infeoff	mib	puy	shend	xyst
col	eth	inkle	mir	pyoid	shiv	ytria
coly	etui	ipomea	mirk	pyx	sid	yupon
corf	feoff	ism	mneme	pyxis	sjambok	zanana
corgi	feu	istle	moa	quag	skeg	zax
coz	fey	ixia	mol	quagga	skua	zemstvo
crambo	fid	ixtle	mot	quean	slojd	zoon
cultch	fique	izzard	moxa	querl	slub	

THE SCRABBLE WORD GUIDE

A

	abiotic	absence	acauline	acetonate	acrasia	acute
	abject	absent	acaulose	acetone	acre	acylic
aalii	abjection	absentee	acaulous	acetonic	acreage	adactylia
aardvark	abjective	absinth	accede	acetonize	acred	adage
aardwolf	abjure	absinthe	accent	acetose	acrid	adamant
abaci	ablactate	absolute	accentual	acetous	acridine	adamite
aback	ablation	absolve	accept	acetum	acridity	adamsite
abacus	ablative	absolvent	acceptant	acetyl	acrimony	adapt
abacuses	ablaut	absonant	access	acetylene	acrobat	adaptive
abaft	ablaze	absorb	accessary	acetylic	acrobatic	adays
abalone	able	absorbent	accession	ache	acrodrome	add
abandon	ablegate	abstain	accessory	achene	acrogen	addax
abase	abloom	absterge	accidence	achenia	acrogenic	addend
abash	abluent	abstinent	accident	achenial	acrolein	addenda
abate	ablush	abstract	accite	achenium	acrolith	addendum
abatis	ablution	abstruse	acclaim	achieve	acromia	adder
abattis	ably	absurd	acclimate	achromic	acromial	addict
abattoir	abnegate	absurdity	acclivity	achromous	acromion	addiction
abaxial	abnormal	abulia	acclivous	acicula	acronic	addictive
abaxile	abnormity	abulic	accolade	aciculae	acronical	addition
abb	aboard	abundance	accompany	acicular	acropetal	additive
abbacy	abode	abundant	accord	aciculate	acropolis	addle
abbatial	abolish	abune	accordant	acid	acrospire	address
abbatical	abolition	abuse	accordion	acidic	across	addressee
abbess	aboma	abusive	accost	acidify	acrostic	adduce
abbey	abomasum	abut	account	acidity	acrotism	adducent
abbot	abominate	abutilon	accouter	acidosis	acrylic	adduct
abbotcy	aboon	abutment	accredit	acidotic	act	adduction
abbotship	aboral	abuttal	accresce	acidulate	actinal	adductive
abdicate	aborigen	abysm	accrete	acidulent	actinia	adeem
abdicable	aborigin	abysmal	accretion	acidulous	actinian	adelphous
abdomen	aborigine	abyss	accretive	acierate	actinic	ademption
abdominal	abort	abyssal	accroach	aciform	actinical	adenoid
abduce	abortion	abyssic	accrual	acini	actinism	adenoidal
abducent	abortive	acacia	accrue	aciniform	actinium	adenology
abduct	aboulia	academic	accumbent	acinose	actinoid	adenoma
abduction	aboulic	academism	accuracy	acinous	action	adept
abeam	abound	academy	accurate	acinus	activate	adequacy
abecedary	about	acajou	accursed	acline	active	adequate
abed	above	acaleph	accusal	aclinic	activity	adfected
abele	abradant	acalephan	accuse	acme	actor	adhere
abelmosk	abrade	acalephe	accustom	acne	actress	adherence
abelmusk	abrasion	acanthi	ace	acnode	actual	adherency
aberrance	abrasive	acanthial	acedia	acock	actuality	adherent
aberrancy	abrastol	acanthine	acentric	acolyte	actualize	adhesion
aberrant	abreact	acanthion	acerate	aconite	actuarial	adhesive
abet	abreast	acanthoid	acerb	aconitine	actuary	adhibit
abettal	abri	acanthous	acerbate	aconitum	actuate	adiabatic
abeyance	abridge	acanthus	acerbity	acorn	actuation	adiantum
abeyancy	abroach	acardia	acerose	acoumeter	acuate	adieu
abeyant	abroad	acardiac	acervate	acoustic	acuity	adieus
abhor	abrogate	acariasis	acervulus	acoustics	aculeate	adieux
abhorrent	abrupt	acarid	acescence	acquaint	aculei	adipic
abidal	abruption	acaroid	acescent	acquest	aculeus	adipocere
abidance	abscess	acarpous	acetamide	acquiesce	acumen	adipoma
abide	abscind	acaudal	acetate	acquire	acuminate	adipomata
ability	abscissa	acaudate	acetic	acquit	acuminous	adipose
abiosis	abscond	acaules	acetify	acquittal	acushla	adiposis

adipous
adit
adjacence
adjacency
adjacent
adjective
adjoin
adjourn
adjudge
adjunct
adjure
adjust
adjustive
adjutage
adjutancy
adjutant
adjuvant
admeasure
adminicle
admirable
admiral
admire
admissible
admission
admissive
admissory
admit
admix
admixt
admixture
admonish
admonitor
adnascent
adnate
adnation
adnoun
adnominal
ado
adobe
adopt
adoption
adoptive
adoration
adore
adorn
adown
adrenal
adrift
adroit
adscript
adsorb
adsorbate
adsorbent
adularia
adulate
adulation
adulatory
adult
adultery
adulterer
adulthood
adumbral
adumbrant
adumbrate
adunc
aduncous
adust

advance
advantage
advection
advent
adventive
adventure
adverb
adverbial
adversary
adverse
adversity
advert
advertent
advertise
advertize
advice
advise
advisory
advocacy
advocate
advowee
advowson
adynamia
adynamic
adyta
adytum
adz
adze
aedeagus
aedaeagus
aedes
aedile
aedileship
aedilian
aedilic
aedoeagus
aegis
aeneous
aeneus
aeolian
aeolipile
aeolipyle
aeon
aeonian
aeonism
aequum
aerarian
aerate
aeration
aerial
aerialist
aeriality
aerie
aeried
aeriform
aerify
aerobe
aerobia
aerobic
aerocurve
aerodyne
aerogen
aerogram
aerograph
aerolite
aerolith
aerolitic

aerologic
aerology
aeromancy
aerometer
aerometry
aeronaut
aerophore
aerophyte
aeroplane
aeroscope
aeroscopy
aerosled
aerosol
aerostat
aerotaxis
aery
aesthesis
aesthete
aesthetic
aestival
aestivate
afar
affable
affair
affect
affection
affective
afferent
affiance
affiant
affidavit
affiliate
affined
affinity
affirm
affirmant
affix
affixture
afflation
afflatus
afflict
affluence
affluent
afflux
afforce
afford
afforest
affray
affricate
affright
affront
affuse
affusion
afghan
afield
afire
aflame
afloat
afoot
afore
aforehand
aforesaid
aforetime
afoul
afraid
afresh
afreet

afrit
aft
after
aftermath
aftermost
afternoon
afterpain
aftertime
afterwale
afterward
aftmost
again
against
agalloch
agama
agamic
agamous
agape
agaric
agate
agateware
agatize
agave
age
agee
ageless
agency
agent
agential
ageratum
ageusia
ageustia
agger
aggrade
aggravate
aggregate
aggress
aggrieve
aghast
agile
agility
aging
agio
agiotage
agist
agitate
agitation
aglet
aglow
agminate
agnail
agnate
agnatic
agnation
agni
agnomen
agnomina
agnominal
agnostic
agnus
ago
agog
agon
agones
agonic
agonist
agonistic

agonize
agony
agouti
agouties
agoutis
agouty
agrafe
agraffe
agraph
agrapha
agraphia
agraphic
agrarian
agree
agrestic
agrimony
agriology
agrology
agrologic
agromania
agronomic
agronomy
aground
ague
agueweed
aguish
ah
aha
ahead
aheap
ahem
ahimsa
ahold
ahoy
ahull
ahungered
ai
aid
aide
aiglet
aigret
aigrette
ail
ailanthic
ailanthus
aileron
ailment
aim
aimless
ain
air
aircraft
airhole
airless
airlock
airlog
airometer
airplane
airport
airproof
airstream
airstrip
airtight
airway
airworthy
airy
aisle

ait
aitch
aitchbone
aithe
ajar
akimbo
akin
akinesia
akinesic
akinesis
ala
alae
alabamine
alabaster
alack
alackaday
alacrity
alan
aland
alant
alanin
alanine
alar
alare
alarm
alarmism
alarmist
alary
alas
alaska
alate
alb
alba
albacore
albata
albatross
albeit
albertite
albescent
albinic
albinism
albino
albite
albitical
albornoz
albuginea
album
albumen
albumin
albumose
alburnum
alcaide
alcalde
alcayde
alcazar
alchemic
alchemist
alchemize
alchemy
alchymy
alcohol
alcoholic
alcove
aldehyde
alder
alderman
aldose

ale
aleatory
alee
alef
alegar
alehouse
alembic
aleph
alert
aleurone
aleuronic
alevin
alewife
alewives
alexia
alexin
alexine
alfaki
alfalfa
alfaqui
alfaquin
alfileria
alforge
alforja
alfresco
alga
algebra
algebraic
algedonic
algae
algerine
algid
algidity
algoid
algology
algometer
algometry
algor
algorism
algorithm
algous
alguazil
alias
alibi
alibility
alible
alidad
alidade
alien
alienable
alienage
alienate
alienee
alienism
alienist
alif
aliform
alight
align
alike
alikeness
aliment
alimenta
alimony
aline
aliped
aliphatic

aliquant	allspice	alter	ambassage	amidin	amphora	analgetic
aliquot	allude	alterant	ambassy	amidogen	amphorae	analgia
alist	allure	altercate	amber	amidol	amphoral	analog
alit	allusion	alternate	ambergris	amidships	amphoric	analogic
alive	allusive	altho	amberoid	amidst	ample	analogist
alizarin	alluvia	althorn	ambery	amine	amplify	analogize
alizarine	alluvial	although	ambient	amino	amplitude	analogous
alkahest	alluvian	altigraph	ambiguity	amir	amply	analogue
alkali	alluvion	altimeter	ambiguous	amiss	ampoule	analogy
alkalic	alluvious	altimetry	ambit	amitosis	ampul	analyses
alkalies	alluvium	altiscope	ambition	amitotic	ampule	analysis
alkalify	alluviums	altitude	ambitious	amity	ampulla	analyst
alkalin	ally	alto	ambivert	ammeter	ampullae	analytic
alkaline	allyl	altrical	amble	ammine	ampullar	analytics
alkalis	allylic	altrices	amblyopia	ammonal	amputate	analyze
alkalize	alma	altricial	amblyopic	ammonia	amreeta	anamnesis
alkaloid	almacen	altruism	amblyopy	ammoniac	amrita	anamnia
alkalosis	almacenes	altruist	ambo	ammonite	amuck	anandria
alkane	almah	aludel	ambones	ammonium	amulet	anandrous
alkanet	almanac	alula	ambos	amnesia	amuse	ananthous
alkene	almandine	alulae	ambroid	amnesic	amusive	anapest
alkyl	almandite	alular	ambrosia	amnestic	amygdule	anapestic
alkyne	almemar	alum	ambrosial	amnesty	amyl	anaphase
all	almighty	alumin	ambrosian	amnia	amylase	anaphora
allantoic	almner	alumina	ambrotype	amnion	amylene	anaplasty
allantoid	almond	alumine	ambry	amnionate	amylic	anaptotic
allantoin	almoner	aluminize	ambsace	amnionic	amylogen	anarch
allantois	almonry	aluminous	ambulacra	amniotic	amyloid	anarchic
allay	almost	aluminum	ambulance	amniote	amyloidal	anarchism
allege	alms	alumna	ambulant	amock	amylopsin	anarchist
allegoric	almsdeed	alumnae	ambulate	amok	amylose	anarchy
allegory	almshouse	alumni	ambuscade	amoke	amylum	anarthria
allegro	almsman	alumnus	ambuscado	amoeba	an	anastroph(e
alleluia	almswoman	alumroot	ambush	amoebic	ana	anatase
alleluiah	almuce	alumstone	ameba	amoeboid	anabaena	anathema
allergen	almud	alunite	amebae	amole	anabas	anathemas
allergic	almude	alveary	amebas	among	anabases	anatomic
allergin	aloe	alveolar	amebic	amongst	anabasis	anatomist
allergy	aloes	alveolary	amebean	amoral	anabatic	anatomize
alleviate	aloetic	alveolate	amebiasis	amorality	anabiosis	anatomy
alley	aloetical	alveolus	ameboid	amorally	anabiotic	anatropal
alliance	aloft	alvine	ameer	amoretto	anabolic	anatto
alligator	aloha	always	amelcorn	amorini	anabolism	ancestor
allision	aloin	alyssum	amen	amorino	anabranch	ancestral
allium	alone	am	amenable	amorist	anadem	ancestry
allocable	along	amain	amenably	amorous	anaemia	anchor
allocate	alongside	amalgam	amend	amorphism	anaemic	anchorage
allocatur	aloof	amanita	amende	amorphous	anaerobe	anchoress
allodia	aloofly	amanous	amends	amort	anaerobia	anchorite
allodial	alopecia	amaracus	amenity	amortize	anaerobic	anchoret
allodium	aloud	amaranth	ament	amotion	anaglyph	anchovy
allogamy	alow	amaroid	amentia	amount	anagoge	anchusa
allomorph	alp	amaryllis	amerce	amour	anagogic	anchusin
allonym	alpaca	amass	americium	amove	anagogy	ancient
allopath	alpenglow	amateur	amethyst	amperage	anagram	ancillary
allopathy	alpha	amative	ametropia	ampere	anal	ancipital
allophane	alphabet	amatol	ametropic	ampersand	analcime	ancon
alloplasm	alphosis	amatorial	amia	amphibian	analcite	ancone
allosome	alphyl	amatory	amiable	amphibion	analect	anconal
allot	alpine	amaurosis	amianthus	amphibole	analecta	anconeal
allocrope	alpinist	amaurotic	amic	amphiboly	analectic	ancoral
allotropy	already	amaze	amicable	amphigory	analects	and
allottee	alsike	amazon	amice	amphioxus	analeptic	andante
allow	also	amzonite	amicrobic	amphipod	analgen	andesite
allowance	alt	ambage	amid	amphipode	analgene	andiron
alloy	altar	ambagious	amide	amphiscii	analgesia	andradite
alloyage	altarage	ambary	amidic	amphiuma	analgesic	androgen

androgyny	animistic	ansa	antipathy	aperture	apologia	approve
android	animosity	ansae	antiphon	apery	apologist	appulse
androidal	animus	answer	antiphony	apetalous	apologize	appulsion
anecdote	anion	ant	antipodal	apex	apologue	apricot
anecdotal	anise	anta	antipode	apexes	apology	apron
anecdotic	aniseed	antacid	antipole	aphanite	apomictic	apronful
anele	anisette	antae	antipyic	aphanitic	apomixis	apronless
anemia	anker	antalgic	antiquary	aphasia	apophasis	apropos
anemic	ankerite	antalkali	antiquate	aphasiac	apophyge	apse
anemology	ankh	antarctic	antique	aphasic	apophysis	apsidal
anemone	ankle	ante	antiquity	aphasy	apoplexy	apsides
anemosis	anklet	antecede	antiscii	aphelia	aport	apsis
anenst	ankus	antechoir	antiserum	aphelian	apostasy	apt
anent	ankush	antedate	antitoxic	aphelion	apostate	apteryx
anergia	ankylose	antefix	antitoxin	aphemia	apostil	aptitude
anergic	ankylosis	antefixa	antitrade	aphemic	apostille	apyretic
anergy	ankylotic	antefixae	antitrust	apheresis	apostle	apyrexia
aneroid	anlace	antefixal	antitypal	apheretic	apostolic	apyrexial
aneurism	anlage	antefixes	antitype	aphesis	apothece	apyrexy
aneurysm	anlas	antelope	antitypic	aphetic	apothecia	aquaplane
anew	annal	antenatal	antivenin	aphid	apothegm	aquaria
angaria	annalist	antenna	antler	aphides	apothem	aquarium
angary	annat	antennula	antonym	aphis	appal	aquariums
angel	annates	antennule	antrorse	aphonia	appall	aquatic
angelhood	annatto	antepast	anuran	aphonic	appanage	aquatical
angelic	anneal	anterior	anuresis	aphorism	apparatus	aquatint
angelica	annex	anteroom	anuretic	aphorist	apparel	aquatinta
angelical	annexive	antes	anuria	aphorize	apparency	aqueduct
angelus	annotate	antetype	anuric	aphotic	apparent	aqueous
anger	announce	antevert	anurous	aphrodite	apparitor	aquiform
angina	annoy	anthelia	anury	aphyllose	appeal	aquilegia
angle	annoyance	anthelion	anvil	aphyllous	appear	aquiline
anglepod	annual	anthelix	anxiety	aphylly	appease	aquose
anglesite	annually	anthem	anxious	apian	appeasive	arabic
angleworm	annuitant	anthemia	any	apiarian	appelable	arability
angry	annuity	anthemion	anybody	apiarist	appelant	arable
angstrom	annul	anther	anyhow	apiary	appellate	araceous
anguine	annular	anthesis	anyone	apical	appellee	araneous
anguish	annulary	anthodia	anything	apices	appellor	arapaima
angular	annulate	anthodium	anyway	apiculate	append	araroba
angulate	annulet	anthoid	anywhere	apiculus	appendage	araucaria
angustate	annulose	anthology	anywise	apiece	appendix	arbalest
anhelous	annulus	anthotaxy	aorist	apiology	appertain	arbiter
anidrosis	anodal	anthozoan	aoristic	apish	appetence	arbitress
anhydrate	anode	anthozoic	aorta	apivorous	appetency	arbitrage
anhydride	anodic	anthrax	aortae	aplanatic	appetite	arbitral
anhydrite	anodize	antiar	aortas	aplasia	appetize	arbitrary
anhydrous	anodyne	antibody	aortal	aplastic	applaud	arbitrate
ani	anoint	antic	aortic	aplomb	applause	arboreal
anigh	anolyte	anticked	aoudad	apnoea	apple	arboreous
anight	anomalous	anticking	apace	apnoeal	appliance	arboretum
anights	anomalism	antichlor	apagoge	apnoeic	applicant	arborous
anil	anomaly	antidim	apagogic	apocarp	appliqué	arbour
anile	anon	antidotal	apanage	apocopate	apply	arbuscle
anilin	anonym	antidote	apart	apocope	appoint	arbuscule
aniline	anonymous	antigen	apartment	apod	appointee	arbute
anility	anonymity	antigene	apatetic	apodal	apportion	arbutean
animal	anopheles	antigenic	apathetic	apodan	appose	arbutus
animalism	anorak	antilogy	apathy	apodictic	apposite	arc
animalist	anorectic	antimask	apatite	apodosis	appraisal	arcade
animality	anorexia	antimere	ape	apogamic	appraise	arcanum
animalize	anorexy	antimeric	apeak	apogamous	apprehend	arcature
animate	anorthite	antimonic	aperient	apogamy	appressed	arch
animation	anosmia	antimony	aperitive	apogeal	apprise	archaic
animative	anosmic	antimonyl	aperiodic	apogean	apprize	archaical
animism	another	antinode	apert	apogee	approach	archaism
animist	anoxaemia	antinomy	apertura	apolog	approbate	archaist

archaize	aridity	arrogate	ascot	assertive	ataunt	attar
archangel	ariel	arrow	ascribe	assertory	atavic	attemper
archducal	arietta	arrowhead	ascus	assess	atavism	attempt
archduchy	ariette	arrowroot	asepsis	asset	atavist	attend
archduke	aright	arrowwood	aseptic	assiduity	atavistic	attendant
archery	aril	arrowy	asexual	assiduous	ataxia	attent
archetype	arillate	arroyo	ash	assign	ataxic	attention
archfiend	arillode	arsenal	ashamed	assignee	ataxy	attentive
archicarp	ariose	arsenate	ashcake	assist	ate	attenuant
archil	arise	arseniate	ashcan	assistant	atelic	attenuate
archimage	arisen	arsenic	ashen	assize	atelier	attest
archiplasm	arista	arsenical	ashery	associate	ateliosis	attic
architect	aristate	arsenide	ashine	associes	athanasia	attire
archival	aristol	arsenite	ashlar	assoil	athart	attitude
archive	ark	arsenous	ashler	assonance	atheism	attorney
archivist	arm	arsine	ashlaring	assonant	atheist	attract
archivolt	armada	arson	ashore	assort	atheistic	attrahens
archon	armadillo	art	ashtray	assuage	atheling	attrahent
archway	armament	arterial	ashy	assuasive	atheneum	attribute
arciform	armature	arteritis	asialia	assume	athetosis	attrite
arctic	armband	artery	aside	assumpsit	athirst	attrited
arcuate	armchair	artful	asinine	assurance	athlete	attrition
arcuation	armet	arthritic	asininity	assure	athletic	attune
ardeb	armful	arthritis	ask	assurgent	athletics	atwain
ardency	armhole	arthropod	askance	astasia	athort	atwirl
ardent	armiger	arthroses	askew	astatic	athwart	atypic
ardour	armigeri	arthrosis	aslant	aster	atilt	atypical
arduous	armillary	artichoke	asleep	asterial	atlantean	auburn
are	armistice	article	aslope	asterisk	antlantes	auction
area	armlet	articular	asocial	asterism	atlas	audacious
areal	armorial	artifact	asp	astern	atmology	audacity
areca	armour	artifice	asparagus	asternal	atmometer	audible
areic	armoury	artificer	aspect	asteroid	atmometry	audibly
arena	armozeen	artillery	aspen	asthenia	atoll	audience
areology	armozine	artisan	asper	asthenic	atom	audient
areola	armpit	artist	asperate	asthma	atomic	audile
areolar	army	artiste	aspergill	asthmatic	atomical	audio
areolate	arnica	artistic	asperity	astir	atomicity	audiogram
areole	arnatto	artistry	aspermous	astonish	atomism	audiphone
areometer	arnotto	artless	asperse	astound	atomist	audit
arethusa	aroid	arty	aspersion	astraddle	atomistic	audition
argala	aroideous	arum	aspersive	astragal	atomize	auditive
argent	aroma	arval	asphalt	astrakhan	atomy	auditory
argental	aromatic	arytenoid	asphaltic	astral	atonal	augen
argentate	aromatize	as	asphodel	astrand	atonality	augend
argentic	arose	asarum	asphyxia	astray	atone	auger
argentine	around	asbestos	asphyxial	astrict	atonic	aught
argentite	arousal	asbolin	asphyxy	astride	atonity	augite
argentol	arouse	ascarid	aspic	astringe	atony	augitic
argentous	arow	ascend	aspirant	astrology	atop	augment
argil	arpeggio	ascendent	aspirate	astronomy	atria	augur
argillous	arquebus	ascension	aspire	astrut	atrichous	augural
argillite	arrack	ascensive	aspirin	astucious	atrip	augurial
arginine	arraign	ascent	aspish	astute	atrium	augury
argol	arrange	ascertain	asquint	astylar	atrocious	august
argon	arrant	ascetic	ass	asunder	atrocity	auk
argonaut	arras	ascetical	assagai	aswim	atrophic	auklet
argosies	arrasene	asci	assail	aswoon	atrophous	aunt
argosy	array	ascidian	assailant	asylum	atrophy	auntie
argot	arrayal	ascidioid	assassin	asymmetry	atropine	aunty
argotic	arrear	ascidium	assault	asymptote	atropism	aura
argue	arrearage	ascites	assay	asyndetic	attach	aural
argument	arrest	ascitic	assemble	asyndeton	attaché	aurate
argus	arret	ascitical	assembly	at	attack	aureate
argute	arris	ascocarp	assent	atalaya	attain	aurei
aria	arrival	ascorbic	assert	ataman	attainder	aureola
arid	arrive	ascospore	assertion	atamasco	attaint	aureole

aureolin	autotruck	awing	babirusa	bag	baluster	barbarian
aureous	autotype	awesome	baboo	bagass	bambini	barbaric
aureus	autotypic	awful	baboon	bagasse	bambino	barbarism
auric	autotypy	awhile	baboonery	bagatelle	bamboo	barbarity
auricle	autumn	awhirl	baboonish	baggage	ban	barbarous
auricula	autumnal	awkward	babu	baggy	banal	barbate
auriculae	autunite	awl	babuism	bagman	banality	barbecue
auricular	auxiliary	awless	babushka	bagnio	banana	barbel
auriform	auximone	awlwort	baby	bagpipe	band	barberry
auriscope	avail	awn	babyhood	baguet	bandage	barbet
auriscopy	avalanche	awned	babyish	baguette	bandana	barbette
aurist	avant	awnless	baccate	baguio	bandanna	barbican
aurochs	avarice	awning	bacchanal	bagworm	bandbox	barbicel
aurora	avast	awny	bacchant	bah	bandeau	barbital
auroral	avatar	awoke	bacchante	bail	bandeaux	barbitone
aurorean	avaunt	awry	bacchic	bailey	banderol	barbule
auroric	avenge	ax	bacchical	bailiff	banderole	barcarole
aurous	avens	axe	bacciform	bailiwick	bandicoot	bard
aurum	avenue	axeman	bachelor	bailsman	bandit	bare
auscultate	aver	axial	bacillar	bait	banditry	bareback
auspex	average	axil	bacillary	bake	bandog	barefoot
auspicate	averse	axile	bacillus	bakehouse	bandoleer	barege
auspice	aversion	axilla	back	bakery	bandolier	baresark
auspices	avert	axillae	backbite	bakeshop	bandoline	bargain
auspicial	avian	axillar	backboard	baksheesh	bandore	barge
austenite	aviarist	axillary	backbone	baku	bandstand	bargeman
austere	aviary	axiom	backcross	bakuin	bandwagon	barghest
austerity	aviate	axiomatic	backdrop	balalaika	bandy	baric
austral	aviation	axis	backfall	balance	bane	barilla
autacoid	aviator	axle	backfire	balas	baneberry	barite
autarchic	aviatress	axletree	backhand	balata	baneful	baritone
autarchy	aviatrice	axman	backhouse	balboa	bang	barium
authentic	aviatrix	axolotl	backlash	balcony	bangle	bark
author	avicular	axon	backlog	bald	bani	barkless
authoress	avid	axone	backmost	baldachin	banian	barky
authorial	avidity	axseed	backrope	baldaquin	banish	barley
authority	avifauna	ay	backset	baldface	banister	barm
authorize	avifaunal	aye	backsight	baldhead	banjo	barmaid
autism	avigation	ayahuasca	backslide	baldpate	banjos	barmy
autistic	aviso	ayin	backstage	baldric	banjoist	barn
autoboat	avocado	azalea	backstay	baldrice	banjorine	barnacle
autobus	avocados	azedarach	backstop	bale	bank	barnstorm
autoclave	avocation	azimuth	backstrap	baleen	bankbook	barnyard
autocracy	avocatory	azimuthal	backswept	balefire	banknote	barogram
autocrat	avocet	azo	backsword	baleful	bankpaper	barograph
autocycle	avocette	azoic	backward	balisaur	bankrupt	barometer
autodyne	avoid	azonic	backwards	balk	banksia	barometry
autogamy	avoidance	azote	backwash	balkanize	banner	baron
autogenic	avoset	azoth	backwater	balky	banneret	baronage
autogeny	avouch	azotic	backwoods	ball	bannock	baroness
autogiro	avow	azotize	bacon	ballad	banquet	baronet
autograph	avowal	azure	bacteria	ballade	banquette	baronetcy
autoharp	avowry	azurite	bacterial	ballast	banshee	baronial
automat	avulsion	azygous	bacterin	ballerina	bant	barony
automata	avuncular	azym	bacterine	ballet	bantam	baroque
automatic	await	azyme	bacterium	ballistic	banter	baroscope
automaton	awake	azymic	bacterize	ballistics	bantling	barouche
autonomic	awaken	azymous	bacteroid	balloon	banyan	barque
autonomy	award		baculine	ballot	baobab	barrack
autopsy	aware		bad	balm	baptism	barracoon
autoptic	awash		bade	balmacaan	baptismal	barracuda
autosomal	away	**B**	badge	balmoral	baptistery	barrage
autosome	awe		badger	balmy	baptistry	barranca
autotomy	aweary		badinage	balneal	baptize	barranco
autotoxin	aweather	babassu	badminton	balsa	bar	barrator
autotoxic	aweigh	babbitt	baffle	balsam	barathea	barratry
autotoxis	aweless	babble	baffy	balsamic	barb	barrel
		babe				

barren	bate	beano	bedspring	behest	benthic	bestowal
barret	bateau	bear	bedstaff	behind	benthonic	bestrew
barrette	bateaux	bearberry	bedstand	behold	benthos	bestride
barricade	batfish	bearcat	bedstaves	beholden	benumb	bestrode
barrier	batfowl	beard	bedstead	behoof	benzene	bet
barrister	bath	beargrass	bedstraw	behoove	benzidin	beta
barroom	bathe	bearish	bedtime	behove	benzidine	betaine
barrow	bathetic	bearskin	bedward	beige	benzin	betake
bartender	bathhouse	bearwood	bedwards	being	benzine	betatron
barter	batholite	beast	bedwarmer	bel	benzoate	betel
bartizan	batholith	beat	bee	belabour	benzoic	betelnut
barye	bathos	beaten	beebread	belated	benzoin	bethel
baryta	bathrobe	beatific	beech	belay	benzol	bethink
barytes	bathroom	beatify	beechen	belch	benzoline	bethought
barytone	bathtub	beatitude	beechdrops	beldam	benzoyl	betide
basal	batik	beau	beechmast	beldame	benzyl	betimes
basalt	batiste	beaus	beechnut	beleaguer	bequeath	betoken
basaltic	baton	beauish	beef	belemnite	bequest	betony
bascule	batrachian	beauteous	beefing	belfry	berate	betook
base	batsman	beautiful	beefsteak	belga	berberin	betray
baseball	batt	beautify	beefy	belie	berberine	betroth
baseboard	battalion	beauty	beehive	belief	bereave	betrotha
baseburner	batten	beaux	beeline	believe	bereft	between
baseless	battery	beaver	been	belittle	beret	bevel
baselevel	battle	bebeerine	beer	bell	berg	beverage
baseman	batty	bebeeru	beery	bellbird	bergamot	bevy
basement	bauble	becalm	beestings	bellboy	beriberi	bewail
basenji	baudekin	became	beeswax	belle	beriberic	beware
bash	baulk	because	beeswing	belleek	berime	bewilder
bashaw	bauson	beccafico	beet	bellhop	berlin	bewitch
bashful	bauxite	bechamel	beetle	bellicose	berline	bey
basic	bawd	bechance	beetree	bellman	berm	beylic
basicity	bawdry	beck	beeves	bellow	berme	beylik
basidial	bawdy	becket	beewolf	bellwort	bernicle	beyond
basidium	bawl	beckon	befall	belly	berry	bezant
basify	bay	becloud	befell	bellyache	berseem	bezel
basil	bayadere	become	befit	bellyband	berserk	bezique
basilar	bayard	bed	befog	belong	berth	bezoar
basilary	bayberry	bedaub	befool	belove	bertha	biangular
basilica	bayman	bedazzle	before	below	berthage	biannual
basilican	bayonet	bedbug	befriend	belt	beryl	bias
basilisk	bayou	bedchair	befoul	beluga	berylline	biases
basin	baytree	bedcover	befuddle	belvedere	beryllium	biasses
basinet	baywood	bedeck	beg	bema	beseech	biaxal
basion	bazaar	bedevil	began	bemata	beseem	biaxial
basis	bazar	bedew	beget	bemean	beset	bib
bask	bazooka	bedfellow	begat	bemire	beshow	bibb
basket	bdellium	bedframe	beggar	bemoan	beside	bibcock
basketry	be	bedgown	beggardom	bemuse	besides	bibelot
basophile	beach	bedight	beggary	bench	besiege	biblical
basque	beachhead	bedim	begin	benchmark	besmear	biblicist
bass	beachy	bedizen	begird	benchroot	besmirch	bibulous
basset	beacon	bedlam	begohm	bend	besom	bicameral
bassinet	bead	bedlamite	begone	beneath	besot	bice
basso	beadhouse	bedmaker	begonia	benedict	besought	biceps
bassoon	beadle	bedmate	begot	benefic	bespangle	biche
basswood	beadledom	bedplate	begotten	benefice	bespatter	bicipital
bast	beadroll	bedpost	begrudge	benefit	bespeak	bicker
bastard	beadwork	bedquilt	beguile	bengaline	bespoke	bicolour
bastardy	beady	bedraggle	begum	benight	bespread	biconcave
baste	beagle	bedrid	begun	benign	best	biconvex
bastille	beak	bedrock	behalf	benignant	bestead	bicorn
bastinade	beam	bedroll	behave	benignity	bestial	bicorne
bastinado	beamish	bedroom	behaviour	benison	bestially	bicornous
bastion	beamy	bedside	behead	benne	bestiary	bicron
bat	bean	bedsore	beheld	bennet	bestir	bicuspid
batch	beancaper	bedspread	behemoth	bent	bestow	bicuspis

bicycle	billion	bipolar	blackish	bliss	blueweed	bolero
bicyclic	billionth	biradial	blackjack	blister	bluewood	boletu
bicyclical	billon	birch	blackleg	blistery	bluff	bolide
bid	billow	birchen	blacklist	blithe	blunder	bolivar
bidactyl	billowy	bird	blackmail	blithely	blunge	bolivars
bidarka	billy	birdcall	blackpoll	blizzard	blunt	bolivia
bidarkee	bilorate	birdgrass	blackwill	bloat	blur	boll
bidden	bilocular	birdhouse	blackwood	blob	blurb	bollard
biddy	bimanous	birdie	bladder	block	blurry	bollworm
bide	bimanual	birdlime	bladdery	blockade	blurt	bolo
bode	bimensal	bireme	blade	blockhead	blush	bolograph
bidentate	bimonthly	biretta	bladebone	blockish	blushful	bolometer
biennial	bimotored	birth	blain	blocklike	bluster	bolshevik
bier	bin	birthday	blame	blocky	blustery	bolster
bifacial	binary	birthmark	blameful	blond	blustrous	bolt
bifarious	binate	birthroot	blameless	blonde	boa	boltel
bifid	bination	birthwort	blanch	blood	boar	bolthead
bifidate	binaural	bis	bland	bloodless	board	boltonia
bifidity	bind	biscuit	blandish	bloodline	boardwalk	boltrope
bifilar	bindery	bisect	blank	bloodroot	boarfish	bolus
biflex	bindweed	bisection	blanket	bloodshed	boarhound	bomb
bifocal	bine	bisector	blare	bloodwood	boarish	bombard
bifold	bing	bisectrix	blarney	bloodworm	boast	bombardor
bifoliate	bingo	biserrate	blasé	bloodwort	boastful	bombast
biform	binnacle	bisexual	blaspheme	bloody	boat	bombastic
bifurcate	binocle	bishop	blasphemy	bloom	boatage	bombazine
bifurcous	binocular	bishopric	blast	bloomery	boatbill	bombe
big	binomial	bismuth	blastema	bloomy	boatman	bombproof
bigamic	binominal	bismuthal	blasthole	blossom	boatswain	bombshell
bigamous	binuclear	bismuthic	blastula	blossomy	bob	bombsight
bigamy	biogen	bison	blastulae	blot	bobbin	bombycid
bigaroon	biogeny	bisque	blastular	blotch	bobbinet	bombyx
bigarreau	biography	bistort	blatancy	blotchy	bobcat	bonaci
biggin	biologic	bistoury	blatant	blouse	bobolink	bonanza
bighorn	biologism	bistre	blather	blow	bobsled	bonasus
bight	biologist	bisulcate	blaze	blowfish	bobstay	bond
bignonia	biology	bit	blazon	blowfly	bobtail	bondage
bigot	biolysis	bitch	blazonry	blowgun	bobtailed	bondmaid
bigotry	biolytic	bite	bleach	blowhole	bobwhite	bondman
bijou	biometry	bitstock	bleachery	blown	bock	bondwoman
bijoux	bionomic	bitt	bleak	blowpipe	boddle	bondsman
bijugate	bionomics	bitten	bleakish	blowsy	bode	bondstone
bijugous	bionomist	bittern	blear	blowtorch	bodement	bondslave
bilabial	bioplasm	bitumen	bleary	blowtube	bodice	bone
bilabiate	biopsic	bivalence	bleat	blowy	bodied	bonedust
bilander	biopsy	bivalency	bleb	blowzy	bodiless	bonehead
bilateral	bioscope	bivalent	blebby	blubber	bodkin	bonemeal
bilbo	bioscopic	bivalve	bled	blubbery	bodyguard	boneset
bilboes	bioscopy	bivalvous	bleed	blucher	bog	boneyard
bile	biosphere	bivalvular	blemish	bludgeon	boggish	bonfire
bilection	biota	bivouac	blench	blue	bogbean	bongo
bilestone	biotic	biweekly	blend	bluish	bogey	bonhomie
bilge	biotical	biyearly	blende	bluebell	boggle	bonito
bilgekeel	biotin	bizarre	blendous	blueberry	boggy	bonnet
bilgy	biotite	blab	blendy	bluebird	bogie	bonny
biliary	biotitic	black	blennioid	bluebook	bogle	bonus
bilinear	biotope	blackball	blenny	bluecap	bogus	bony
bilingual	biotype	blackbird	bless	bluecoat	bogwood	bonze
bilious	biotypic	blackboy ·	blet	bluecurls	bogy	boo
biliteral	biparous	blackcap	blew	bluefish	bohea	booby
bilk	bipartite	blackcock	blight	bluegill	boil	boodling
billhook	biped	blackdamp	blind	bluegum	boiler	book
billboard	bipedal	blacken	blindage	bluejack	bolar	bookish
billet	biphenyl	blackfish	blindfish	bluenose	bolary	bookland
billfish	bipinnate	blackgum	blindfold	blueprint	bold	bookmaker
billhead	biplane	blackhaw	blindworm	bluestone	boldface	bookman
billiards	bipod	blackhead	blink	bluet	bole	bookplate

bookworm	botonée	brabble	brawn	bridewell	bromate	buccal
boom	botony	braccate	brawny	bridge	brome	buccaneer
boomerang	botryoid	brace	braxy	bridle	bromic	buck
boon	botryose	bracelet	bray	bridoon	bromide	buckaroo
boor	bots	brachia	brayer	brief	bromine	buckbean
boorish	bott	brachial	brayera	briefcase	bromism	buckberry
boost	bottle	brachiate	braza	briefless	bromize	buckboard
boot	bottom	brachium	braze	brier	bronchi	bucket
bootblack	bottomry	bracken	brazen	brierwood	bronchia	bucketful
bootee	botulism	bracket	brazier	briery	bronchial	buckeye
booth	bouclé	brackish	brazil	brig	bronchus	buckhorn
bootjack	boudoir	bract	breach	brigade	bronco	buckhound
bootleg	bouffe	bracteal	breachy	brigadier	bronze	buckle
bootless	bough	bracteate	bread	brigand	bronzy	bucko
booty	bought	bracteole	breadline	bright	brooch	buckram
booze	bougie	bractlet	breadnut	brighten	brood	bucksaw
boracic	bouillon	brad	breadroot	brill	broody	buckshee
boracite	boulder	brag	breadth	brilliant	brook	buckshot
borage	boule	braggart	break	brim	brooklet	buckskin
borate	boulevard	bragget	breakage	brimful	brookweed	buckthorn
borax	bounce	braid	breakbone	brimstone	broom	bucktooth
border	bound	brail	breakfast	brindle	broomcorn	buckwagon
bordure	boundary	braille	breakneck	brine	broomrape	buckwheat
bore	bounden	brain	bream	brinish	broth	bucolic
boreal	boundless	brainless	breast	bring	brothel	bud
boredom	bounty	brainpan	breastpin	brink	brother	buddle
boric	bouquet	brainstem	breath	briny	brougham	buddleia
boride	bourdon	brainy	breathe	briolette	brought	budge
born	bourg	braise	breathy	briquet	brow	budget
borne	bourgeois	braize	breccia	briquette	browband	budgetary
borneol	bourgeon	brake	bred	brisance	browbeat	buff
bornite	bourn	brakeage	breech	brisk	brown	buffalo
boron	bourne	brakeman	breeches	brisket	brownish	buffet
borough	bourrelet	brakesman	breeching	brisling	brownie	buffoon
borrow	bourse	braky	breed	bristle	browntail	buffy
bort	bouse	bramble	breeze	brit	browse	bug
borty	bout	brambly	breezy	britannia	brucine	bugbane
bortz	bovine	bran	bregma	brittle	bruise	bugbear
borzoi	bow	branch	bregmata	britska	bruit	bugeye
boscage	bowel	branchia	bregmate	britzka	brumal	buggy
boschbok	bower	branchiae	brehon	britzska	brume	bugle
boschvark	bowerbird	branchial	brethren	broach	brumous	bugleweed
bosh	bowfin	brand	breve	broad	brunet	bugloss
boshbok	bowhead	brandish	brevet	broadbill	brunette	bugseed
boshvark	bowpin	brandy	brevetcy	broadbrim	brunt	buhach
bosk	bowknot	branle	breviary	broadcast	brush	buhl
boskage	bowl	branny	brevier	broaden	brushwood	build
bosky	bowlder	brant	brevity	broadish	brushy	built
bosket	bowman	brantail	brew	broadleaf	brusk	bulb
bosquet	bowpin	brash	brewage	broadside	brusque	bulbar
bosom	bowshot	brashy	brewery	broadtail	brut	bulbel
boss	bowsprit	brass	brewis	brocade	brutal	bulbiform
bossy	bowstring	brassard	briar	brocatel	brutality	bulbil
bosun	bowyer	brassie	briard	broccoli	brutalize	bulbous
bot	box	brassière	briarwood	broch	brute	bulbul
botanic	boxberry	brassy	briary	brochure	brutify	bulge
botanical	boxcar	brat	bribe	brocket	brutish	bulgy
botanist	boxen	brattice	bribery	brogan	bryology	bulimia
botanize	boxhaul	brattle	brick	brogue	bryonin	bulimic
botany	boxthorn	bravado	brickbat	broil	bryony	bulk
botch	boxwood	bravadoes	brickkiln	brokage	bryophyte	bulkage
botchery	boy	bravados	brickwork	broke	bubal	bulkhead
botchy	boyar	brave	brickyard	broken	bubaline	bulky
botfly	boyard	bravery	bricole	broker	bubble	bull
both	boycott	bravo	bridal	brokerage	bubo	bulla
bother	boyhood	bravura	bride	broma	bubonic	bullate
botoné	boyish	brawl	bridesman	bromal		bullbat

bulldog	burgrave	butterfly	cachepot	cajeput	calisaya	campaign
bulldozer	burial	butterine	cachet	cajole	calix	campanero
bullet	burin	butternut	cachexia	cajolery	calk	campanile
bulletin	burke	buttery	cachexy	cajun	call	campanula
bullfight	burl	buttock	cacholong	cake	calla	campfire
bullfinch	burlap	button	cachou	cakewalk	callboard	camphene
bullfrog	burlesque	buttony	cacique	calabar	callboy	camphire
bullhead	burley	buttress	cackle	calabash	calliope	camphogen
bullion	burly	buttweld	cacodemon	caladium	callitype	camphol
bullish	burn	butyl	cacodyl	calamanco	callose	camphor
bullneck	burnet	butylene	cacodylic	calamary	callosity	camphoric
bullock	burnish	butyrate	cacoethes	calami	callous	campion
bullpen	burnoose	butyric	cacology	calamine	callow	camshaft
bullpout	burnt	butyrin	cacophony	calamint	calli	camwood
bullring	burr	buxom	cacti	calamite	callus	can
bullweed	burro	buy	cactus	calamity	calluses	canaille
bully	burrow	buzz	cactuses	calamus	calm	canal
bullyrag	burrstone	buzzard	cacumen	calash	calmative	canalage
bullytree	burry	buzzwig	cacuminal	calathi	calomel	canalize
bulrush	bursa	by	cad	calathus	caloric	canape
bulwark	bursal	bye	cadaster	calcanea	calorie	canard
bumble	bursar	bygone	cadastral	calcaneum	calorific	canary
bumblebee	bursarial	bylaw	cadaver	calcaneus	calotte	canaster
bumboat	bursary	bypass	cadaveric	calcar	caloyer	cancan
bumkin	burse	bypast	caddie	calcarate	caltrap	cancel
bump	burseed	byre	caddis	calcaria	caltrop	cancelli
bumpkin	bursiform	byroad	caddish	calceate	calumet	cancer
bumptious	bursitis	byssus	caddy	calces	calumny	cancerate
bumpy	burst	bystander	cade	calcic	calvaria	cancerous
bun	burthen	bywater	cadelle	calcific	calvarium	cancroid
bunch	burton	byway	cadence	calciform	calvary	candent
buncombe	burweed	byword	cadency	calcify	calve	candid
bund	bury	bywork	cadent	calcimine	calvities	candidacy
bundle	busby	byzant	cadenza	calcine	calx	candidate
bung	bush		cadet	calcinize	calxes	candle
bungalow	bushbuck		cadetship	calcite	calyces	candlenut
bungle	bushgoat		cadetcy	calcitic	calycinal	candlepin
bunion	bushel	**C**	cadette	calcium	calycine	candour
bunk	bushrider		cadge	calcspar	calycle	candy
bunkhouse	bushwhack	cab	cadgy	calctufa	calypso	candytuft
bunkmate	bushy	caba	cadmium	calctuff	calypter	cane
bunt	busk	cabal	cadre	calculate	calyptra	canebrake
buntline	buskin	cabala	caducean	calculous	calyx	canella
buoy	buskit	cabalism	caducei	calculus	cam	canephora
buoyage	busman	cabalist	caduceus	caldera	camail	canescent
buoyance	bust	caballine	caducity	caldron	camas	cangue
buoyancy	bustard	cabana	caducous	calendal	camber	canicular
buoyant	bustic	cabane	caeca	calendar	cambist	canikin
buprestid	bustle	cabaret	caecal	calender	cambium	canine
bur	busy	cabas	caecum	calends	cambric	canions
burble	busybody	cabbage	caesarian	calendula	came	canister
burbot	but	cabin	caesarist	calenture	camel	canities
burden	butadiene	cabinet	caesural	calescent	cameleer	canjar
burdock	butane	cable	café	calf	camelish	canjiar
bureau	butanol	cablegram	caffeic	calibrate	camellia	canker
bureaus	butanone	cablet	caffeine	calibre	cameo	cankery
bureaux	butcher	cabman	cafeteria	calices	camera	canna
burette	butchery	caboched	caftan	calicle	camerae	cannabin
burg	butler	caboose	cage	calico	cameral	cannel
burgage	butlery	caboshed	cagy	calicoes	cameraman	cannelure
burgee	butment	cabotage	caique	calicos	cameras	cannery
burgeon	butt	cabriole	cairn	caliginous	camion	cannibal
burgess	butte	cabriolet	cairned	caligraphy	camise	cannikin
burgher	butter	cacao	cairngorm	calipash	camisole	cannon
burglar	butterbur	cachalot	caisson	calipee	camlet	cannonade
burglary	buttercup	cache	caitiff	caliper	camomile	cannoneer
burgoo	butterfat	cachectic	cajaput	caliph	camp	cannonry

cannot	capriccio	carcinoma	carotin	casern	catbrier	causalgia
cannula	caprice	card	carotte	caseworm	catcall	causality
cannular	capriform	cardamom	carousal	cash	catch	causation
cannulate	capriole	cardamon	carouse	cashaw	catchfly	causative
canny	caproic	cardamum	carousel	cashbook	catchment	cause
canoe	capsaicin	cardboard	carp	cashew	catchpole	causerie
canon	capsicum	cardcase	carpal	cashier	catchword	causeway
canonic	capsize	cardia	carpale	cashmere	catchy	caustic
canonical	capstan	cardiac	carpalia	cashoo	catechism	caustical
canonist	capstone	cardiacal	carpel	casino	catechist	cauterant
canonize	capsular	cardialgy	carpellum	cask	catechize	cauterism
canonries	capsulate	cardigan	carpenter	casket	catechu	cauterize
canonry	capsule	cardinal	carpentry	casque	catechuic	cautery
canonship	captain	cardioid	carpet	cassareep	category	caution
canopy	captaincy	carditis	carpetbag	cassation	catenary	cautious
canorous	caption	cardoon	carpology	cassava	catenate	caval
cant	captious	care	carpi	casse	cater	cavalcade
cantabile	captivate	careen	carpus	casserole	caterwaul	cavalier
cantaloup	captive	careenage	carrack	cassia	catfall	cavalla
cantar	captivity	career	carrageen	cassimere	catfish	cavally
cantata	captor	careerist	carrell	cassock	catgut	cavalry
cantdog	capture	carefree	carreta	cassowary	catharsis	cavan
canteen	capuche	careful	carriage	cast	cathartic	cavatina
canter	capuchin	careless	carriole	castanet	cathead	cave
cantharis	caput	caress	carrion	caste	cathedra	caveat
canthus	car	caret	carrom	castellan	cathedral	cavern
canticle	carabid	caretaker	carronade	castelry	catheter	cavernous
cantle	caracal	cargador	carrot	castigate	cathexis	cavesson
canto	caracara	cargo	carroty	castle	cathode	cavetto
canton	carack	caribe	carry	castlery	cathodic	caviar
cantonal	caracole	caribou	cart	castor	catholic	caviare
cantor	carafe	caries	cartage	castoreum	cation	cavicorn
cantus	caramel	carillon	carte	castrate	catkin	cavil
canvas	carangoid	carina	cartel	casual	catlike	cavity
canvass	carapace	carinal	cartilage	casualism	catling	cavort
cany	carapacic	carinate	cartogram	casualist	catmint	cavy
canyon	carapax	cariole	carton	casualty	catnap	caw
canzone	carat	carious	cartoon	casuist	catnip	cay
canzonet	caravan	cariosity	cartouche	casuistic	catoptric	cayman
canzoni	caravel	carline	cartridge	casuistry	cattalo	cease
cap	caraway	carload	cartulary	cat	cattle	ceaseless
capable	carbamic	carman	cartwheel	catabasis	cattleman	cedar
capably	carbazole	carmelite	caruca	catabatic	catty	cedarbird
capacious	carbide	carmine	carucage	catabolic	catwalk	cedarn
capacity	carbine	carminic	carucate	cataclysm	caucus	cede
caparison	carbineer	carnage	caruncle	catacomb	cauda	cedilla
cape	carbinol	carnal	carvacrol	catalase	caudad	cedula
capelin	carbolate	carnalist	carve	catalepsy	caudae	ceiba
capeline	carbolic	carnalite	carvel	catalo	caudal	ceil
caper	carbolize	carnation	carven	catalogue	caudate	ceiling
capias	carbon	carnelian	caryatid	catalpa	caudated	celadon
capiases	carbonado	carnify	caryopses	catalysis	caudex	celandine
capillary	carbonate	carnival	caryopis	catalyst	caudexes	celebrant
capita	carbonic	carnivora	caryotin	catalytic	caudices	celebrate
capital	carbonis	carnivore	cascabel	catalyze	caudle	celebrity
capitally	carbonize	carnosity	cascade	catamaran	caught	celerity
capitate	carbonyl	carnotite	cascara	catamenia	caul	celery
capitol	carbora	carob	case	catamount	cauldron	celesta
capitula	carboxyl	caroche	casease	cataplasm	caules	celestial
capitular	carboy	carol	caseate	cataplexy	caulicle	celestine
capitulum	carbuncle	caroli	caseation	catapult	cauliform	celestite
capon	carburet	carolus	caseic	cataract	cauline	celiac
caponier	carburize	caroluses	casein	catarrh	caulis	celibacy
caporal	carcajou	carom	casemate	catarrhal	caulk	celibate
capot	carcanet	carontene	casement	catbird	caulome	cell
capote	carcass	carotid	caseose	catblock	caulomic	cella
capric	carcel	carotidal	caseous	catboat	causal	cellar

cellarage	ceramics	chainman	char	cheerless	chignon	chock
cellaret	ceramist	chair	charabanc	cheery	chigoe	chocolate
cellist	cerastes	chairman	character	cheese	chilblain	choice
cello	cerate	chaise	charade	cheesy	child	choir
celloidin	ceratodus	chalaza	charbon	cheetah	childbed	choke
cellular	ceratoid	chalazae	charcoal	chef	childhood	chokebore
cellule	cercaria	chalcid	chard	chela	childing	chokedamp
cellulose	cercarial	chalder	charge	chelae	childish	choky
cellulous	cercarian	chaldron	charily	chelate	childless	cholagogue
celt	cerci	chalet	chariot	cheliform	childlike	cholecyst
celtium	cercus	chalice	charity	chemical	children	cholemia
cement	cere	chaliced	charivari	chemise	chile	choler
cementite	cereal	chalk	chark	chemism	chili	cholera
cementum	cerebella	chalkitis	charka ˅	chemist	chiliad	choleric
cemetery	cerebra	chalky	charkha	chemistry	chiliarch	choline
cenobia	cerebral	challenge	charlatan	chemurgic	chiliasm	chondrify
cenobite	cerebrate	challie	charlock	chemurgy	chiliast	chondroid
cenobitic	cerebric	challis	charlotte	chenille	chill	chondroma
cenobium	cerebrin	chalumeau	charm	chenopod	chime	choose
cenoby	cerebrum	chalybite	charnel	cherish	chimer	chop
cenotaph	cerecloth	chamber	charpoy	cheroot	chimera	chophouse
cense	cered	chambray	charqued	cherry	chimere	chopine
censer	cerement	chameleon	charry	chert	chimeric	choplogic
censor	ceremony	chamfer	chart	cherub	chimney	choppy
censorial	cereus	chamfrain	charta	cherubic	chin	choragi
censual	ceria	chamois	chartless	cherubim	china	choragic
censure	cerise	champ	chary	cherubs	chinaware	choragus
census	cerite	champac	chase	chervil	chinch	choral
cent	cerium	champacol	chasm	chess	chine	chord
cental	cernuous	champagne	chasmal	chest	chink	chordal
centare	cero	champaign	chasse	chestnut	chinkapin	chore
centaur	cerograph	champak	chassepot	cheval	chinky	chorea
centaury	ceros	champerty	chasseur	chevalet	chinook	choreal
centavo	cerotic	champion	chassis	chevalier	chintz	choria
centenary	cerotype	chañar	chaste	chevals	chintzy	choriamb
centesimi	cerous	chance	chasten	chevaux	chip	choric
centesimo	certain	chanceful	chastise	cheviot	chipmunk	chorion
centigram	certainty	chancel	chastity	chevon	chipper	chorist
centile	certify	chancery	chasuble	chevron	chippy	chorister
centime	certitude	chancre	chat	chew	chirm	choristic
centiped	cerulean	chancroid	chateau	chewink	chiromant	choroid
centipede	cerumen	chancrous	chateaux	chi	chiropody	chorology
centner	ceruse	chandler	chatelain	chiasm	chiropter	chortle
cento	cerusite	chandlery	chatoyant	chiasma	chirp	chorus
centra	cervical	change	chattel	chiasmal	chirr	chose
centrad	cervices	changeful	chatter	chiasmic	chirre	chosen
central	cervine	channel	chatty	chiasmus	chirrup	chough
centre	cervix	chanson	chauffer	chibouk	chirrupy	chow
centrebit	cesious	chant	chauffeur	chic	chisel	chowder
centric	cesium	chantage	chaunt	chicane	chit	chrism
centrical	cespitose	chantey	chausses	chicanery	chitin	chrismal
centriole	cessation	chantry	chazan	chick	chitinous	chrisom
centroid	cession	chaos	cheap	chickadee	chiton	christen
centrum	cesspit	chaotic	cheapen	chickaree	chivalric	chroma
centumvir	cesspool	chaotical	cheat	chicken	chivalry	chromate
centuple	cesta	chaparral	chebec	chickpea	chive	chromatic
centurial	cestode	chapbook	check	chickweed	chlamydes	chromatin
centurion	cestoid	chape	checkmate	chicle	chlamys	chrome
century	cestus	chapeau	checkrein	chico	chloral	chromic
ceorl	cetane	chapeaux	checkrow	chicory	chlorate	chromism
ceorlish	chacma	chapel	cheddite	chid	chloric	chromite
cephalad	chafe	chaperon	cheek	chidden	chloride	chromium
cephalic	chaff	chaperone	cheeky	chide	chlorine	chromo
cephalin	chaffinch	chaplain	cheep	chief	chlorite	chromogen
cephalous	chaffy	chaplet	cheeper	chieftain	chlorosis	chromous
ceraceous	chagrin	chapman	cheer	chiffon	chlorotic	chronaxia
ceramic	chain	chapter	cheerful	chigger	chlorous	chronaxie

chronaxy	cinder	civet	clay	cloaca	clypeus	cockade
chronic	cindery	civic	claybank	cloacal	clyster	cockaded
chronical	cinema	civicism	clayey	cloak	coach	cockateel
chronicle	cinematic	civics	claymore	cloakroom	coachman	cockatiel
chrysalid	cineraria	civil	claytonia	cloche	coact	cockatoo
chrysalis	cinerator	civilian	clean	clock	coaction	cockboat
chthonian	cinerous	civility	cleanse	clockwise	coactive	cockcrow
chthonic	cingula	civilize	clear	clockwork	coadjutor	cocker
chub	cingulate	civisni	clearance	clod	coadunate	cockerel
chubasco	cingulum	clabber	clearcut	cloddish	coagency	cockfight
chubby	cinnabar	clack	clearweed	cloddy	coagent	cockhorse
chuck	cinnamic	clad	clearwing	clog	coagula	cocking
chuckhole	cinnamon	cladode	cleat	cloggy	coagulant	cockle
chuckle	cinnamyl	clag	cleavage	cloisonné	coagulate	cocklebur
chuffy	cinque	claim	cleave	cloister	coagulin	cockloft
chug	cion	claimant	cledonism	cloistral	coagulum	cockmatch
chukka	cipher	clam	clef	clon	coal	cockney
chum	cipolin	clamant	cleft	clone	coalesce	cockneyfy
chummy	circinate	clambake	clematis	clonic	coalfish	cockpit
chump	circle	clamber	clemency	clonicity	coalhole	cockroach
chunk	circlet	clammy	clement	clonus	coalition	cockscomb
chunky	circuit	clamorous	clench	close	coalpit	cockshead
church	circuity	clamour	clepsydra	closet	coalsack	cockspur
churchman	circular	clamp	clergy	closure	coaltit	cocksure
churl	circulate	clamshell	clergyman	clot	coaming	cockswain
churlish	circus	clamworm	cleric	clotty	coarctate	cocktail
churn	cirque	clan	clerical	cloth	coarse	coco
churr	cirrate	clang	clerisy	clothe	coarsen	cocoa
chute	cirri	clangour	clerk	clothier	coast	cocoanut
chutney	cirriped	clank	clerkship	cloture	coastal	cocobolo
chyle	cirrous	clannish	cleveite	cloud	coastward	cocograss
chylous	cirrus	clanship	clever	cloudland	coastways	coconut
chyme	cirsoid	clansman	clevis	cloudless	coastwise	cocoon
chymify	cirsotomy	clap	clew	cloudlet	coat	cocotte
chymosin	cisalpine	clapboard	cliché	cloudy	coati	coction
chymous	cisco	claque	click	clough	coatless	cod
cibol	cissoid	clarence	cliency	clout	coax	coda
ciboria	cist	clarendon	client	clove	coaxal	coddle
ciborium	cistern	claret	clientage	cloven	coaxial	code
cicada	cistus	clarify	cliental	clover	cob	codeia
cicadae	cistvaen	clarinet	clientele	clovetree	cobalt	codein
cicadas	citadel	clarion	cliff	clown	cobaltic	codex
cicatrice	cital	clarionet	climatal	clownery	cobaltite	codices
cicatrix	citation	clarity	climate	clownish	cobaltous	codicil
cicatrize	citatory	clary	climatic	clownism	cobble	codify
cicely	cite	clash	climax	cloy	coble	codling
cicerone	cithara	clasp	climactic	club	cobnut	codpiece
cicerones	cither	class	climb	clubfoot	cobra	coenzym
ciceroni	cithern	classic	clime	clubgrass	cobweb	coenzyme
cichlid	citied	classical	clinch	clubhand	cobwebby	coequal
cider	citified	classify	cline	clubhaul	cobwork	coerce
cigar	citizen	classis	cling	clubmoss	cocain	coercion
cigaret	citizenry	classmate	clinic	cluck	cocaine	coercive
cigarette	citral	classroom	clinical	clue	cocainism	coeternal
cilia	citrange	clastic	clinician	clump	cocainize	coeval
ciliary	citrate	clatter	clinique	clumpish	cocci	coexist
ciliate	citreous	clause	clink	clumpy	coccoid	coextend
cilice	citric	claustral	clinquant	clumsy	coccus	coffee
cilicious	citrin	clausura	clintonia	clung	coccygeal	coffer
ciliolate	citrine	clavate	clip	clupeid	coccyges	cofferdam
cilium	citron	clavated	clique	clupeoid	coccyx	coffin
cimices	citrous	clavecin	cliquey	cluster	cochineal	coffle
cimex	citrus	clavicle	cliquish	clustery	cochlea	cog
cinch	cittern	clavicorn	cliquy	clutch	cochleae	cogency
cinchona	city	clavier	clistase	clutter	cochlear	cogent
cinchonic	cityfied	claviform	clitoris	clypeate	cochleate	cogitable
cincture	cityward	claw	clivers	clypei	cock	cogitate

cognac	college	coly	communize	concerto	congeal	constrict
cognate	collegial	colza	commutual	conch	congener	construct
cognation	collegian	coma	commutate	concha	congenial	contrue
cognition	collet	comal	commute	conchoid	conger	consul
cognitive	collide	comate	comose	concierge	congeries	consular
cognizant	collie	comatose	comous	concise	congest	consulate
cognize	collier	comatous	compact	concision	conglobe	consult
cognomen	colliery	comatula	compadre	conclave	congo	consume
cognomens	colligate	comatulid	companion	conclude	congou	contact
cognomina	collimate	comb	company	concoct	congress	contagia
cogon	collinear	combat	compare	concord	congreve	contagion
cogwheel	collinsia	combatant	compart	concordat	congruent	contagium
cohabit	collision	combative	compass	concourse	congruity	contain
cohere	collocate	combine	compeer	concrete	congruous	contemn
coherence	collodion	combust	compel	concubine	congu	contempt
coherency	collodium	comby	compend	concur	conic	contend
coherent	colloid	come	compendia	concuss	conical	content
cohesion	colloidal	comedian	compete	condemn	conid	contented
cohesive	collop	comedo	competent	condense	conidial	contest
cohobate	colloquy	comedones	compile	condign	conidium	context
cohort	collotype	comedy	complain	condiment	conifer	continent
cohosh	collotypy	comely	complaint	condition	coniferin	continua
cohune	collude	comet	complect	condole	coniine	continual
coif	collusion	cometary	complete	condone	conium	continue
coiffure	collusive	cometic	complex	condor	conjoin	continuum
coign	collyrium	comfit	complexus	conduce	conjoint	contort
coil	colocynth	comfiture	compliant	conducent	conjugal	contour
coin	cologne	comfort	complin	conducive	conjugant	contract
coinage	colon	comfrey	compline	conduct	conjugate	contralti
coincide	colonic	comic	complot	conduit	conjunct	contralto
coinsure	colonel	comical	compluvia	condylar	conjure	contrary
coir	colonelcy	comitatus	comply	condyle	conjury	contrast
coition	colonial	comitia	compo	condyloid	connate	contrite
coitus	colonist	comitial	component	condyloma	connation	contrive
coke	colonitis	comitium	compony	cone	connaught	control
col	colonize	comity	comport	conepate	connect	contumacy
cola	colonnade	comma	compose	conepatl	connive	contumely
colander	colony	command	composite	coney	connivent	contuse
colanut	colophon	commandry	compost	confer	connotate	contusion
colcannon	colophony	commence	composure	conferee	connote	contusive
colchicum	colorado	commend	compote	conferva	connubial	conundrum
colcothar	colorific	commensal	compound	conferval	conoid	convector
cold	colossal	comment	comprador	confess	conoidal	convene
coldframe	colossi	commerce	compress	confest	conoidic	convent
cole	colossus	commerge	comprisal	confetti	conquer	converge
coleslaw	colostrum	commingle	comprise	confidant	conquest	converse
colessee	colotomy	comminute	compute	confide	conquian	convert
colessor	colour	commissar	computist	confident	conscious	convex
coleus	colourful	commit	comrade	configure	conscript	convexity
colewort	colourist	committal	comradery	confine	consensus	convey
colic	colourless	committee	con	confirm	consent	convict
colicky	colt	commix	conation	confirmee	conserve	convince
colin	colter	commode	conative	confiture	consider	convivial
colitis	coltish	commodity	conatural	conflate	consign	convoke
collage	coltsfoot	commodore	conatus	conflict	consignee	convolute
collagen	colubrine	common	concave	conflux	consist	convolve
collapse	colugo	commonage	concavity	confluent	consocies	convoy
collar	columbiad	commoner	conceal	confocal	console	convulse
collard	columbine	commons	concede	conform	consommé	cony
collaret	columbite	commotion	conceit	confound	consonant	coo
collargol	columbium	commove	conceited	confrère	consonous	cooee
collate	columella	communal	conceive	confront	consort	cooey
collation	column	commune	concentre	confuse	conspire	cook
collative	columnar	communion	concept	confusion	constable	cookery
colleague	columned	communism	concern	confute	constancy	cookey
collect	columnist	communist	concert	conga	constant	cookie
colleen	colure	community	concerted	congé	constrain	cooky

cool	corbeil	corporate	cost	courage	coxa	crave
coolant	corbel	corporeal	costa	courant	coxalgia	craven
cooler	cord	corposant	costae	courante	coxalgic	craw
coolish	cordage	corps	costal	couranto	coxcomb	crawfish
coolie	cordate	corpse	costate	courier	coxcombry	crawl
coom	cordial	corpulent	costive	courlan	coxswain	crayfish
coomb	cordiform	corpus	costmary	course	coy	crayon
coon	cordite	corpuscle	costume	court	coyish	craze
cooncan	cordoba	corrade	cosy	courteous	coyote	crazed
coontie	cordon	corral	cot	courtesan	coyotillo	crazy
coop	cordovan	corrasion	cotangent	courtesy	coypu	creak
cooper	corduroy	correct	cote	courtezan	coypou	creaky
cooperage	cordwain	correlate	cotenancy	courtier	coz	cream
cooperate	cordwood	corridor	cotenant	courtleet	cozen	creamcups
coopery	cordy	corrival	cotenure	courtlike	cozenage	creamer
coopt	core	corrode	coterie	courtly	cozy	creamery
cooptate	coreless	corrodent	cothurn	courtroom	craal	creamy
coordinal	coreopsis	corrody	cothurnal	courtship	crab	crease
coot	coreplasty	corrosion	cothurni	courtyard	crabby	creasy
cooter	corf	corrosive	cothurnus	cousin	crabgrass	create
cop	corgi	corrugant	cotidal	cousinry	crabstick	creatine
copaiba	coriander	corrugate	cotillion	couteau	crack	creation
copaiva	coria	corrupt	cotillon	couteaux	crackle	creative
copal	corium	corsage	cotta	coutel	cracknel	creatural
copalm	cork	corsair	cottae	couvade	cradle	creature
cope	corkage	corselet	cottas	covalence	craft	crèche
copeck	corkscrew	corset	cottabus	covalent	craftsman	credence
copepod	corkwood	corslet	cottage	cove	crafty	credenda
copepodan	corkiness	cortège	cottager	covenant	crag	credendum
copestone	corky	cortex	cotter	cover	cragged	credible
copious	corm	cortical	cottier	coverage	craggy	credit
copped	cormi	corticate	cottise	coverlet	cragsman	credo
copper	cormorant	cortices	cottised	coverlid	crake	credulity
copperas	cormus	corticose	cotton	covert	cram	credulous
coppice	corn	corticous	cottony	coverture	crambo	creed
copra	cornbread	cortina	cotyledon	covet	cramp	creek
copraemia	corncob	cortinae	cotyloid	covetous	crampfish	creel
copraemic	corncrib	corundum	couch	covey	crampon	creep
copremia	cornea	coruscate	couchant	coving	cranberry	creepy
copremic	corneal	coruscant	coucher	cowage	cranch	cremate
coprolite	cornel	corvée	couching	cowalker	crandall	cremation
copse	cornelian	corves	cougar	coward	crane	crematory
copula	corneous	corvet	cough	cowardice	cranebill	cremocarp
copular	corner	corvette	could	cowbane	cranefly	crenate
copulate	cornet	corvine	coulee	cowbell	crania	crenated
copy	cornetcy	corymb	coulisse	cowberry	cranial	crenation
copybook	cornfield	corymbose	couloir	cowbind	craniate	crenature
copycat	cornice	corymbous	coulomb	cowbird	cranium	crenel
copygraph	cornmeal	coryphei	coulter	cowboy	crank	crenelate
copyhold	cornus	corypheus	coumaric	cower	crankcase	crenelle
copyist	cornute	coryza	coumarin	cowfish	crankle	crenulate
copyright	cornuted	cosecant	coumarine	cowhage	crankpin	creodont
coquet	corny	coseismal	council	cowherb	crannied	creosol
coquetry	corody	coseismic	counsel	cowherd	crannog	creosote
coquette	corol	cosher	count	cowhide	cranny	crepe
coquille	corolla	cosinage	counter	cowl	crape	crepitant
coquina	corollate	cosine	countess	cowlick	crapefish	crepitate
coquito	corollary	cosmetic	countless	cowlstaff	crappie	crept
coracle	corona	cosmic	countrify	cowman	craps	crepuscle
coracoid	coronach	cosmism	country	cowpea	crapulent	crescendo
coral	coronal	cosmist	county	cowpilot	crapulous	crescent
coralline	coronary	cosmogony	coup	cowpox	crapy	cresol
corallite	coroner	cosmology	coupé	cowrie	crash	cress
coralloid	coronet	cosmorama	coupee	cowry	crasis	cresset
corallum	corpora	cosmos	couple	cowskin	crass	cressy
coralroot	corporal	coss	couplet	cowslip	crate	crest
corban	corporale	cosset	coupon	cowtree	cravat	crestless

cresyl	croft	crucifix	cubiform	cumulous	current	cutlet
cresylate	crofter	cruciform	cubism	cumulus	curricle	cutpurse
cresylic	cromlech	crucify	cubist	cunctator	curriery	cuttie
cretic	cromorna	crude	cubit	cuneal	curry	cuttle
cretin	crone	crudity	cubital	cuneate	currish	cutwater
cretinism	crony	cruel	cuboid	cuneated	currycomb	cutworm
cretonne	crook	cruelty	cuboidal	cuneatic	curse	cyanamid
crevasse	crookback	cruet	cuckold	cuneus	cursive	cyanamide
crevice	crooked	cruise	cuckoldy	cuneiform	cursorial	cyanate
creviced	crookneck	cruller	cuckoldry	cuniculus	cursory	cyanic
crew	crool	crumb	cuckoo	cunner	curt	cyanide
crewel	croon	crumble	cucullate	cunning	curtail	cyanin
crib	crop	crumbly	cucumber	cup	curtain	cyanine
cribbage	croquet	crumby	cucurbit	cupbearer	curtate	cyanite
cribbite	croquette	crump	cucurbite	cupboard	curtation	cyanize
cribbiter	crore	crumpet	cud	cupcake	curtilage	cyanogen
cribble	crosier	crumple	cudbear	cupel	curtsey	cyanopia
cribwork	cross	crunch	cuddle	cupful	curtsy	cyanopsia
crick	crossbar	crunodal	cuddy	cupidity	curule	cyanopsis
cricket	crossbill	crunode	cudgel	cupola	curvate	cyanotic
cricoid	crossbow	crupper	cudweed	cuppy	curvated	cyanotype
cried	crossbred	crura	cue	cupreous	curvation	cyanuric
crime	crossbun	crural	cuerpo	cupric	curvature	cybotaxis
criminal	crosscut	crus	cuff	cuprite	curve	cycad
criminate	crossfire	cruisade	cuirass	cuprous	curvet	cyclamen
crimmer	crossfoot	cruse	cuish	cupshake	curvity	cycle
crimp	crosshair	cruset	cuisine	cupule	cusec	cyclic
crimpage	crosshead	crush	culch	cur	cushat	cyclical
crimpy	crossjack	crust	culet	curacy	cushaw	cyclist
crimson	crosslet	cruster	culets	curara	cushion	cyclogiro
cringe	crossroad	crustose	culettes	curare	cushiony	cycloid
cringle	crossruff	crusty	culinary	curari	cusk	cycloidal
crinite	crosstree	crutch	cull	curarize	cusp	cyclone
crinkle	crossway	crutched	cullender	curassow	cusped	cyclonic
crinoid	crosswise	crux	cullet	curate	cuspated	cyclorama
crinoidea	crotali	cruxes	cullion	curative	cuspidal	cyclosis
crinoline	crotaline	cruzado	cullis	curator	cuspidate	cyclotron
crinum	crotalus	cry	cully	curb	cuspid	cygneous
cripple	crotch	cryogen	culm	curbstone	cuspidor	cygnet
crises	crotched	cryogenic	culmen	curculio	cusso	cylinder
crisis	crotchet	cryolite	culminal	curculios	custard	cylindric
crisp	crotchety	cryometer	culminate	curcuma	custodial	cylix
crispate	croton	cryoscope	culotte	curcumin	custodian	cyma
crispated	crouch	cryoscopy	culottes	curcumine	custody	cymae
crissal	croup	cryostat	culpa	curd	custom	cymatia
crissum	croupe	crypt	culpable	curdle	customary	cymatium
cristate	croupier	cryptic	culprit	curdly	customer	cymbal
cristated	croupous	cryptical	cult	curdy	custodes	cymbalist
criteria	croupy	cryptogam	cultch	cure	custos	cymbling
criterion	crouton	cryptonym	cultigen	cureless	custumal	cyme
critic	crow	crystal	cultivate	curettage	cut	cymene
critical	crowbar	crystallic	cultrate	curette	cutaneous	cymlin
criticism	crowberry	crystule	cultrated	curfew	cutaway	cymling
criticize	crowd	ctenoid	cultural	curialism	cutback	cymol
critique	crowfoot	cuarenta	culture	curialist	cutch	cymogene
crizzling	crown	cub	culturist	curie	cutchberry	cymograph
croak	crownless	cubage	culver	curiegram	cute	cymoid
croaky	crownlet	cubature	culverin	curio	cutgrass	cymometer
crocein	crowquill	cubbish	culvert	curiosity	cuticle	cymophane
crochet	croze	cubbyhole	cumber	curious	cuticula	cymoscope
crocin	crozer	cube	cumbrance	curium	cuticular	cymose
crock	crozier	cubic	cumbrous	curl	cutin	cymous
crockery	cruces	cubical	cumin	curlew	cutinize	cynic
crocket	crucial	cubicle	cumquat	curlicue	cutlas	cynical
crocodile	cruciate	cubicula	cumshaw	curlycue	cutlass	cynicism
crocoite	crucible	cubicular	cumulate	currant	cutler	cynophobe
crocus	crucifer	cubiculum	cumuli	currency	cutlery	cynosure

cypher	daimio	darksome	deaf	deciare	deerberry	deicide
cypress	daimyo	darling	deafen	decibel	deerfly	deictic
cyprinid	dainty	darn	deal	decide	deergrass	deific
cyprinoid	dairy	darnel	dealt	decidua	deerhound	deifical
cypsela	dairymaid	dart	dealfish	deciduous	deerlet	deiform
cyst	dairyman	dartars	dean	decigram	deerskin	deify
cystic	dais	dartle	deanery	decile	deerweed	deign
cystous	daisied	dartrous	deanship	deciltre	deface	deipotent
cystidium	daisy	dash	dear	decillion	defalcate	deism
cystine	dakerhen	dashboard	dearborn	decimal	defame	deistic
cystitis	dale	dasheen	dearth	decimate	default	deistical
cystitome	dalesman	dashy	death	decimetre	defeat	deity
cystocarp	dalet(h)	dastard	deathbed	decipher	defeatism	deject
cystocele	dalles	dastardy	deathblow	decision	defeatist	dejecta
cystoid	dalliance	dasyure	deathcup	decisive	defecate	dejection
cystolith	dally	data	deathful	decistere	defect	dekagram
cystotomy	dalmatic	dataria	deathless	deck	defection	dekalitre
cytase	daltonism	datary	deathlike	deckle	defective	dekametre
cytaster	dam	date	deathmask	declaim	defence	dekastere
cytogenic	damage	dateless	deathy	declare	defend	delaine
cytologic	damar	dative	debacle	declinable	defendant	delate
cytology	damascene	datolite	debar	decline	defensive	delation
cytolysin	damaskeen	datum	debark	declivity	defer	delay
cytolysis	damask	datura	debase	declutch	deference	dele
cytolytic	dame	daub	debate	decoct	deferent	deleble
cytometer	damewort	daubery	debauch	decoction	defiance	delible
cytophagy	damiana	daubry	debauchee	decode	defiant	delectate
cytophil	dammar	dauby	debenture	decollate	deficit	delegacy
cytoplasm	dammer	daughter	debility	decolour	defilade	delegant
cytoplast	damn	daunt	debit	decompose	defile	delegate
czar	damnation	dauntless	debonair	decorate	define	delete
czardom	damnatory	dauphin	debonaire	decorous	definite	deletion
czarevna	damnify	dauphine	debouch	decorum	deflate	delft
czarina	damp	davenport	debris	decoy	deflation	delicacy
czaritza	dampen	davit	debt	decrease	deflect	delicate
czarism	dampish	daw	debtor	decree	deflector	delicious
	damsel	dawdle	debut	decrement	deflex	delict
	damson	dawn	decade	decrepit	deflexion	delight
	dance	day	decadence	decretal	deflexure	delimit
D	dandelion	daybook	decadent	decretive	deflorate	delineate
	dander	daybreak	decagon	decretory	deflower	deliriant
dab	dandify	daydream	decagonal	decry	defluxion	delirious
dabble	dandle	dayfly	decagram	decuman	defoliate	delirium
dabchick	dandruff	daylight	decalcify	decumbent	deforce	deliver
dace	dandy	daylily	decalitre	decuple	deforest	delivery
dachshund	dandyish	daylong	decameter	decurion	deform	dell
dacite	dandyism	dayspring	decamp	decurrent	deformity	delouse
dactyl	danewort	daystar	decanal	decurve	defoul	delphinic
dactylate	danger	daytime	decane	decury	defraud	delta
dactylic	dangerous	daze	decant	decussate	defray	deltaic
dactylion	dangle	dazzle	decapod	dedans	defrock	deltoid
dactylium	dank	deacon	decapodal	dedicate	defrost	delude
dad	dankish	deaconry	decare	deduce	deft	deluge
daddy	danseuse	deaconess	decastere	deducive	deftness	delusion
dado	dap	dead	decathlon	deduct	defunct	delusive
dadoes	daphne	deadbeat	decay	deduction	defy	delusory
daduchi	dapple	deaden	decease	deductive	degas	delve
daduchus	dare	deadeye	decedent	dee	degauss	demagog
daffodil	daredevil	deadfall	deceit	deed	degrade	demagogic
daft	dareful	deadhead	deceitful	deedful	degree	demagogue
dag	daric	deadhouse	deceive	deedless	degum	demagogy
dagger	daring	deadlight	decemvir	deem	degust	demand
daggle	dark	deadline	decemviri	deemster	degustate	demandant
daglock	darken	deadlock	decency	deep	dehisce	demarch
dahlia	darkish	deadly	decent	deepmost	dehiscent	deme
dahoon	darkle	deadman	decentre	deepen	dehorn	demean
daily	darkroom	deadwood	decern	deer	dehydrate	demeanou r

dement	dentist	derm	detentive	dextrad	diaphysis	dieback
dementia	dentistry	derma	deter	dextral	diarchy	diecious
demerit	dentition	dermal	deterrent	dextrin	diarist	diereses
demersed	dentoid	dermatoid	deterge	dextrine	diarrh(o)ea	dieresis
demesne	denture	dermic	detergent	dextrose	diarrh(o)eal	dieretic
demigod	denudate	dermis	determine	dextrous	diarrh(o)eic	diesis
demijohn	denude	dermoid	detersion	dey	diary	diestock
demilune	deny	derogate	detersive	dharna	diaspore	diet
demise	deodand	derrick	detest	dhoti	diastase	dietary
demission	deodar	derrid	dethrone	dhoora	diastasic	dietetic
demit	deodorant	derringer	detinue	dhooti	diastatic	dietetics
demitasse	deodorize	derris	detonate	dhourra	diaster	dietetist
demiurge	deoxidize	derry	detorsion	dhow	diastole	dietician
demivolt	deoxidate	dervish	detour	dhu	diastolic	differ
demiwolf	depart	descant	detract	diabase	diathermy	different
democracy	departure	descend	detrain	diabasic	diathesis	difficile
democrat	depasture	descent	detriment	diabetes	diathetic	difficult
demolish	depend	describe	detrition	diabetic	diatom	diffident
demon	dependant	descry	detritus	diablerie	diatomic	diffract
demoniac	dependent	desecrate	detrital	diablery	diatomite	diffuse
demonian	depict	deseret	detruck	diabolic	diatonic	diffusion
demonic	depiction	desert	detrude	diabolism	diatribe	diffusive
demonism	depicture	desertion	detrusion	diabolist	diazine	dig
demonist	depilate	deserve	detrusive	diabolize	diazole	digamist
demonize	depilator	desiccate	deuce	diabolo	diazonium	digamma
demotic	depilatory	design	deuteric	diachylon	diazotize	digamous
demotics	deplete	designate	deuterium	diacid	dibasic	digamy
demount	depletion	desinence	deuteron	diaconal	dibber	digastric
dempster	depletive	desipient	deuton	diaconate	dibble	digenesis
demulcent	depletory	desirable	devaluate	diacritic	dicast	digenetic
demur	deplore	desire	devalue	diactinic	dicastic	digest
demure	deploy	desirous	develop	diadem	dice	digestant
demurrage	deplumate	desist	devest	diagnose	dicentra	digestion
demurral	deplume	desk	deviate	diagnosis	dicerous	digestive
demy	depolarize	desman	deviation	diagonal	dichasial	digit
den	depone	desmid	deviatory	diagram	dichasium	digital
denarrii	deponent	desmidian	device	diagraph	dichlorid	digitalin
denarius	depopulate	desmoid	devil	dial	dichogamy	digitalis
denary	deport	desolate	devilfish	dialect	dichotomy	digitate
denature	deportee	despair	devilish	dialectal	dichroic	digitoxin
dendrite	deposal	despatch	devilkin	dialectic	dichroism	diglot
dendritic	depose	desperado	devilry	dialist	dichroite	dignify
dendroid	deposit	desperate	deviltry	diallage	dichromic	dignitary
dendron	depot	despise	devilwood	diallist	dicker	dignity
denehole	deprave	despite	devious	dialogic	dickey	digraph
dengue	depravity	despoil	devisal	dialogism	dicky	digraphic
denial	deprecate	despond	devise	dialogist	diclinous	digress
denigrate	depredate	despot	devisee	dialogize	dicrotal	dihedral
denim	depress	despotic	devitrify	dialogue	dicrotic	dike
denitrate	deprive	despotism	devoid	dialysis	dicrotism	dilantin
denitrify	depth	despotize	devoir	dialyses	dicrotous	dilatant
denitrize	depurant	despumate	devolve	dialytic	dicta	dilatancy
denizen	depurate	dessert	devote	dialyze	dictate	dilatate
denote	depute	destine	devotee	diameter	dictation	dilatator
denounce	deputize	destiny	devotion	diametral	diction	dilate
dense	deputy	destitute	devour	diametric	dictum	dilater
density	deraign	destroy	devout	diamine	dictynid	dilation
dent	derail	desuetude	dew	diamond	did	dilative
dental	derange	desultory	dewan	diandrous	didactic	dilator
dentate	derby	detach	dewberry	dianoetic	didactics	dilatory
dentation	derelict	detail	dewclaw	dianthus	didapper	dilemma
dentel	deride	detain	dewdrop	diapason	diddle	diligence
denticle	derisible	detect	dewlap	diaper	didrachma	diligent
dentiform	derision	detection	dewy	diaphony	didym	dill
dentil	derisive	detective	dexter	diaphonic	didymium	dillantin
dentinal	derisory	detent	dexterity	diaphragm	didymous	dilly
dentine	derive	detention	dexterous	diaphyses	die	diluent

dilute	diplopic	discount	disorder	distort	dobla	dolour
dilution	diplopy	discourse	disoreint	distract	doblon	dolphin
diluvial	dipnoan	discover	disown	distrain	dobra	dolt
diluvian	dipody	discovert	disparage	distraint	dobson	doltish
dim	dipole	discovery	disparate	distrait	docent	domain
dime	dipolar	discreate	disparity	distraite	docile	domanial
dimension	dipsades	discredit	dispart	distress	docility	dome
dimer	dipsas	discreet	dispatch	district	dock	domesday
dimerism	dipsey	discrete	dispel	distrust	dockage	domestic
dimerous	dipteral	discrown	dispense	disturb	docket	domical
dimeter	dipterous	discus	dispeople	distyle	doctoral	domicil
dimethyl	diptych	discuses	dispermic	disunion	doctorate	domicile
dimetric	dire	discuss	dispermy	disunite	doctrinal	dominance
dimidiate	direct	disdain	dispersal	disusage	doctrine	dominancy
diminish	direction	disease	disperse	disuse	document	dominant
dimissory	directive	disembed	dispirit	disvalue	dodder	dominate
dimity	directly	disenable	displace	disyoke	dodge	domine
dimorphic	directory	disendow	displant	ditch	doe	domineer
dimple	directrix	disengage	display	ditheism	doeskin	dominical
din	direful	disentail	displease	ditheist	doff	dominie
dinar	dirge	disentomb	disport	dither	dog	dominion
dine	dirigible	disesteem	disposal	dithery	dogbane	dominium
dineric	diriment	disfavour	dispose	dithionic	dogberry	domino
dinero	dirk	disfigure	dispraise	dithyramb	dogbrier	dominoes
ding	dirndl	disforest	dispread	dittany	doge	dominos
dingey	dirt	disfrock	disprize	ditto	dogedom	donate
dinghy	dirty	disgorge	disproof	dittos	dogeship	donation
dingle	disable	disgrace	disproval	dittogram	dogfennel	donative
dingo	disabuse	disguise	disprove	ditty	dogfight	done
dingy	disaccord	disgust	disputant	diuresis	dogfish	donee
dinner	disaffect	dish	dispute	diuretic	dogger	donga
dinoceras	disaffirm	dishful	disquiet	diurnal	doggerel	dongola
dinosaur	disagree	dishcloth	disrate	diva	doggish	donjon
dinothere	disallow	dishclout	disregard	divagate	doggy	donkey
dint	disannul	dishelm	disrelish	divalent	doggie	donna
diobol	disanoint	disherit	disrepair	divan	dogie	donor
diobolon	disappear	dishevel	disrepute	dive	dogma	doodle
diocesan	disarm	dihonest	disrobe	diverge	dogmas	doom
diocese	disarray	dishonour	disroot	divergent	dogmata	doomsday
diode	disaster	dishpan	disrupt	divers	dogmatic	doomster
dioicous	disavow	dishwater	diss	diverse	dogmatics	door
diopside	disavowal	disinfect	disseat	diversify	dogmatism	doorman
dioptase	disband	disinfest	dissect	diversion	dogmatize	doornail
diopter	disbar	disinhume	dissemble	diversity	dogmatist	doorplate
dioptre	disbelief	disinter	dissent	divert	dogtail	doorpost
dioptric	disbosom	disject	dissever	divest	dogwood	doorsill
dioptrics	disbranch	disjoin	dissident	divide	dogy	doorstep
dioptry	disburden	disjoint	dissipate	dividend	doily	doorway
diorama	disburse	disjunct	dissocial	divine	doings	dope
dioramic	disc	disk	dissolute	divinity	doit	dopey
diorite	discal	dislike	dissolve	divinize	dolce	dor
dioritic	discalced	dislocate	dissonant	divisibly	doldrums	dorine
dioryte	discant	dislodge	disspread	division	dole	doris
diosmosis	discard	disloyal	dissuade	divisive	doleful	dormancy
dioxid	discase	dismal	distaff	divisor	dolerite	dormant
dioxide	discept	dismantle	distain	divorce	doleritic	dormer
dip	discern	dismast	distal	divorcee	dolesome	dormice
diphase	discharge	dismay	distance	divulgate	doll	dormie
diphenyl	disci	dismember	distant	divulge	dollar	dormitory
diphasic	disciple	dismiss	distaste	divulsion	dollish	dormouse
diphthong	disclaim	dismissal	distemper	divulsive	dolman	dormy
diplex	disclose	dismount	distend	dixit	dolmans	dornick
diploid	discoid	disnature	distich	dizen	dolmen	dornock
diploma	discolour	disobey	distil	dizzy	dolomite	dorp
diplomacy	discomfit	disoblige	distinct	do	dolomitic	dorsa
diplomat	discommon	disodic	distingué	doaty	dolorous	dorsad
diplopia	discord	disodium	distome	dobber	dolose	dorsal

dorsum	doze	dreamful	drow	dude	duplexity	dysentery
dory	dozen	dreamland	drown	dudeen	duplicate	dysgenic
dosage	dozenth	dreamless	drowse	dudgeon	duplicity	dysgenics
dose	dozy	dreamt	drowsy	due	dura	dyspepsia
dosimeter	drab	dreamy	drub	duel	durable	dyspeptic
dosimetry	drabble	drear	drudge	duelist	duramen	dysphagia
dossal	dracaena	dreary	drudgery	duellist	durance	dysphagic
dosser	drachm	dredge	drugget	duenna	duration	dysphasia
dossier	drachma	dreggish	druggist	duet	duresse	dysphonia
dossil	drachmae	dreggy	drugstore	duff	durian	dysphonic
dotage	drachmas	dregs	druid	duffel	during	dysphoria
dotant	draff	drench	druidess	duffer	durion	dysphotic
dotard	draffish	dress	druidic	duffle	durmast	dyspnea
dotation	draffy	dressy	druidical	dug	durr	dyspneal
dote	draft	drib	druidism	dugong	durra	dyspneic
dottel	draftsman	dribble	druidry	duiker	durst	dyspnoea
dotterel	drag	dribblet	drum	duikerbok	durum	dystaxi
dottle	draggle	driblet	drumbeat	duke	dusk	dystrophy
dotty	draghound	drift	drumfire	dukedom	duskish	dysuria
double	draghunt	driftage	drumfish	dulce	dusky	dysuric
doublet	dragline	driftwood	drumhead	dulcet	dust	dziggetai
doubloon	draglink	drifty	drumlin	dulciana	dustless	
doubt	dragnet	drill	drumstick	dulcify	dustman	
doubtful	dragoman	drink	drunk	dulcimer	dustpan	
doubtless	dragon	drip	drunkard	dulcinea	duststorm	E
douceur	dragonet	dripstone	drunken	dulia	dusty	
douche	dragonfly	drive	drupe	dull	duteous	each
dough	dragoon	driveway	drupel	dullard	dutiful	eager
doughnut	dragrope	drivebolt	drupelet	dullish	duty	eagle
doughty	dragsail	drivel	drupeole	dully	duumvir	eaglet
douzeper	dragsheet	driven	druse	dulosis	duumviral	eaglewood
dove	drain	drizzle	drused	dulotic	duumviri	eagre
dovecot	drainage	drizzly	drusy	dulse	duumvirs	ear
dovecote	drainpipe	drogue	dry	duly	duvetine	earache
dovekey	drake	droitural	dryad	dumb	duvetyn	eardrop
dovekie	drakefly	droll	dryadic	dumbell	duvetyne	eardrum
dovetail	dram	drollery	dryclean	dumbfound	dwarf	earl
dowager	drama	drolly	drydock	dummy	dwarfish	earldom
dowcet	dramatic	dromedary	dryfoot	dump	dwell	earlock
dowdy	dramatics	dromoi	drynurse	dumpish	dwelt	early
dowel	dramatist	dromon	drypoint	dumpling	dyad	earmark
dower	dramatize	dromond	dryrot	dumpy	dyadic	earn
dowerless	dramshop	dromos	drysalt	dun	dyarchy	earnest
dowery	drank	drone	drywash	dunce	dye	earphone
dowitcher	drape	drongo	duad	dune	dyestuff	earring
dowl	drapery	dronism	dual	dunfish	dyeweed	earshot
dowle	drastic	drool	dualism	dungaree	dyewood	earstone
down	draught	droop	dualist	dungeon	dying	earth
downcast	draughts	droopy	dualistic	dunghill	dyke	earthen
downcome	draughty	drop	dub	dunk	dynameter	earthling
downfall	draw	dropforge	dubh	dunlin	dynamic	earthnut
downhaul	drawback	dropkick	dubiety	dunnage	dynamical	eathstar
downhill	drawbar	dropleaf	dubiosity	dunnite	dynamics	earthward
downpour	drawbore	droplet	dubious	duo	dynamism	earthwork
downright	drawee	droplight	dubitate	duodecimo	dynamist	earthworm
downstage	drawl	dropsical	ducal	duodenal	dynamite	earthy
downtake	drawn	dropsied	ducat	duodenary	dynamo	earwax
downthrow	drawplate	dropsy	duchess	duodenum	dynamotor	earwig
downward	drawshave	dropwort	duchy	duograph	dynast	ease
downwards	drawtube	droshky	duck	duologue	dynastic	easel
downy	dray	drosky	duckbill	duos	dynasty	east
dowry	drayage	dross	duckling	duotone	dyne	eastbound
dowse	dread	drought	duckmole	duotype	dynograph	easterly
doxology	dreadful	droughty	duckweed	dupe	dysaemia	eastern
doyen	dreadless	drouth	duct	dupery	dyscrasia	easting
doyley	dream	drouthy	ductile	duple	dyscrasic	eastward
doyly	dreamed	drove	ductility	duplex	dysemia	eastwards

easy	ectogenic	effectual	élan	elk	embosom	empiric
eat	ectomere	effendi	eland	elkhound	emboss	empirical
eau	ectomeric	efferrent	elaphine	ell	embow	emplastic
eaux	ectopia	effete	elapse	ellipse	embowel	employ
eave	ectopic	efficacy	elastic	ellipses	embrace	employé
eavedrop	ectoplasm	efficient	elastin	ellipsis	embracery	employee
eaves	ectosarc	effigy	elastomer	elliptic	embranch	emporia
eavesdrip	ectrogeny	efflation	elate	ellwand	embrasure	emporium
eavesdrop	ectropium	effluence	elater	elm	embrittle	emporiums
ebb	ectropion	effluency	elaterid	elmy	embrocate	empower
ebon	ectypal	effluent	elaterin	elocution	embroider	empress
ebonite	ectype	effluvium	elaterite	eloign	embroil	empty
ebonize	ecumenic	efflux	elaterium	eloin	embrown	empurple
ebony	eczema	effluxion	elation	elongate	embryal	empyema
ebullient	edacious	effluvial	elbow	elope	embryo	empyreal
eburnated	edacity	effort	elder	eloquence	embryon	empyrean
eburnean	edaphic	effulge	eldership	eloquent	embryonal	empyreuma
eburnian	eddo	effulgent	eldest	else	embryonic	emu
ecad	eddoes	effuse	elect	elsewhere	embryos	emulate
écarté	eddy	effusion	election	elucidate	embusqué	emulation
eccentric	edelweiss	effusive	elective	elude	emeer	emulative
ecclesia	edema	eft	electoral	elusion	emend	emulgent
ecclesiae	edemata	egad	electress	elusive	emendate	emulous
ecdemic	edematose	egest	electric	elusory	emerald	emulsify
ecdysis	edematous	egesta	electrine	elute	emerge	emulsion
ecdyses	edentate	egestion	electrize	elutriate	emergence	emulsive
ecesis	edge	egestive	electrode	elvan	emergency	emunctory
echard	edgeways	egg	electron	elver	emergent	emyd
echelon	edgewise	eggcup	electrum	elves	emeritus	emyde
echidna	edgy	eggnog	electuary	elvish	emersed	emys
echidnae	edh	eggplant	elegance	elytra	emersion	en
echinal	edible	eggshell	elegancy	elytroid	emery	enable
echinate	edibility	egis	elegant	elytron	emesis	enact
echinoid	edict	eglantine	elegiac	elytrum	emetic	enactive
echinus	edictal	ego	elegiacal	em	emetine	enactory
echini	edifice	egoism	elegiast	emaciate	emeu	enalid
echo	edificial	egoist	elegist	emanant	émeute	enallage
echoes	edify	egoistic	elegit	emanate	emew	enamel
echoic	edile	egotism	elegize	emanation	emigrant	enamelist
echoism	edileship	egotist	elegy	emanative	emigrate	enamour
echolalia	edilian	egregious	element	embalm	eminence	enate
eclampsia	edilic	egress	elemental	embank	eminency	enation
éclat	edit	egret	elemi	embar	eminent	encage
eclectic	edition	egression	elench	embargo	emir	encamp
eclipse	editorial	eh	elenchi	embargoes	emirate	encase
eclipsis	educable	eider	elenchic	embark	emissary	encaustic
ecliptic	educate	eidetic	elenchus	embarrass	emission	encave
eclogite	education	eidograph	eleoblast	embassage	emissive	enceinte
eclogue	educative	eidola	eleolite	embassy	emmenin	encenia
eclosion	educatory	eidolon	elephant	embathe	emollient	encephala
ecmnesia	educe	eight	elevate	embattle	emolument	enchain
ecologic	educt	eighteen	elevation	embay	emotion	enchant
ecologist	eduction	eightfold	elevator	embed	emotional	enchase
ecology	eductive	eighth	eleven	embellish	emotive	enchoric
economic	eel	eightieth	eleventh	ember	emotivity	enchorial
economics	eelgrass	eighty	elf	embezzle	empale	enchyma
economist	eelpot	eikon	elfchild	embitter	empanel	encipher
economize	eelpout	einkorn	elfin	emblaze	empathy	encircle
economy	eelworm	either	elfish	emblazon	empennage	enclasp
écraseur	eely	ejaculate	elicit	emblem	emperor	enclave
écru	eery	eject	elide	emblemize	empery	enclavure
ecstasize	eerie	ejection	eligible	embody	emphases	enclitic
ecstasy	effable	ejective	eliminate	embolden	emphasis	enclose
ecstatic	efface	ejido	elinguid	emboli	emphasize	enclosure
ectoblast	effacive	eke	elision	embolism	emphatic	encode
ectoderm	effect	ekka	élite	embolus	emphysema	encomia
ectoenzym	effective	elaborate	elixir	emborder	empire	encomiast

encomium	endwise	enrage	entrance	ephah	epinosic	equisetum
encomiums	enema	enrapt	entrant	epharmone	epinosis	equitably
encompass	enemas	enrapture	entrap	epharmony	epiphysis	equitant
encore	enemata	enravish	entreat	ephebi	epiphyte	equites
encounter	enemy	enrich	entreaty	ephebic	epiphytic	equity
encourage	energesis	enring	entrée	epheboi	epirogeny	equivocal
encrimson	energetic	enrobe	entremets	ephebos	episcopal	equivoke
encrinite	energid	enrol	entrench	ephebus	episcope	equivoque
encroach	energize	enroll	entrepôt	ephedrin	episode	era
encrust	energumen	enroot	entresol	ephedrine	episodal	eradiate
encumber	energy	ens	entropy	ephemera	episodial	eradiation
encyclic	enervate	ensconce	entruck	ephemerae	episodic	eradicate
encyst	enervate	ensemble	entrust	ephemeral	episperm	erase
end	enface	enshrine	entry	ephemeras	epispore	erasion
endamage	enfeeble	enshroud	entryman	ephemerid	epistasis	erasure
endamoeba	enfeoff	ensiform	entryway	ephemeris	epistatic	erbium
endanger	enfetter	ensign	entwine	ephemeron	epistaxis	erect
endbrain	enfilade	ensigncy	entwist	ephod	epistle	erectile
endbrush	enfold	ensilage	enucleate	ephor	epistler	erection
endear	enforce	ensile	enumerate	ephori	epistoler	erective
endeavour	enframe	enskied	enunciate	epi	epistolic	erector
endecagon	engage	ensky	enure	epiblast	epistyle	erectores
endemial	engarland	enslave	enuresis	epibolic	epitaph	erelong
endemic	engender	ensnare	envelop	epibolism	epitaphic	eremic
endemical	engild	ensoul	envelope	epiboly	epitasis	eremite
endemism	engine	ensphere	envenom	epic	epithet	eremitic
endermic	engineer	ensue	envious	epicalyx	epithetic	eremitish
endermism	enginery	ensure	environ	epicarp	epitheton	erenow
endive	engird	entail	environs	epicedium	epitome	erepsin
endless	engirt	entangle	envisage	epicene	epitomic	ereptase
endlong	engirdle	entasia	envision	epicenism	epitomist	ereptic
endmost	englacial	entasis	envoi	epicentral	epitomize	erethism
endoblast	engorge	entastic	envoy	epicentre	epitrite	erg
endocarp	engraft	entelechy	envy	epicentrum	epizeuxis	ergo
endocrine	engrail	entellus	enwind	epicotyl	epizoon	ergograph
endocyte	engrain	entente	enwomb	epicritic	epizootic	ergometer
endocytic	engram	enter	enwrap	epicure	epizooty	ergon
endoderm	engrave	enteric	enwreathe	epicurean	epoch	ergophile
endogamic	engross	enteritis	enzootic	epicurism	epochal	ergot
endogamy	engulf	entera	enzym	epicycle	epode	ergotism
endogen	enhance	enteron	enzymatic	epidemic	eponym	erigeron
endogeny	enigma	entertain	enzyme	epiderm	eponymic	eringo
endolymph	enigmatic	enthalpy	eoclimax	epidermal	eponymist	eriometer
endometry	enisle	enthetic	eohippus	epidermis	eponymous	eristic
endomixis	enjoin	enthral	eolian	epidote	eponymy	erlking
endomorph	enjoy	enthrall	eolipile	epidotic	epopee	ermine
endopathy	enkindle	enthrone	eolipyle	epifocal	epopoeia	ermined
endophyte	enlace	enthymeme	eolith	epigamic	epopt	erode
endoplasm	enlarge	entia	eolithic	epigeal	epoptic	erodent
endoreic	enlighten	entice	eon	epigean	epos	erogenic
endorse	enlink	entire	eonian	epigene	epsilon	erogenous
endorsee	enlist	entirety	eonism	epigenous	equable	erose
endorser	enliven	entitle	eosere	epigeous	equably	erosion
endoscope	enmesh	entity	eosin	epigram	equal	erosive
endoscopy	enmity	entoblast	eosine	epigraph	equalize	erotic
endosmose	ennead	entoderm	eosinic	epigraphy	equate	erotical
endosperm	enneagon	entomb	epact	epigynous	equation	eroticism
endospore	ennoble	entophyte	eparch	epigyny	equator	erotics
endostea	ennui	entopic	eparchial	epilepsia	equerry	err
endosteum	enologist	entoptic	eparchy	epilepsy	equery	errancy
endotoxic	enology	entoptics	epaulet	epileptic	eques	errand
endotoxin	enormity	entosarc	epaulette	epilogic	equilenin	errant
endow	enormous	entotic	epaulière	epilogize	equine	errantry
endplate	enough	entourage	ependyma	epilogue	equinox	errata
endue	enounce	entrails	ependymal	epinastic	equip	erratic
endurance	enplane	entrain	epergne	epinasty	equipage	erratical
endure	enquiry	entrammel	epha	epineuria	equipoise	erratum

errhine	essoin	ethologic	eupnoea	evolve	exegesis	exoticism
erroneous	essonite	ethology	eureka	evolvent	exegeses	exotoxic
error	establish	ethos	eurhythmy	evulsion	exegete	exotoxin
ers	estacade	ethyl	euripi	evzone	exegetic	expand
ersatz	estacado	ethylate	euripus	ewe	exegetist	expanse
eruct	estafet	ethylene	europium	ewer	exegetics	expansile
eructate	estafette	ethylic	euryon	exact	exemplar	expansion
erudite	estate	etiolate	eurythmic	exaction	exemplary	expansive
erudition	esteem	etiology	eurythmy	exalt	exemplify	expatiate
eruginous	ester	etiologist	eusol	examen	exempt	expect
erupt	esterase	etiquette	eutaxic	examinant	exemption	expectant
eruption	esterify	etna	eutaxy	examine	exequatur	expedient
eruptive	esterize	étude	eutectic	examinee	exequy	expedite
eryngo	esthesia	etui	eutectoid	example	exercise	expel
erythema	esthesis	etwee	euthenics	exanimate	exergue	expellant
erythemic	esthete	etyma	euthenist	exanthema	exert	expellent
erythrean	esthetic	etymology	euxenite	exarch	exertion	expend
erythrene	esthetics	etymon	evacuant	exarchate	exertive	expense
erythrism	estimable	etymons	evacuate	excaudate	exesion	expensive
erythrite	estimably	eucain	evacuee	excavate	exfoliate	expert
erythrol	estimate	eucaine	evade	exceed	exhalant	expiable
escalade	estival	eucalpyt	evaginate	excel	exhale	expiate
escalate	estivate	eucalypti	evaluate	excellent	exhaust	expiation
escallop	estoile	eucharis	evanesce	excelsior	exhibit	expiatory
escalop	estop	euchre	evangel	excentric	exhort	expire
escapade	estoppage	euclase	evanish	except	exhume	explain
escape	estoppel	eudaemon	evaporate	exception	exigence	explant
escapist	estrange	eudemon	evasion	exceptive	exigency	expletive
escarp	estray	eudemonia	evasive	excerpt	exigent	expletory
eschalot	estriol	eudemonic	eve	excess	exigible	explicate
eschar	estrogen	eugenic	evection	excessive	exiguous	explicit
escheat	estrone	eugenical	even	exchange	exiguity	explode
eschew	estrum	eugenics	evenfall	exchequer	exile	explodent
escopet	estrus	eugenist	evensong	excipient	exilic	exploit
escopeta	estuarial	eugenol	event	excise	exist	explore
escopette	estuarian	eulogia	eventful	excision	existence	explosion
escort	estuarine	eulogious	eventide	excitant	existent	explosive
escrol	estuary	eulogism	eventless	excite	exit	exponent
escroll	esurient	eulogist	eventual	exclaim	exocardia	exponible
escrow	esurience	eulogium	eventuate	exclave	exocarp	export
escuage	esuriency	eulogize	ever	exclude	exoderm	exposal
escudo	eta	eulogy	everglade	exclusion	exodic	expose
esculent	etagère	eunuch	evergreen	exclusive	exodontia	expositor
eserine	etamine	eunuchoid	evermore	excoriate	exodus	exposure
eskar	étape	euonymus	eversible	excrement	exogamic	expound
esker	etch	eupatrid	eversion	excreta	exogamy	express
esne	eternal	eupepsia	eversive	excretal	exogen	expulsion
esophagal	eternity	eupepsy	evert	excrete	exonerate	expunge
esophagus	eternize	eupeptic	evertile	excretion	exopathic	expurgate
esoteric	etesian	euphemism	every	excretive	exorable	exquisite
espalier	eth	euphemist	everybody	excretory	exorcise	exscind
esparto	ethane	euphemize	everyday	exculpate	exorcism	exsect
especial	ethanol	euphonic	everyone	excurrent	exorcist	exsert
espionage	ether	euphonium	evict	excursion	exorcize	exsection
esplanade	ethereal	euphonize	eviction	excursive	exordia	exsertile
espontoon	etherify	euphony	evidence	excursus	exordial	exsertion
espousal	etherize	euphorbia	evident	excuse	exordium	exsiccate
espouse	ethic	euphoria	evil	execrable	exoreic	exsiccant
esprit	ethical	euphoric	evince	execrate	exosmic	exstrophy
espy	ethicize	euphotic	evincive	executant	exosmose	extant
esquire	ethics	euphrasy	evocation	execute	exosmosis	extend
ess	ethnarch	euphroe	evocative	execution	exosmotic	extensile
essay	ethnarchy	euphuism	evoe	executive	exospore	extension
essayist	ethnic	euphuist	evohe	executrix	exostosis	extensity
essence	ethnical	euphuize	evoke	executory	exostoses	extensive
essential	ethnogeny	euplastic	evolute	exedra	exoteric	extensor
essoign	ethnology	eupnea	evolution	exedrae	exotic	extent

extenuate	eyestone	faille	fang	fatidical	federacy	fenny
exterior	eyestrain	failure	fangled	fatigable	federal	fenugreek
extern	eyestring	fain	fanion	fatigue	federate	feod
external	eyetooth	faineance	fanlight	fatling	fedora	feodal
extinct	eyewash	faineancy	fano	fatten	fee	feoff
extirpate	eyewater	faineant	fanon	fattish	feeble	feoffee
extol	eyewinker	faint	fantail	fatty	feeblish	feracious
extort	eying	faintish	fantasia	fatuity	feed	feracity
extortion	eyrie	fair	fantasm	fatuitous	feedback	feral
extortive	eyry	fairground	fantasmal	fatuoid	feedbag	feretory
extra		fairish	fantasmic	fatuous	feedhead	ferial
extract		fairway	fantast	faubourg	feel	ferine
extradite		fairy	fantastic	faucal	feet	ferity
extrados	**F**	fairyhood	fantasy	fauces	feetless	ferment
extravert		fairyism	fantom	faucet	feign	fern
extreme	fa	fairyland	fanum	faucial	feignedly	fernery
extremism	fabaceous	faith	fanwort	faugh	feint	fernlike
extremist	fable	faithful	far	fault	feist	fernwort
extremity	fabliau	faithless	farad	faultless	feldspar	ferny
extricate	fabliaux	fake	faradaic	faulty	feldspath	ferocious
extrinsic	fabric	fakeer	faradic	faun	felicific	ferocity
extrorsal	fabricate	faker	faradism	fauna	felicity	ferrate
extrorse	fabulist	fakir	faradize	faunae	felid	ferret
extrovert	fabulize	falcate	farce	faunal	feline	ferrety
extrude	fabulous	falcated	farceur	faunas	felinity	ferriage
extrusion	face	falcation	farcial	faveolate	fell	ferric
extrusive	faceplate	falchion	farcical	favose	fellah	ferrite
exuberant	facet	falciform	farcy	favour	fellaheen	ferrotype
exuberate	facetiae	falcon	fare	favourite	felloe	ferrous
exudate	facetious	falconet	farewell	favus	fellow	ferrule
exudation	facette	falconry	farina	fay	felly	ferry
exudative	facial	falcula	farinose	fayalite	felon	ferryboat
exude	faciend	falderal	farm	faze	felonious	ferryman
exult	facies	faldstool	farmhand	fazenda	felonry	fertile
exultance	facile	fall	farmhouse	fealdike	felony	fertility
exultancy	facility	fallacia	farmstead	fealty	felsite	fertilize
exultant	facsimile	fallacy	farmyard	fear	felsitic	ferula
exuviae	fact	fallal	faro	fearful	felspar	ferulae
exuvial	factice	fallalery	farrago	fearless	felstone	ferule
exuviate	faction	fallen	farrier	fearsome	felt	fervent
eyas	factional	fallfish	farriery	feasance	felting	fervency
eye	factious	fallow	farrow	feasible	felucca	fervid
eyeball	factitive	false	fasces	feasibly	female	fervidity
eyebar	factor	falsehood	fascia	feasor	feme	fervour
eyebeam	factorage	falsetto	fasciae	feast	feminacy	fescue
eyebolt	factorial	falsework	fascial	feastful	femineity	fess
eyebright	factorize	falsify	fasciate	feat	feminine	fesse
eyebrow	factory	falsity	fascicle	feather	feminish	fesswise
eyecup	factotum	faltboat	fascinate	feathery	feminism	fessewise
eyeglass	factual	falter	fascine	feature	feminist	festal
eyeground	facula	fame	fascism	feaze	feminity	fester
eyehole	faculae	familial	fascist	febricity	feminize	festival
eyeing	faculty	familiar	fashion	febricula	femora	festive
eyelash	fad	family	fast	febrific	femoral	festivity
eyeless	faddist	famine	fasten	febrifuge	femur	festoon
eyelet	faddle	famish	fat	febrile	fen	festoony
eyeleteer	fade	famous	fatal	fecal	fence	fetal
eyelid	fadeless	fan	fatalism	feces	fenceless	fetation
eyepiece	faecal	fanatic	fatalist	feckless	fencible	fetch
eyeserver	faeces	fanciful	fatality	fecula	fend	fête
eyeshot	fag	fanciless	fatback	feculence	fenestra	feterita
eyesight	fagaceous	fancy	fate	feculency	fenestrae	fetial
eyesome	fagot	fancywork	fateful	feculent	fenestral	fetich
eyesore	faggot	fandango	fathead	fecund	fenestrate	fetichism
eyesplice	fahlband	fane	father	fecundate	fennec	feticide
eyespot	faience	fanfare	fathom	fecundity	fennel	feticidal
eyestalk	fail	fanfarade	fatidic	fed	fennish	fetid

fetish	fidge	filtrate	fireroom	fixate	flatware	flimsies
fetishism	fidget	fimbriate	fireside	fixation	flatways	flimsy
fetishist	fidgety	fin	firestone	fixative	flatwise	flinch
fetlock	fiducial	finable	firetrap	fixity	flatwork	flinder
fetor	fiduciary	final	firewall	fixture	flatworm	fling
fetter	fie	finale	firewater	fizgig	flaunt	flint
fettle	fief	finalist	fireweed	fizz	flaunty	flinty
fetus	field	finality	firewood	fizzle	flautist	flip
fetuses	fieldfare	finance	fireworks	fizzy	flavin	flippant
feu	fieldsman	financial	fireworm	fjord	flavism	flippancy
feuar	fieldwork	financier	firkin	flabby	flavone	flipper
feud	fiend	finback	firlot	flaccid	flavorous	flirt
feudal	fiendish	finch	firm	flag	flavour	flirty
feudalism	fierce	find	firmament	flagella	flavous	flit
feudalist	fiery	findings	firman	flagellum	flaw	flitch
feudality	fiesta	fine	firmaun	flageolet	flawless	float
feudalize	fife	finery	firn	flaggy	flawy	floatage
feudary	fifteen	finesse	firry	flagman	flax	floccule
feudatory	fifteenth	finetop	first	flagon	flaxen	flocculi
feudist	fifth	finfish	firstly	flagpole	flaxseed	flocculus
fever	fiftieth	fingent	fiscal	flagrance	flaxwort	floccus
feverbush	fifty	finger	fish	flagrancy	flaxy	flock
fevered	fig	finial	fishbolt	flagrant	flay	floe
feverfew	fight	finic	fishbone	flagship	flea	flog
feverish	figment	finical	fisherman	flagstaff	fleabane	flood
feverous	figuline	finikin	fishery	flagstone	fleam	floodgate
feverroot	figural	finis	fishgig	flail	fleawort	floor
feverweed	figurant	finises	fishgrass	flair	fleck	floorage
feverwort	figurante	finish	fishmeal	flak	fleckless	flooring
few	figurate	finite	fishnet	flake	flecky	flop
fey	figure	finitude	fishpond	flakship	flection	floppy
fez	figurine	finnicky	fishpot	flaky	fled	flora
fezzed	figwort	finny	fishpound	flam	fledge	floral
fiacre	fike	fiord	fishskin	flambeau	fledgling	florence
fiancé	filagree	fipple	fishspear	flambeaux	fledgy	floret
fiancée	filament	fique	fishway	flame	flee	floriated
fiasco	filar	fir	fishwife	flamen	fleece	florid
fiat	filaria	fire	fishy	flamenco	fleecy	floridity
fib	filarial	firearm	fissate	flamingo	fleer	florin
fibre	filarian	fireback	fissile	flamingos	fleet	florist
fibriform	filature	fireball	fissility	flammable	flench	floss
fibril	filbert	firebird	fission	flamy	flense	flossy
fibrilla	filch	fireboard	fissiped	flan	flesh	flotage
fibrillae	file	firebox	fissure	flanch	fleshpot	flotation
fibrillar	filefish	firebrand	fist	flange	fleshy	flotilla
fibrin	filet	firebrat	fistic	flank	fletch	flotsam
fibrinous	filial	firebreak	fisticuff	flannel	fletcher	flotsan
fibroid	filiate	firebrick	fistula	flannelet	fleured	flotson
fibroin	filiation	firedamp	fistular	flanque	fleury	flounce
fibroma	filibeg	firedog	fistulate	flap	flew	flounder
fibromata	filicide	firedrake	fistulous	flapjack	flewed	flour
fibrosis	filicidal	firefang	fistwise	flare	flews	flourish
fibrous	filicoid	firefly	fit	flash	flex	floury
fibula	filiform	firefoam	fitch	flashy	flexile	flout
fibulae	filigree	fireguard	fitchet	flask	flexion	flow
fibular	fillagree	firehouse	fitchew	flasket	flexional	flowage
fice	fillet	fireirons	fitchole	flat	flexor	flower
fichu	fillip	fireless	fitful	flatboat	flexuose	flowerage
fickle	fillister	firelock	fiumara	flatfish	flexuous	floweret
fico	filly	fireman	fiumaras	flatfoot	flexural	flowery
fictile	film	firenew	fiumare	flatten	flexure	flown
fiction	filmy	firepan	five	flatter	fliaum	fluctuant
fictional	filose	firepink	fivefold	flattery	flick	fluctuate
fictive	filter	fireplace	fivepence	flattish	flicker	flue
fid	filth	fireplug	fivepenny	flatulent	flickery	fluent
fiddle	filthy	firepower	fiver	flatuous	flight	fluey
fidelity	filtrable	fireproof	fix	flatus	flighty	fluency

fluff	foe	footage	forebode	forethink	forte	foxwood
fluffy	foeman	football	forebrace	foretime	fortes	foxy
fluid	foetal	footboard	forebrain	foretoken	forth	foyer
fluidal	foetation	footboy	forecast	foretold	forthwith	fracas
fluidic	foeticide	footcloth	forecited	foretop	fortieth	fraction
fluidity	foetid	footfall	foreclose	forever	fortify	fractious
fluidram	foetor	footgear	foredate	forewarn	fortis	fractural
fluke	foetus	footguard	foredeck	forewent	fortitude	fracture
flukey	fog	foothill	foredo	forewoman	fortress	fragile
fluky	fogey	foothold	foredoom	foreword	fortuity	fragility
flume	fogbow	footle	forefeel	foreyard	fortunate	fragment
fluminous	fogfruit	footless	forefelt	forfeit	fortune	fragrance
flummery	foggage	footling	forefend	forfend	forty	fragrancy
flung	foggy	footlog	forefoot	forficate	forum	fragrant
flunkey	foghorn	footloose	forefront	forgather	forward	frail
flunky	fogie	footman	forego	forgave	forwent	frailty
fluor	fogram	footmark	foregone	forge	forworn	framb(o)esia
fluoresce	fogy	footnote	foregut	forgery	foss	frame
fluoric	fogyish	footpace	forehand	forget	fossa	framework
fluorid	fogyism	footpad	forehead	forgetful	fossae	franc
fluoride	foh	footpath	foreign	forgetive	fosse	franchise
fluorin	foible	footprint	foreigner	forgive	fossick	francolin
fluorine	foil	footrest	forejudge	forgo	fossil	frangible
fluorite	foilsman	footrope	foreknow	forgone	fossilist	frank
fluorosis	foist	foots	foreknew	forgot	fossilize	franklin
fluorspar	fold	footsore	foreknown	forgotten	fossorial	frantic
flurry	folderol	footstalk	forelaid	forjudge	foster	frap
flush	folia	footstall	foreland	fork	fosterage	fraternal
fluster	foliage	footstep	forelay	forked	fostress	fraud
flustrate	foliaged	footstock	foreleg	forky	fouadin	fraudful
flute	foliar	footstone	forelock	forlorn	fought	fraudless
fluted	foliate	footstool	foreman	form	foul	fraught
fluting	foliation	footstove	foremast	formal	foulard	fray
flutist	foliature	footway	foremost	formalism	foulimart	frazil
flutter	folio	footwear	forename	formalist	foumart	frazzle
fluttery	foliolate	footwork	forenenst	formality	found	freak
fluty	foliose	foozle	forenoon	formalize	foundery	freakish
fluvial	folium	fop	forensic	formally	foundling	freaky
fluviatic	folk	fopling	forepart	format	foundry	freckle
flux	folkfree	foppery	forepast	formate	fount	freckly
fluxation	folkland	foppish	forepeak	formation	fountain	free
fluxion	folklore	for	foreran	formative	four	freeboard
fluxional	folkmoot	fora	forerank	former	fourfold	freeboot
fly	folkmote	forage	forereach	formic	fourpence	freebooty
flyblow	folkright	foramen	forerun	formicant	fourscore	freedman
flyblown	follicle	foramina	foresaid	formicary	foursome	freedom
flyboat	follow	foray	foresail	formicate	fourteen	freehand
flyframe	folly	forbad	foresaw	formless	fourth	freehold
flyleaf	foment	forbade	foresee	formula	foveate	freeman
flynet	fomes	forbear	foreseen	formulae	foveola	freesia
flypaper	fomites	forbid	foreseer	formulary	foveolae	freeze
flyspeck	fond	forbidden	foresheet	formulate	foveolate	freight
flystone	fondant	forbore	foreshew	formulism	foveole	freighter
flytrap	fondle	forborne	foreshore	formulize	foveolet	frenetic
flyweight	fondue	force	foreshow	formyl	fowl	frenum
flywheel	font	forceful	foreside	forsake	fox	frena
foal	fontal	forcemeat	foresight	forsaken	foxbane	frenzied
foam	fontanel	forceps	forest	forsook	foxberry	frenzy
foamless	food	ford	forested	forsooth	foxfire	frequence
foamy	foodstuff	fordless	forestage	forspeak	foxfish	frequency
fob	fool	fordid	forestall	forspent	foxglove	frequent
focal	foolery	fordo	forestay	forswear	foxhole	fresco
focalize	foolhardy	fordoing	forester	forswore	foxhound	frescoes
foci	foolish	fordone	forestral	forsworn	foxhunt	frescoist
focus	foolproof	fore	forestry	forsythia	foxskin	frescos
focuses	foolscap	forearm	foretaste	fort	foxtail	fresh
fodder	foot	forebear	foretell	fortalice	foxtrot	freshen

freshet	frostbite	fulfill	furfuran	**G**	galleass	ganglioid
freshman	frostfish	fulgency	furfurane		galleon	gangplank
fret	frostweed	fulgent	furfures	gab	gallery	gangrene
fretful	frostwork	fulgid	furfurol	gabardine	gallfly	gangster
fretty	frostwort	fulgurate	furibund	gabble	galliard	gangue
fretwork	frosty	fulgurite	furious	gabbro	gallic	gangway
friable	froth	fulgurous	furl	gabbroid	gallinazo	ganister
friar	frother	fulham	furlong	gabel	gallinule	gannet
friarbird	frothy	full	furlough	gabelle	galliot	gannister
friary	frounce	fullam	furmenty	gabelled	gallipot	ganoid
fribble	frouzy	fuller	furmety	gaberdine	gallium	gantlet
fricassee	frow	fullery	furmity	gabion	galliwasp	gantline
fricative	froward	fully	furnace	gabionade	gallnut	gantlope
friction	frown	fulmar	furnish	gable	gallon	gantry
friend	frowzled	fulminant	furniture	gad	gallonage	gap
frieze	frowzy	fulminate	furor	gadabout	galloon	gape
frigate	froze	fulmine	furore	gadbee	gallop	gapeseed
fright	frozen	fulminic	furrier	gadfly	gallopade	gapeworm
frighten	fructify	fulminous	furriery	gadid	gallows	gappy
frightful	fructose	fulsome	furrow	gadoid	gallowses	gapy
frigid	fructuous	fulvous	furry	gadroon	gallstone	gar
frigidity	frugal	fumaric	further	gadsman	gallus	garage
frijol	frugality	fumarole	furthest	gadwall	galop	garb
frijole	frugally	fumatoria	furtive	gaff	galopade	garbage
frijoles	fruit	fumatory	furuncle	gaffer	galore	garbel
frill	fruitage	fumble	fury	gaffle	galosh	garble
frilly	fruiter	fume	furze	gag	galoshe	garboard
fringe	fruitful	fumet	furzy	gage	galvanic	gardant
fringy	fruition	fumette	fusain	gaggle	galvanism	garden
fripper	fruitless	fumigant	fuscous	gagman	galvanist	gardenia
frippery	fruity	fumigate	fuse	gahnite	galvanize	garderobe
frisette	frumenty	fumitory	fusee	gaiety	galyak	garfish
friseur	frump	fumulus	fusel	gaily	gam	garganey
frisk	frumpish	fumy	fuselage	gain	gamb	garget
frisky	frumpy	fun	fusiform	gainful	gamba	gargle
frit	frusta	function	fusil	gainless	gambade	gargoyle
frith	frustrate	fund	fusilade	gainly	gambado	gargoyled
fritter	frustule	fundament	fusile	gainsaid	gambadoes	garibaldi
frivolity	frustum	funeral	fusillade	gainsay	gambados	garish
frivolous	frustums	funereal	fusion	gairish	gambit	garishly
friz	fruticose	funest	fusionism	gait	gamble	garland
frizette	fry	fungal	fusionist	gaited	gamboge	garlic
frizz	fuadin	fungi	fuss	gala	gambol	garlicky
frizzle	fub	fungible	fussy	galactic	gambrel	garment
fro	fubsy	fungicide	fust	galactose	game	garner
frock	fuchsia	fungiform	fustian	galangal	gamesome	garnet
froe	fuchsin	fungoid	fustic	galantine	gamester	garnish
frog	fuchsine	fungous	fustigate	galax	gamete	garnishee
frogbit	fucoid	fungus	fusty	galaxy	gametic	garniture
frogfish	fucoidal	funguses	futhorc	galbanum	gamic	garotte
froggery	fucous	funicle	futhork	gale	gamin	garpike
froggy	fucus	funicular	futile	galea	gaming	garret
frolic	fucuses	funiculus	futility	galeae	gamma	garreteer
frolicky	fuddle	funnel	futtock	galeate	gammacism	garrison
from	fuder	funny	future	galeated	gammadia	garrote
fromenty	fudge	fur	futurism	galeiform	gammadion	garrotte
frond	fuel	furan	futurity	galena	gammation	garruline
fronded	fugacious	furane	fuze	galenite	gammon	garrulity
front	fugacity	furbelow	fuzee	galenical	gamomania	garrulous
frontage	fugio	furbish	fuzil	galingale	gamp	garter
frontal	fugitive	furcal	fuzz	galiot	gamut	gas
frontier	fugle	furcate	fuzzy	galipea	gamy	gascon
frontless	fugleman	furcraea	fyke	galipot	gang	gasconade
frontlet	fugue	furcula	fylfot	gall	ganglia	gaselier
fronton	fulcra	furculum		gallant	gangliate	gaseous
frore	fulcrum	furfur		gallantry	ganglion	gases
frost	fulfil	furfural		gallberry		gash

gasifier	gear	genotypic	gerundive	ginger	glandular	glomerate
gasiform	gearcase	genro	gesso	gingery	glandule	glomerule
gasify	gearshift	gens	gest	gingili	glandes	glonoin
gasket	gearwheel	genteel	gestate	gingival	glans	glonoine
gaskin	geck	gentes	gestation	ginglymi	glare	gloom
gasking	gecko	gentian	gestatory	ginglymus	glary	glooming
gasman	geckoes	gentile	geste	ginkgo	glass	gloomy
gasogene	gee	gentilism	gestic	ginseng	glassful	gloria
gasolene	geepound	gentility	gestical	gip	glassine	glorify
gasolier	geese	gentle	gesture	gipon	glassman	gloriole
gasoline	gel	gentleman	get	gipsify	glassware	glorious
gasometer	gelatin	gentry	gettable	gipsy	glasswool	glory
gasometry	gelatine	genuflect	geyser	gipsyish	glasswork	gloss
gasp	gelation	genuine	geyserite	gipsyism	glasswort	glossa
gassing	geld	genus	ghastly	giraffe	glassy	glossae
gassy	gelding	geobion	gherkin	girandole	glaucedo	glossal
gastric	gelid	geobotany	ghetti	girasol	glaucoma	glossary
gastrin	gelidity	geode	ghetto	girasole	glaucous	glossator
gastritic	gelsemine	geodesic	ghettos	gird	glaze	glossitic
gastritis	gelsemium	geodesist	ghost	girder	glaziery	glossitis
gastropod	gem	geodesy	ghostlike	girderage	glazy	glossy
gastrula	gemel	geodetic	ghoul	girdle	gleam	glost
gastrulae	geminate	geodic	giant	girl	gleamy	glottal
gastrular	gemmate	geognosy	giantess	girlhood	glean	glottic
gat	gemmation	geography	giantism	girlish	glebe	glottides
gate	gemmeous	geoid	giaour	giro	gled	glottis
gateage	gemmology	geologer	gib	girosol	glede	glove
gatehouse	gemmule	geologic	gibber	girt	glee	glow
gateman	gemmy	geologist	gibberish	girth	gleeful	glower
gatepost	gemot	geologize	gibbet	gisement	gleesome	glowfly
gateway	gemote	geology	gibbon	gist	gleet	glowworm
gather	gemsbok	geomancer	gibbose	gitano	gleety	gloxinia
gating	gender	geomancy	gibbosity	gitanos	glen	gloze
gauche	gene	geomantic	gibbous	gittern	glenoid	glucinium
gaucherie	genealogy	geometer	gibe	gittith	gliadin	glucinum
gaud	genera	geometric	giblet	giunta	glib	glucose
gaudery	generable	geometrid	gibus	give	glide	glucosic
gaudy	general	geometry	gid	gizzard	glimmer	glucoside
gauffer	generalcy	geophagy	giddy	glabella	glimpse	gluey
gauge	generalty	geophyte	gift	glabellae	glint	glum
gaunt	generate	geoponic	gifted	glabrate	glioma	glume
gauntlet	generic	geoponics	gig	glabrous	gliomata	glut
gauntree	generical	georgette	gigantean	glacé	gliosis	glutamic
gauntry	generous	georgic	gigantic	glacial	glissade	glutamine
gaur	geneses	georgical	gigantism	glaciate	glissandi	gluteal
gauss	genesis	geostatic	giggle	glacier	glissando	glutelin
gauze	genet	geotaxis	gigolo	glacis	glisten	gluten
gauzy	genetic	geotropic	gigolos	glad	glister	glutenous
gave	genetical	geranial	gigot	gladden	glitter	glutei
gavel	genetics	geranium	gilbert	glade	glittery	gluteus
gavelkind	genette	gerbil	gild	gladiate	gloam	glutinous
gavial	geneva	gerbille	gildhall	gladiator	gloaming	glutton
gavot	geniality	gerent	gildry	gladiola	gloat	gluttony
gavotte	genic	gerenuk	gill	gladiole	global	glyceric
gawk	genie	gerfalcon	gilsonite	gladioli	globate	glycerid
gawky	genii	gerkin	gilt	gladiolus	globated	glyceride
gay	genion	germ	gilthead	gladsome	globe	glycerin
gayety	genitival	german	gimbals	glair	globefish	glycerine
gaywings	genitive	germander	gimcrack	glaire	globin	glycerol
gaze	genitor	germane	gimel	glaireous	globoid	glyceryl
gazebo	geniture	germanium	gimlet	glairy	globose	glycin
gazeboes	genius	germicide	gimp	glamorous	globosity	glycine
gazebos	geniuses	germinant	gin	glamour	globous	glycocoll
gazehound	genocide	germinate	gingal	glance	globular	glycogen
gazelle	genom	gerontal	gingall	gland	globule	glycol
gazette	genome	gerund	gingeli	glandered	globulin	glycoside
gazetteer	genotype	gerundial	gingelly	glanders	globulous	glyph

glyphic	godparent	goosefoot	gradient	grass	grego	grivet
glyptic	godroon	gooseherd	gradin	grassland	greige	grizzle
glyptics	godrooned	gooseneck	gradine	grassplot	greisen	grizzly
gnar	godsend	goosy	gradual	grasstree	gremial	groan
gnarl	godship	goosey	graduate	grassy	gremlin	groat
gnarly	godson	gopher	gradus	grate	grenade	groats
gnarr	godwit	goral	graft	grateful	grenadier	grocer
gnash	goethite	gorge	graftage	gratify	grenadine	grocery
gnat	goffer	gorgeous	grail	gratinate	grew	grog
gnathic	goggle	gorgerin	grain	gratis	grewsome	groggery
gnathion	goglet	gorget	graine	gratitude	grey	groggy
gnathonic	goitre	gorgon	grainy	gratuity	greyback	grogram
gnaw	goitrous	gorgonea	gram	gratulant	greybeard	grogshop
gneiss	gold	gorgoneum	grama	gratulate	greyfish	groin
gneissic	goldbrick	gorgonia	gramary	graul	greyhound	grommet
gneissoid	goldbug	gorgoniae	gramarye	graupel	greyish	gromwell
gnome	golden	gorgonian	gramma	gravamen	greylag	groom
gnomic	goldeneye	gorgonias	grammar	gravamina	greyling	groomsman
gnomical	goldenrod	gorgonize	grammatic	grave	greywacke	groove
gnomish	goldfinch	gorhen	gramme	gravel	gribble	grope
gnomology	goldfinny	gorilla	grampus	graven	grid	grosbeak
gnomon	goldfish	gormand	granary	graves	griddle	grosgrain
gnomonic	goldsmith	gorse	grand	graveyard	gride	gross
gnomonics	goldstick	gorsy	grandam	gravid	gridiron	grot
gnosis	goldstone	gory	grandame	gravidity	grief	grotesque
gnostic	golf	gosh	grandaunt	gravitate	grievance	grotto
gnostical	golgotha	goshawk	grandee	gravity	grieve	grottoes
gnu	goliard	gosling	grandeur	gravure	grievous	grottos
go	goliardic	gospel	grandiose	gravy	griff	grouch
goa	golliwog	gossamer	grandma	gray	griffe	grouchy
goad	gombroon	gossamery	grandmama	grayback	griffin	ground
goadsman	gomphosis	gossip	grandsire	graybeard	griffon	groundage
goal	gonad	gossipry	grandson	grayfish	grig	groundnut
goalie	gonadal	gossipy	grange	grayish	grigri	groundsel
goanna	gonadial	got	graniform	graylag	grill	group
goat	gonadic	gothic	granite	grayling	grillage	grouse
goatbeard	gonadial	gotten	granitic	graywacke	grille	grout
goatee	gondola	gouache	granitoid	graze	grillroom	grouty
goatfish	gondolier	gouge	granivore	grazier	grilse	grove
goatherd	gone	goulash	grannie	grease	grim	grovel
goatish	goneness	goumier	grannies	greasy	grimace	grow
goatlike	gonfalon	gourd	granny	great	grimalkin	growl
goatsrue	gonfanon	gourmand	grant	greatcoat	grime	grown
gob	gong	gourmet	grantee	greaten	grimy	growth
goban	gonia	gout	grantor	greaves	grin	grub
gobang	gonidia	gouty	granular	grebe	grind	grubby
gobbe	gonidial	govern	granulate	greed	grindelia	grubstake
gobbet	gonidium	governess	granule	greedy	grindery	grudge
gobble	gonion	gown	granulite	greegree	grindle	gruel
gobies	gonium	gownman	granulose	green	gringo	gruesome
goblet	gonocci	gownsman	granulous	greenback	gringos	gruff
goblin	gonof	gownsmen	grape	greenbelt	grip	gruffish
gobstick	gonoph	graal	grapery	greenery	gripe	gruffy
goby	gonophore	grab	grapeshot	greenfly	gripy	grum
gocart	gony	grabble	grapevine	greengage	grippe	grumble
god	good	graben	graph	greenhead	grippy	grume
godchild	goodbye	grace	graphic	greenhorn	gripsack	grummet
goddess	goodish	graceful	graphical	greening	grisaille	grumose
godfather	goods	graceless	graphics	greenish	griseous	grumous
godhead	goody	gracile	graphite	greenlet	grisette	grumpy
godhood	googly	gracility	graphitic	greenling	grisly	grunion
godless	googul	gracious	graplin	greenroom	grison	grunt
godlike	gooney	grackle	grapline	greensand	grist	gryllid
godling	goop	gradate	grapnel	greenth	gristle	gryllidae
godly	gooral	gradation	grapple	greenwood	gristmill	guacharo
godmother	goosander	gradatory	grapy	greet	grit	guaiac
godown	goose	grade	grasp	gregarine	gritty	guaiacol

guaiacum	gulf	gymnast	hade	halcyon	handiwork	harmful
guan	gulfweed	gymnastic	hadj	hale	handle	harmless
guanaco	gulfy	gynaecea	hadjee	haler	handlebar	harmonic
guanase	gull	gynaeceum	hadji	half	handless	harmonica
guanidin	gullet	gynander	h(a)emin	halfback	handmaid	harmonics
guanidine	gullies	gynandry	h(a)emoid	halfbeak	handsel	harmonist
guanin	gully	gynarchic	h(a)emolsin	halfcrown	handset	harmonium
guanine	gulp	gynarchy	h(a)emolsis	halfpenny	handsome	harmonize
guano	gum	gynics	h(a)molytic	halibut	handspike	harmony
guanos	gumboil	gynobase	h(a)emophile	halic	handwork	harmotome
guarantee	gumdrop	gynobasic	h(a)emostat	halid	handy	harness
guarantor	gumma	gynoecium	hafiz	halide	hang	harp
guaranty	gummata	gynophore	hafnium	halidom	hangar	harpings
guard	gummatous	gyp	haft	halite	hangbird	harpins
guardian	gummosis	gypseous	hag	halitosis	hangdog	harpist
guardrail	gummous	gypsum	hagadic	hall	hangfire	harpoon
guardroom	gummy	gypsy	hagberry	halliard	hangman	harpy
guardsman	gumshoe	gyral	hagbush	hallmark	hangnail	harquebus
guava	gumwood	gyrant	hagbut	hallo	hangwire	harridan
guayule	gun	gyrate	hagdel	halloa	hank	harrow
gudgeon	gunboat	gyration	hagden	halloo	hanker	harrowing
guenon	guncotton	gyratory	hagdon	hallow	hanse	harry
guerdon	gunfire	gyre	hagfish	halluces	hansel	harsh
guernsey	gunflint	gyrfalcon	haggadic	hallux	hansom	harshen
guerrilla	gunlock	gyro	haggadist	hallway	hanuman	harslet
guess	gunman	gyron	haggard	halm	hap	hart
guesswork	gunnel	gyroplane	haggis	halma	haphazard	hartal
guest	gunnery	gyroscope	haggish	halo	hapless	hart(e)bees
guff	gunny	gyrostat	haggle	halobios	haplite	hartshorn
guffaw	gunpaper	gyri	hagiarchy	halogen	haplitic	haruspex
gugal	gunpowder	gyrus	hagiology	haloid	haploid	haruspicy
gugul	gunroom	gyve	haglet	halophyte	haploidic	harvest
guha	gunrunner		haglin	halt	haploidic	has
guidance	gunshot		hagseed	halting	haplosis	hash
guide	gunsmith		hah	halter	haply	hasheesh
guidebook	gunstock	**H**	haik	halteres	happen	hashish
guidepost	gunwale		hail	halve	happy	haslet
guiderope	guppy	ha	haily	halves	haptera	haslock
guideway	gurge	haaf	hailstone	halyard	haptere	hasp
guidon	gurgle	haak	hailstorm	ham	hapteron	hassock
guild	gurglet	habanera	hair	hamadryad	harangue	hast
guilder	gurnard	habendum	hairbird	hamburger	harass	hastate
guildhall	gurnet	habergeon	hairbrush	hame	harbinger	haste
guildry	gush	habile	haircloth	hamlet	harbour	hasten
guildship	gushy	habit	haircut	hammer	hard	hasty
guildsman	gusset	habitancy	hairless	hammertoe	harden	hat
guile	gust	habitant	hairline	hammock	hardhack	hatband
guileful	gustation	habitat	hairpin	hammy	hardhead	hatbox
guileless	gustative	habitual	hairseal	hamper	hardihood	hatch
guillemot	gustatory	habituate	hairshirt	hamster	hardly	hatchway
guilloche	gusto	habitude	hairspace	hamstring	hardpan	hatchel
guillotine	gusty	habitué	hairworm	hamulate	hards	hatchery
guilt	gut	habu	hairy	hamuli	hardshell	hatchet
guiltless	gutta	hachure	haj	hamulus	hardship	hate
guilty	guttae	hacienda	haje	hanaper	hardtack	hateful
guimpe	guttate	hack	haji	hance	hardware	hath
guinea	guttated	hackberry	hajj	hand	hardwood	hatred
guipure	gutte	hackbut	hajji	handbag	hardy	hatteria
guise	guttee	hackee	hake	handball	hare	hauberk
guitar	gutty	hackery	hakeem	handbill	harebell	haughty
guitguit	guttery	hackle	hakem	handbook	harelip	haul
gula	guttural	hackly	hakim	handcuff	harem	haulage
gulae	guy	hackman	halachist	handed	haricot	haulm
gulash	guzzle	hackney	halation	handfast	hark	haulmy
gulch	gybe	hacksaw	halbard	handful	harken	haulyard
gulden	gymbals	had	halberd	handgrip	harl	haunch
gules	gymnasium	haddock	halbert	handicap	harm	haunched

haunt
haustella
haustoria
hautboy
hauteur
have
havelock
haven
haverel
haversack
haversine
havoc
havocked
havocking
haw
hawfinch
hawk
hawkbill
hawkweed
hawse
hawser
hawthorn
hay
haycock
hayfork
hayloft
haymaker
haymow
hayrack
hayrick
hayseed
haystack
hayward
hazard
hazardous
haze
hazel
hazelly
hazelnut
hazy
he
head
headache
headachy
headband
headboard
headdress
headfirst
headgear
headland
headless
headlight
headline
headliner
headlock
headlong
headmost
headphone
headpiece
headpin
headrace
headrest
headright
headsail
headset
headship
headsman

headspin
headstall
headstock
headstone
headwater
headway
headwork
heady
heal
heald
health
healthful
healthy
heap
hear
heard
hearken
hearsay
hearse
heart
heartache
heartbeat
heartburn
hearted
hearten
hearth
heartless
heartseed
heartsick
heartsore
heartsome
heartwood
heartworm
hearty
heat
heath
heathen
heathenry
heather
heathery
heathy
heaume
heave
heaven
heavy
hebdomad
hebetate
hebetic
hebetude
hecatomb
heckle
hectare
hectic
hectical
hectogram
hector
heddle
hedge
hedgy
hedgehog
hedgehop
hedgerow
hedonic
hedonics
hedonism
hedonist

heed
heedful
heedless
heel
heelpiece
heelpost
heeltap
heft
hegemonic
hegemony
hegira
hegumen
hegumene
hegumenos
hegumeny
heifer
heigh
height
heighten
heinous
heir
heirdom
heiress
heirless
heirloom
heirship
hejira
hektare
hektogram
helcosis
helcotic
heliac
heliacal
heliast
helical
helices
helicline
helicoid
helicon
heliogram
heliology
heliostat
heliotype
heliotypy
helium
helix
helixes
hell
hellbroth
hellcat
hellebore
heller
hellfire
hellhound
hellion
hellish
hellkite
hello
helm
helmet
helmeted
helminth
helmsman
helophyte
helot
helotism
helotry

help
helpful
helpless
helpmate
helpmeet
helve
hem
h(a)emal
h(a)ematal
h(a)ematein
h(a)ematic
h(a)ematin
h(a)ematinic
h(a)ematite
h(a)ematitic
h(a)ematoid
h(a)ematoma
h(a)ematose
h(a)emotosis
h(a)ematozea
h(a)ematuria
hemelytra
hemialgia
hemic
hemicrany
hemicycle
hemihedra
hemiplegy
hemipter
hemistich
hemitrope
hemlock
hemp
hempen
hempseed
hempy
hemstitch
hen
henbane
henbit
hence
henchman
hencoop
hendiadys
henequen
henequin
henhussy
henna
hennery
henpeck
henroost
henry
hepar
hepatin
hepatic
hepatica
hepaticae
hepatical
hepaticas
hepatitis
heptad
heptaglot
heptagon
heptane
heptarchy
heptode
her

herald
heraldic
heraldry
herb
herbage
herbal
herbalist
herbaria
herbarium
herbary
herbicide
herbist
herbivore
herby
herculean
herd
herdic
herdgrass
herdman
herdsman
here
hereabout
hereafter
hereat
hereby
heredity
herein
hereinto
hereof
hereon
heresy
heretic
heretical
hereto
hereunto
hereupon
herewith
heriot
heritable
heritably
heritage
heritor
heritrix
herl
herma
hermae
hermes
hermetic
hermit
hermitage
hermitic
hern
hernia
hernial
hernshaw
hero
heroic
heroical
heroin
heroine
heroism
heron
heronbill
heronry
herpes
herpetic
herpetism

herring
herse
herself
hesitance
hesitancy
hesitant
hesitate
hesp
hessian
hessite
hessonite
het
hetaera
hetaerism
hetaira
hetairai
hetairism
heterodox
heteronym
heterosis
hetman
hetmans
heuristic
hew
hewn
hexabasic
hexachord
hexad
hexadic
hexagon
hexagonal
hexagram
hexahedra
hexameral
hexameter
hexane
hexapod
hexapody
hexarchy
hexastich
hexastyle
hexone
hexosan
hexose
hexyl
hey
heyday
hiaqua
hiatus
hiatuses
hibernal
hibernate
hibiscus
hiccough
hiccup
hickey
hickory
hickup
hid
hidalga
hidalgo
hidden
hiddenite
hide
hidebound
hideous
hidrosis

hidrotic
hie
hielaman
hiemal
hierarch
hierarchy
hieratic
hieratica
hierodule
hieogram
hierology
higgle
high
highball
highboy
highland
highlight
highroad
hight
highway
hike
hila
hilarious
hilarity
hill
hillman
hillo
hilloa
hillock
hillocky
hillside
hilltop
hilly
hilt
hilum
hilus
him
himself
hind
hindbrain
hinder
hindgut
hindmost
hindrance
hindsight
hinge
hinny
hint
hip
hipparch
hippiatry
hippocras
hippus
hircine
hire
hireling
hirsute
hirudine
hirudo
hirundine
his
hispid
hispidity
hiss
hist
histamine
histidine

histioid	hoigh	homograph	hordein	hostage	huffy	hurtless
histoid	hoist	homologic	hordenine	hostel	hug	husband
histogeny	holard	homologue	horehound	hosteler	huge	husbandry
histogram	holcodont	homology	horizon	hostelry	hula	hush
histology	hold	homonym	hormonal	hostess	hulk	husk
histone	holdback	homonyme	hormone	hostile	hulking	husky
historian	holdfast	homonymic	hormonic	hostility	hulky	hussar
historic	holdover	homonymy	horn	hostler	hull	hussy
historied	hole	homophone	hornbeam	hot	hullo	husting
historify	holey	homophony	hornbill	hotbed	hum	hustle
history	holibut	homoplasy	hornbook	hotbox	human	hut
hit	holiday	homopolar	hornet	hotchpot	humane	hutch
hitch	holiness	homospory	hornless	hotel	humanism	huzza
hither	holla	homostyly	hornpipe	hotfoot	humanist	huzzah
hitherto	holland	homotaxic	hornstone	hothead	humanity	huzzay
hive	hollo	homotaxis	horntail	hothouse	humanize	hyacinth
ho	holloa	homy	hornworm	hotpot	humankind	hyaline
hoa	hollow	hone	hornwort	hotpress	humble	hyalite
hoactzin	holly	honest	horny	hotspur	humblebee	hyalogen
hoar	hollyhock	honesty	horologe	houdah	humbly	hyaloid
hoard	holm	honewort	horologer	hound	humbug	hybrid
hoarfrost	holmia	honey	horologic	hour	humdrum	hybridism
hoarhound	holmic	honeycomb	horology	hourglass	humeral	hybridity
hoarse	holmium	honeydew	horoscope	houri	humeri	hybridize
hoarsen	holocain	honeymoon	horoscopy	hourly	humerus	hybridous
hoary	holocaine	honeypot	horrent	house	humic	hydathode
hoatzin	holocaust	hong	horrible	housecarl	humid	hydatid
hoazin	holograph	honk	horrid	houseful	humidify	hydra
hoax	holophote	honoraria	horrific	household	humidity	hydracid
hob	holophyte	honorary	horrify	houseleek	humidor	hydrae
hobble	holotype	honorific	horror	houseline	humiliate	hydrangea
hobby	holozoic	honour	horse	housemaid	humility	hydrant
hobgoblin	holster	hoo	horseback	houseroom	hummock	hydranth
hobnail	holt	hooch	horseboat	housetop	hummocky	hydras
hobnob	holy	hoochinoo	horseboot	houseware	humoral	hydrate
hobo	holystone	hood	horsebot	housewife	humorism	hydration
hoboes	holytide	hoodlum	horseboy	housework	humorist	hydraulic
hobos	homage	hoodman	horsefish	hove	humorous	hydrazine
hoboism	home	hoodoo	horsefly	hovel	humour	hydrazoic
hock	homeless	hoodwink	horsefoot	hover	humous	hydric
hockey	homelike	hoof	horsehair	how	hump	hydrid
hockshop	homely	hoofprint	horsehead	howbeit	humpback	hydride
hocus	homemaker	hook	horseless	howdah	humph	hydriodic
hod	homeopath	hooka	horseman	howe	humpy	hydrocele
hodiernal	homesick	hookah	horsemint	howel	humus	hydrogen
hodograph	homespun	hookworm	horseplay	however	hunch	hydroid
hodometer	homestead	hooky	horsepond	howitzer	hunchback	hydrology
hodoscope	homeward	hooligan	horserake	howl	hundred	hydromel
hoe	homework	hoop	horseshoe	howsoever	hundredth	hydropath
hoecake	homey	hoople	horsetail	hoy	hung	hydropic
hog	homicidal	hoopoe	horseweed	hoyden	hunger	hydrops
hogan	homicide	hoopoo	horsewhip	huanaco	hungry	hydropsia
hogback	homilist	hooray	horsey	huarache	hunk	hydropsy
hogchain	homily	hoot	horst	huaracho	hunt	hydrosere
hogfish	hominy	hooves	horsy	hub	hunter	hydrosol
hoggish	hommock	hop	hortative	hubble	huntress	hydrosoma
hognose	hommocky	hopcalite	hortatory	hubbly	huntsman	hydrosome
hognut	homo	hope	hosanna	hubbub	hurdle	hydrostat
hogscore	homocercy	hopeful	hose	huck	hurds	hydrous
hogshead	homodyne	hopeless	hosier	huckaback	hurl	hydroxide
hogsucker	homogamic	hoplite	hosiery	huckabuck	hurra	hydroxy
hogtight	homogamy	hopple	hospice	huckle	hurrah	hydroxyl
hogswallow	homogen	hopscotch	hospital	huckster	hurricane	hyena
hogwash	homogene	horal	hospitia	huddle	hurry	hyetal
hogweed	homogeny	horarious	hospitium	hue	hurt	hyetology
hoicks	homogony	horary	hospodar	huff	hurtful	hygiene
hoiden	homograde	horde	host	huffish	hurtle	hygienic

hygienics	hypophyge	ideate	illation	immingle	impious	inapt
hygeist	hypoploid	ideation	illative	immission	impish	inarable
hygieist	hyposcope	ideatum	illegal	immit	implant	inarch
hygienist	hypostyle	idem	illegible	immix	implead	inarm
hyla	hypotaxis	identical	illiberal	immixture	impledge	inasmuch
hyle	hypothec	identify	illicit	immobile	implement	inaudible
hylic	hypotonic	identity	illinium	immodest	impletion	inaugural
hylicism	hyracoid	ideograph	illiquid	immodesty	implicate	inbeing
hylicist	hyrax	ideogram	illocal	immolate	implicit	inboard
hylism	hyson	ideologic	illogic	immoral	implode	inborn
hylozoic	hyssop	ideology	illogical	immortal	implore	inbound
hylozoism	hysteria	ideomotor	illume	immotile	implosion	inbreathe
hylozoist	hysteric	ideophone	illumine	immovable	implosive	inbred
hymen	hysteroid	ides	illusion	immune	impluvia	inbreed
hymeneal	hyther	idioblast	illusive	immunity	impluvium	inburst
hymenean		idiocrasy	illusory	immunize	imply	inby
hymenia		idiocy	illy	immure	impolicy	inbye
hymenium		idiograph	ilmenite	immusical	impolite	incage
hymeniums	**I**	idiom	image	immutable	impolitic	incapable
hymn		idiomatic	imagery	imp	imporous	incarnant
hymnal	iamb	idiopathy	imaginal	impact	import	incarnate
hymnist	iambi	idioplasm	imaginary	impaction	important	incase
hymnodist	iambic	idiot	imagine	impair	importune	incaution
hymnody	iambus	idiotic	imagism	impale	impose	incense
hymnology	iatric	idiotical	imagist	impall	impost	incentive
hyoid	iatrical	idiotism	imago	impalla	impostor	incept
hyoscine	ibex	idle	imagoes	impanate	imposture	inception
hypallage	ibis	idly	imam	impanel	impotence	inceptive
hyperacid	iboga	idocrase	imamate	impar	impotency	incertain
hyperbola	ice	idol	imaret	imparity	impotent	incessant
hyperbole	iceberg	idolater	imbalance	impark	impound	incest
hyper(a)emia	iceblink	idolatry	imbalm	impart	imprecate	inch
hyper(a)emic	iceboat	idolism	imbecile	impartial	impress	inchmeal
hyperpn(o)ea	icebone	idolize	imbibe	impasse	imprest	inchoate
hyp(a)ethral	icebox	idoneous	imbricate	impassive	imprimis	inchworm
hypha	icefall	idyl	imbroglio	impaste	imprint	incidence
hyphae	icehouse	idylist	imbrue	impatiens	imprison	incident
hyphal	iceman	idyll	imbrute	impatient	improbity	incipient
hyph(a)ema	icequake	idyllist	imbue	impavid	impromptu	incise
hyph(a)emia	ichneumon	idyllic	imid	impawn	improper	incision
hyphen	ichnite	idyllical	imidazole	impeach	improve	incisive
hyphenate	ichnolite	if	imide	impearl	improvise	incisor
hyphenize	ichorous	igloo	imidogen	impeccant	imprudent	incisory
hypnic	ichthyic	iglu	imine	impedance	impudence	incisure
hypnoid	ichthyoid	ignatia	imitable	impede	impudency	incitant
hypnology	icicle	igneous	imitate	impedient	impudent	incite
hypnoses	icily	ignescent	imitation	impel	impugn	incivility
hypnosis	icon	ignify	imitative	impellent	impulse	incivism
hypnotic	icones	ignite	immanacle	impend	impulsion	inclasp
hypnotism	iconic	ignition	immanence	impendent	impulsive	inclement
hypnotist	iconical	ignoble	immanency	impennate	impunity	incline
hypnotize	iconology	ignominy	immanent	imperator	impure	inclose
hypoblast	icons	ignoramus	immature	imperfect	impurity	inclosure
hypocaust	icteric	ignorance	immediacy	imperial	impurple	include
hypocotyl	icterical	ignorant	immediate	imperil	impute	inclusion
hypocrisy	icterus	ignore	immense	imperious	in	inclusive
hypocrite	ictus	iguana	immensity	imperia	inability	incogent
hypoderm	ictuses	iguanodon	immerge	imperium	inaction	incognita
hypoderma	icy	ileac	immerse	impetigo	inactive	incognito
hypogea	id	ileitis	immersion	impetrate	inaffable	income
hypogeal	ide	ileostomy	immesh	impetuous	inaidable	incomer
hypogene	idea	ileum	immew	impetus	inamorata	incommode
hypogeous	ideal	ilex	immigrant	imphee	inamorato	incompact
hypogeum	idealism	iliac	immigrate	impi	inane	incorrect
hypogyny	idealist	ilia	imminence	impiety	inanimate	incorrupt
hypomania	ideality	ilium	imminency	imping	inanition	increase
hyponasty	idealize	ill	imminent	impinge	inanity	increate

incremate	indiscrete	infantine	ingrowth	innuendo	inspirit	interject
increment	indispose	infantry	inguen	innuendos	instable	interjoin
incretion	indite	infarct	inguinal	inoculate	install	interknit
incrust	indium	infatuate	ingulf	inoculum	instance	interknot
incubate	indocile	infect	inhabit	inodorous	instancy	interlace
incubi	indole	infection	inhalant	inorganic	instant	interlap
incubus	indolence	infective	inhale	inosite	instanter	interlard
incubuses	indolency	infecund	inhalent	inositol	instar	interlay
incudal	indolent	infelt	inhaul	inotropic	instate	interleaf
incudes	indoor	infeoff	inhere	inoxidize	instead	interline
inculcate	indorse	infer	inherence	inpatient	instep	interlock
inculpate	indorsee	inference	inherency	inphase	instigate	interlope
incult	indorser	inferior	inherent	input	instil	interlude
incumbent	indow	infernal	inherit	inquest	instill	interment
incumber	indoxyl	inferno	inhesion	inquiet	instinct	intermit
incur	indraft	infertile	inhibit	inquiline	institute	intermix
incurable	indraught	infest	inhuman	inquinate	instroke	intern
incurious	indrawn	infidel	inhumane	inquire	instruct	internal
incurrent	indri	infield	inhume	inquiry	insula	interne
incursion	induce	infilter	inimical	inro	insulae	internee
incursive	inducible	infinite	inia	inroad	insular	internode
incurvate	induct	infinity	inion	inrush	insulate	interplay
incurve	inductee	infirm	iniquity	insane	insulin	interpose
incus	inductile	infirmary	initial	insanity	insulize	interpret
incuse	induction	infirmity	initiate	insatiate	insult	interrex
indaba	inductive	infit	inject	insatiety	insurance	interrule
indagate	indue	infix	injection	inscribe	insurant	interrupt
indamin	indulge	infixion	injure	insect	insure	intersect
indamine	indulgent	inflame	injurious	insectary	insurgent	intersex
indebted	induline	inflate	injury	insectean	inswathe	interstice
indecency	indult	inflation	injustice	insection	inswept	interval
indecent	indulto	inflect	ink	insecure	intact	intervale
indecorous	indurate	inflexed	inkberry	insensate	intagli	intervein
indeed	indusia	inflexion	inkhorn	insert	intaglio	intervene
indelible	indusial	inflict	inkle	insertion	intaglios	interview
indemnify	indusium	inflow	inkling	inset	intake	interwind
indemnitor	industry	influence	inkstand	insheathe	intarsia	interwork
indemnity	indwell	influent	inkwell	inshore	integer	interwove
indene	inearth	influenza	inkwood	inshrine	integral	intestacy
indent	inebriant	influx	inky	inside	integrand	intestate
indention	inebriate	infold	inlace	insider	integrant	intestine
indenture	inebriety	inform	inlaid	insidious	integrate	inthral
indevout	inebrious	informal	inland	insight	integrity	inthrall
index	inedible	informant	inlander	insigne	intellect	inthrone
indexes	inedited	infract	inlaw	insignia	intend	intima
indexical	ineffable	infringe	inlawry	insincere	intendant	intimacy
indicant	inelastic	infuriate	inlay	insinuate	intendent	intimae
indicate	inelegant	infuscate	inlet	insipid	intense	intimal
indices	inequable	infuse	inly	insipient	intensify	intimate
indicia	inept	infusion	inmate	insist	intension	intine
indicium	inequity	infusive	inmesh	insistent	intensity	intitle
indict	inerrable	ingather	inmost	insnare	intensive	intitule
indictee	inerrancy	ingenious	inn	insocial	intent	into
indiction	inerrant	ingenuity	innate	insolate	intention	intomb
indigen	inert	ingenuous	inner	insole	inter	intonate
indigenal	inertia	ingest	innermost	insolence	interact	intone
indigence	inerudite	ingesta	innervate	insolent	intercede	intrados
indigene	inexact	ingestion	innerve	insoluble	intercept	intrant
indigency	inexpert	ingestive	innholder	insolvent	intercrop	intrench
indigent	infamize	inglenook	inning	insomnia	interdict	intrepid
indignant	infamous	ingoing	innkeeper	insomniac	interest	intricacy
indignity	infamy	ingot	innocence	insomuch	interface	intricate
indigo	infancy	ingraft	innocency	insoul	interfere	intrigant
indigoid	infant	ingrain	innocent	inspan	interfold	intrigue
indigotin	infanta	ingress	innocuous	inspect	interfuse	intrinsic
indirect	infante	ingrow	innovate	insphere	interim	introduce
indiscreet	infantile	ingrown	innoxious	inspire	interior	introit

introject	inwrap	irrigable	isometric	ixodiasis	japan	jessamine
intromit	inwreathe	irriguous	isometry	ixtle	jape	jessant
introrse	inwrought	irritable	isomorph	ixtli	japery	jessed
introvert	io	irritant	isonomic	izzard	japonica	jest
intrude	iodate	irritancy	isonomy		japonism	jet
intrusion	iodation	irritate	isopathic		jar	jetsam
intrusive	iodic	irruption	isopathy		jarabe	jettison
intrust	iodide	irruptive	isophane	**J**	jarfly	jetton
intubate	iodimetry	is	isophene		jargon	jetty
intuit	iodin	isagoge	isophotic	jabber	jargonal	jewel
intuition	iodine	isagogic	isophylly	jabot	jargonize	jeweller
intuitive	iodism	isallobar	isopleth	jaboty	jargoon	jewellery
intumesce	iodize	isandrous	isopod	jacal	jarina	jewelry
inturn	iodoform	isanomaly	isopodan	jacales	jarl	jewelweed
intwine	iodol	isanthous	isopolity	jacamar	jarosite	jewfish
intwist	iodometry	isatin	isopract	jacana	jasmine	jib
inuendo	iodous	isatine	isoprene	jacaranda	jaspé	jibe
inulase	iolite	isatinic	isopropyl	jacinth	jasper	jig
inulin	ion	ischaemia	isopyre	jack	jasperite	jigget
inunction	ionic	ischaemic	isosceles	jackal	jasperize	jiggle
inundant	ionize	ischemia	isosmotic	jackass	jaspidean	jigsaw
inundate	ionone	ischemic	isospore	jackboots	jaundice	jihad
inurbane	iota	ischia	isospory	jackdaw	jaunt	jill
inure	iotacism	ischiac	isostasy	jacket	jauntily	jilt
inurn	ipecac	ischiatic	isostatic	jackey	jaunty	jimmy
inutile	ipomea	ischion	isotheral	jackie	javelin	jingal
inutility	ipomoea	ischium	isothere	jackknife	jaw	jingall
invade	iracund	isinglass	isotherm	jacko	jay	jingko
invalid	irascible	island	isothermic	jackplane	jaywalk	jingle
invariant	irate	isle	isotonic	jackpot	jaywalker	jinglet
invasion	ire	islesman	isotope	jackscrew	jazerant	jingo
invasive	ireful	islet	isotopic	jackshaft	jazz	jinn
invected	irenic	ism	isotopy	jackstay	jazzy	jinnee
invective	irenical	isobar	isotrope	jackstone	jealous	jinni
inveigh	irenics	isobaric	isotropic	jackstraw	jealousy	jinny
inveigle	irenist	isocheim	isotropy	jacky	jean	jinriksha
inveil	iridic	isochime	issuance	jacobus	jebel	jinx
invent	iridium	isochor	issuant	jaconet	jee	jipijapa
invention	iridotomy	isochore	issue	jactation	jeep	jitter
inventive	irides	isochoric	isthmian	jaculate	jeer	jitterbug
inventory	iris	isochrone	isthmus	jade	jehad	jive
inverness	irisated	isoclinal	istle	jadish	jejuna	job
inverse	irisation	isocline	it	jadite	jejune	jobbery
inversion	irised	isoclinic	italic	jady	jujunum	jockey
invert	irisitis	isocracy	italicize	jaeger	jellify	jockeyism
invertase	iritic	isocrat	itch	jag	jelly	jocko
invertin	iritis	isocratic	itchy	jaggary	jellyfish	jocose
invest	irk	isocyclic	item	jaggery	jelutong	jocosity
invidious	irksome	isogamete	itemize	jaghery	jemmy	jocular
inviolacy	iron	isogamy	iterable	jagra	jennet	jocund
inviolate	ironbark	isogenous	iterance	jaggy	jenny	jocundity
invisible	irone	isogeny	iterant	jaguar	jeofail	jodhpurs
invite	ironic	isogon	iterate	jail	jeopard	jog
invoice	ironside	isogonal	iteration	jailbird	jeopardy	joggle
invoke	ironsmith	isogonic	iterative	jalap	jequerity	join
involucel	ironstone	isogram	itineracy	jalapic	jequirity	joinder
involucra	ironware	isograph	itinerant	jalapin	jerboa	joinery
involucre	ironweed	isohel	itinerary	jalousie	jereed	joint
involute	ironwood	isohydric	itinerate	jam	jeremiad	jointress
involve	ironwork	isohyet	its	jamb	jerid	jointure
inwall	ironworks	isolate	itself	jambe	jerk	jointweed
inward	ironwort	isologous	ivied	jambeau	jerky	jointworm
inwards	irony	isologue	ivory	jambeaux	jerkin	joist
inweave	irradiant	isomer	ivorybill	jangle	jerreed	joke
inwind	irradiate	isomeric	ivorytype	janitor	jerrid	jole
inwove	irregular	isomerism	ivy	janizary	jersey	jollify
inwoven	irrigate	isomerous	ivyberry	janty	jess	jollity

jolly	jungle	kalsomine	kept	kilometre	knavish	kremlin
jolt	jungly	kalyptra	ker	kilowatt	knead	kreutzer
jonquil	junior	kamala	keramic	kilt	knee	kreuzer
jonquille	juniority	kame	keramics	kilter	kneecap	krimmer
jordanon	juniper	kampong	keratin	kimono	kneehole	krona
joram	junk	kana	keratitis	kimonos	kneel	krone
jorum	junket	kangaroo	keratoid	kin	kneepan	kronen
joseph	junkman	kaolin	keratose	kinase	kneepiece	kroner
jostle	junta	kaoline	kerb	kind	knell	kronor
jot	jupon	kaolinite	kerbstone	kindle	knelt	kroon
jougs	jura	kaph	kerchief	kindred	knew	krubi
joule	jural	kapok	kerf	kinematic	knickers	krubut
jounce	jurant	karakul	kermes	kinescope	knife	kruller
journal	jurat	karat	kermess	kinetic	knight	kryolite
journey	juratory	karma	kermis	kinetics	knightage	krypton
joust	jures	karroo	kern	king	knit	kudu
jovial	juridic	karyomere	kerne	kingbird	knives	kumiss
joviality	juridical	karyosome	kernel	kingbolt	knob	kumquat
jovialize	jurist	karyotin	kerosene	kingcraft	knobby	kunzite
jovialty	juristic	karyotype	kersey	kingdom	knobstick	kurbash
jowl	juror	kas	kestrel	kingfish	knock	kurrajong
jowled	jury	kasher	ketch	kinglet	knockdown	kuvasz
jowler	juryman	katabasis	ketchup	kingpalm	knockout	kvas
joy	jus	katabatic	ketene	kingpin	knoll	kvass
joyful	jussive	katabolic	ketone	kingpost	knop	kyanite
joyless	just	katalysis	ketonic	kingship	knosp	kyanize
joyous	justice	katalytic	ketosis	kingtruss	knot	kylix
juba	justicer	katharsis	kettle	kingwood	knotgrass	kymograph
jubate	justiciar	kathartic	kevel	kink	knothole	kyphosis
jube	justify	kathode	kex	kinky	knotty	kyphotic
jubilance	justle	kation	key	kinkajou	knotweed	
jubilancy	jut	katydid	keyboard	kino	knout	
jubilant	jute	kauri	keyhole	kinsfolk	know	**L**
jubilate	jutty	kaury	keynote	kinship	knowledge	
jubile	juvenile	kava	keystone	kinsman	known	la
jubilee	juvenilia	kavass	keyway	kiosk	knubbly	labara
judge	juxtapose	kayak	khaki	kip	knuckle	labarum
judgeship		kazoo	khalif	kipper	knur	label
judicable		keck	khamseen	kipskin	knurl	labella
judicator	**K**	keckle	khamsin	kirmess	knurly	labellum
judicial		kedge	khan	kirtle	kob	labia
judiciary	ka	keef	khanate	kish	koba	labial
judicious	kaas	keel	khirkah	kismet	kobold	labialism
jug	kab	keelhaul	kibblings	kiss	koel	labialize
jugal	kabab	keelson	kibe	kist	kohemp	labiate
jugate	kabala	keen	kiblah	kistvaen	kohl	labile
juggle	kabar	keep	kick	kit	kohlrabi	lability
jugglery	kabbala	keepsake	kickshaw	kitchen	kola	labium
jugular	kadi	keeshond	kickshaws	kite	kolanut	laborious
jugulate	kaffir	keeve	kid	kith	kolinsky	labour
juice	kaftan	kef	kidnap	kithara	komondor	labret
juiceless	kago	kefir	kidney	kitten	koodoo	labroid
juicy	kaiak	keg	kidskin	kittenish	kopeck	laburnum
jujitsu	kain	keir	kief	kittiwake	kopek	labyrinth
juju	kainite	keitloa	kier	kittool	koph	lac
jujube	kaiser	keloid	kieserite	kittul	kor	laccate
jujutsu	kakapo	kelp	kilderkin	kitty	koruna	laccolith
julep	kaki	kelter	kilim	klepht	kos	laccolite
julienne	kale	kench	kill	knack	kosher	lace
jumble	kalends	kennel	killdeer	knag	koumiss	lacerate
jumbo	keno	keno	killfish	knaggy	koumyss	lacertian
jump	kali	kenosis	killkid	knap	kousso	lacewing
jumpy	kalian	kenotic	killock	knapsack	kowtow	lacewood
junco	kalif	kentledge	kiln	knapweed	kraal	laches
junco(e)s	kalium	kephalin	kilocycle	knar	kraft	laciniate
junction	kalmia	kephir	kilogram	knave	krait	laciniose
juncture	kalong	kepi	kilolitre	knavery	kraken	

lack	lake	lande	larcener	latria	leach	legate
lackaday	laker	landfall	larcenist	latrine	leachy	legatine
lackey	lakh	landgrave	larcenous	latten	lead	legatee
lacmus	laky	landlady	larceny	latter	leadsman	legation
laconic	lallation	landless	larch	lattice	leadwort	legato
laconical	lama	landloper	lard	laud	leady	legator
laconism	lamasery	landlord	lardacein	laudanum	leaf	legend
lacquer	lamb	landman	larder	laudation	leafage	legendary
lacrimal*	lambaste	landmark	lardon	laudative	leafless	leger
lacrimary*	lambdoid	landowner	lardoon	laudatory	leaflet	leges
lacrimose*	lambency	landscape	lardy	laugh	leafstalk	leggy
lacrosse	lambent	landside	large	laughter	leafy	leghorn
lactam	lambert	landslide	largess	launce	league	legible
lactary	lambie	landslip	largesse	launch	leak	legion
lactase	lambish	landsman	larghetto	launder	leakage	legionary
lactate	lambkill	landward	largo	laundress	lean	legislate
lactation	lambkin	landwards	lariat	laundry	leant	legist
lacteal	lamblike	lane	larine	laura	leap	legless
lactean	lamboys	langrage	larithmic	laureate	leapfrog	legume
lacteous	lambskin	langrel	larithmics	laurel	leapt	legumin
lactic	lame	langridge	lark	lava	lear	lehr
lactone	lamella	language	larksome	lavabo	learn	lehua
lactonic	lamellar	languet	larkspur	lavage	learnt	lei
lactose	lamellate	languette	larrigan	lavalier	lease	leister
lacuna	lamelloid	languid	larrikin	lavalière	leash	leisure
lacunae	lamellose	languidly	larva	lavation	least	leitmotif
lacunal	lament	languish	larvae	lavatory	leather	leitmotiv
lacunar	lamia	languor	larval	lave	leathern	lemma
lacunary	lamina	laniard	larvate	lavender	leave	lemmata
lacune	laminable	laniary	laryngal	lavish	leaven	lemming
lacunose	laminae	lanital	laryngeal	lavolt	leavy	lemnisci
lacustral	laminal	lank	laryngean	lavolta	leben	lemniscus
lacy	laminar	lanky	larynges	lavolto	lecher	lemon
lad	laminaria	lanner	larynx	law	lecherous	lemonade
ladanum	laminary	lanneret	larynxes	lawful	lechery	lempira
ladder	laminate	lanolin	lascar	lawgiver	lecithin	lemur
laddie	laminitis	lanoline	lash	lawing	lectern	lemures
lade	laminose	lanose	lass	lawless	lection	lemurine
laden	laminous	lansdowne	lassitude	lawmaker	lector	lemuroid
ladino	lamp	lant	lasso	lawmaking	lectual	lend
ladle	lampad	lantana	last	lawn	lecture	lene
ladrone	lampas	lantern	lat	lawnmower	led	lenetic
ladronism	lampblack	lanthanum	latania	lawny	ledge	length
lady	lamper	lanugo	latch	lawsome	ledger	lengthen
ladybird	lampereel	lanyappe	latchet	lawsuit	ledgy	lengthy
ladybug	lampers	lanyard	latchkey	lawyer	lee	lenience
ladykin	lampion	lap	late	lax	leeangle	leniency
ladylike	lampoon	lapboard	lated	laxation	leeboard	lenient
ladylove	lamprel	lapel	lateen	laxative	leech	lenitive
ladypalm	lamprey	lapful	latency	laxity	leek	lenity
ladyship	lanary	lapidary	latent	lay	leer	lens
lag	lanate	lapidate	lateral	layer	leery	lent
lagan	lanated	lapides	laterite	layerage	leesome	lenten
lager	lance	lapidific	latescent	layette	leet	lenticel
laggard	lancelet	lapidify	latex	layman	leeward	lentigo
lagnappe	lanceolar	lapillus	lath	laywoman	leeway	lentil
lagniappe	lancer	lapis	lathe	lazar	left	lentoid
lagoon	lancers	lappet	lather	lazaret	leg	lentor
lagune	lancet	lapsation	lathery	lazaretto	legacy	lenvoy
laic	lanceted	lapse	lathwork	lazarlike	legal	leonine
laical	lancewood	lapstone	lathy	lazarly	legalism	leopard
laid	lanciers	lapstrake	latices	laze	legalist	leper
lain	land	lapstreak	laticlave	lazulite	legality	leperous
lair	landau	lapwing	latish	lazy	legalize	lepidote
laity	landaulet	larboard	latitude	lazybones	legantine	leporid

*Also spelt lachry-.

leporide	lewisite	lifeguard	limpidity	lipotropy	liturgy	lock
leporine	lex	lifeless	limpkin	lippen	lituus	lockage
leprose	lexical	lifelike	limpsy	lipstick	livable	locket
leprosy	lexicon	lifelong	limuloid	liquate	live	lockfast
leprous	li	lifetime	limulus	liquation	liveable	lockjaw
lepta	liability	lift	limy	liqueur	livelong	lockram
leptome	liable	ligament	linage	liquid	liven	locksman
lepton	liana	ligan	linalool	liquidate	liver	locksmith
leptotene	lianae	ligate	linchpin	liquidity	liveried	loco
lesion	liangle	ligation	linden	liquify	liverish	locoweed
less	liaison	ligature	line	liquor	liverleaf	locomotor
lessee	liar	ligeance	lineage	liquorice	liverwort	locular
lessen	libation	light	lineal	lira	livery	loculate
lesser	libeccio	lighten	lineament	lire	liveryman	loculi
lesson	libel	lightning	linear	liripipe	livestock	loculus
lessor	libellist	lightsome	lineate	liripoop	livid	locus
lest	libellant	lightwood	lineation	lisle	lividity	locust
let	libellee	lignaloes	lineman	lisp	livre	locution
lethal	libeller	ligneous	linen	lissom	lixivial	locutory
lethargic	libellous	ligniform	lineolate	lissome	lixiviate	lode
lethargy	libellula	lignify	liney	list	lixivium	lodestar
letter	liberal	lignin	ling	listel	lizard	lodestone
lettuce	liberate	lignite	linga	listen	llama	lodge
leu	libertine	lignose	lingam	listless	llano	lodgemen
leucaemia	liberty	ligroin	linger	lit	lo	lodgment
leucaemic	libidinal	ligula	lingerie	litai	loach	loess
leucemia	libido	ligulate	lingo	litany	load	loft
leucemic	libra	ligule	lingoes	litas	loadstar	lofty
leucin	librarian	ligure	lingua	litchi	loadstone	log
leucocyte	library	like	linguae	literal	loaf	logan
leucite	librate	liken	lingual	literary	loam	logaoedic
leucocyte	libration	likewise	linguist	literate	loamy	logarithm
leucoma	libratory	lilac	lingulate	literati	loan	logbook
leucosin	libretti	lilt	lingy	literatim	loasis	loge
leud	libretto	lily	liniment	literator	loath	loggan
leudes	librettos	lilywort	linin	literatus	loathe	loggia
leuds	libriform	limacine	link	litharge	loathful	logia
leukaemia	lice	limb	linkage	lithaemia	loathsome	logic
leukaemic	licence	limbate	linkboy	lithaemic	loaves	logical
leukemia	licencee	limber	linkwork	lithemia	lob	logician
leukemic	license	limbic	linn	lithemic	lobar	logion
leukocyte	licensee	limbless	linnet	lithesome	lobate	logistic
leukoma	lichee	limbo	linoleic	lithia	lobation	logistics
leukosin	lichen	limbus	linoleum	lithiasis	lobby	logogram
lev	lichenin	lime	linsang	lithic	lobbyism	logograph
leva	lichenose	limekiln	linseed	lithium	lobbyist	logogriph
levant	lichenous	limelight	linstock	lithoid	lobe	logomach
levanter	lichgate	limen	lint	lithoidal	lobelia	logopathy
levantine	licit	limerick	lintel	lithology	lobeline	logothete
levator	lick	limestone	linter	lithopone	loblolly	logotype
levatores	licorice	limetree	lintwhite	lithotint	lobscouse	logotypy
levators	lictor	limewater	liny	lithotomy	lobster	logway
levee	lid	liminal	lion	lithy	lobule	logwood
level	lidless	limit	lioness	litigable	lobular	logwork
lever	lidded	limitary	lionet	litigant	lobulate	loiasis
leverage	lie	limn	lionheart	litigate	lobworm	loin
leveret	lief	limnetic	lionize	litigious	local	loincloth
leviable	liege	limnology	lip	litmus	locale	loiter
leviathan	liegeman	limonene	liparoid	litotes	localism	loll
levigate	lien	limonite	lipase	litre	locality	lollipop
levirate	lientery	limonitic	lipid	litter	localize	lollypop
levitate	lierne	limosis	lipide	littery	locate	loment
levity	lieu	limousine	lipocaic	little	location	lomentum
levulin	life	limp	lipoid	littoral	locative	lone
levulose	lifeboat	limpet	lipolysis	liturgic	lochia	lonesome
levy	lifebuoy	limpid	lipolytic	liturgist	lochial	long
levyist	lifeful		lipoma		loci	longan

longboat	lounge	lug	lustrate	macaronic	magilp	majordomo
longbow	loup	luggage	lustre	macaroon	magilph	majority
longcloth	loupe	lugsail	lustrous	macaw	magistery	majuscule
longéron	lour	lugworm	lustrum	maccabaw	magistral	make
longevity	loury	lukewarm	lusty	maccaboy	magma	makebate
longevous	louse	lull	lutantrist	macchia	magmata	makepeace
longhand	lousewort	lullaby	lutation	maccoboy	magmatic	makeshift
longhead	lousy	lumachel	lute	mace	magnaflux	malaceous
longhorn	lout	lumbago	lutecium	macerate	magnate	malachite
longicorn	loutish	lumbar	lutein	machete	magnesia	malacoid
longish	louver	lumber	luteolin	machinal	magnesian	maladroit
longitude	lovage	lumberman	luteous	machinate	magnesic	malady
longshore	love	lumbrical	lutist	machine	magnesite	malaise
longsome	lovebird	lumen	lux	machinery	magnesium	malamute
longspur	loveknot	lumina	luxate	machinist	magnet	malanders
longwise	loveless	luminance	luxmeter	machree	magnetic	malapert
loo	lovelock	luminary	luxuriant	mac(k)intosh	magnetics	malar
loof	lovelorn	luminesce	luxuriate	mackerel	magnetism	malaria
loofah	lovesick	luminous	luxurious	mackinaw	magnetite	malarial
look	lovesome	lummox	luxury	mackle	magnetize	malarian
loom	lovevine	lump	lyceum	macle	magneto	malarious
loon	low	lumpfish	lychnis	macramé	magnetron	malate
loony	lowermost	lumpish	lycopod	macrocosm	magnific	malax
loop	lowery	lumpy	lyddite	macroyst	magnifico	malaxate
loophole	lowland	luna	lye	macrodome	magnify	male
loopy	lowly	lunacy	lymph	macrogamy	magnitude	malefic
loose	lown	lunar	lymphatic	macron	magnolia	maleic
loosen	loxodromy	lunarian	lymphoid	macropia	magnum	malemute
loot	loyal	lunary	lyncean	macropsia	magot	malformed
looves	loyalism	lunate	lynch	macrural	magpie	malic
lop	loyalist	lunatic	lynx	macruran	maguey	malice
lope	loyalty	linatical	lyophil	macruroid	maharaja	malicious
loppy	lozenge	lunation	lyophile	macrurous	maharajah	malign
loquat	lozenger	lunch	lyophilic	mactation	maharanee	malignant
lord	lubber	luncheon	lyophobe	macula	maharani	malignity
lordling	lubricant	lune	lyophobic	maculae	mahatma	maline
lordoma	lubricate	lunet	lyotropic	maculate	mahlstick	malines
lordosis	lubricity	lunette	lyrate	macule	mahogany	malinger
lordotic	lubricous	lung	lyre	mad	mahout	malison
lordship	lucarne	lunge	lyrebird	madam	maid	mall
lore	luce	lungfish	lyric	madcap	maiden	mallard
lorgnette	lucency	lungee	lyrical	madden	maidhood	malleable
lorica	lucent	lungi	lyricism	maddish	maieutic	malleate
loricae	lucern	lungworn	lyriform	made	maieutics	mallei
loricate	lucernal	lungwort	lyrism	madman	maigre	mallein
lorikeet	lucerne	lunitidal	lyrist	madras	maihem	malleine
loris	luces	lunkhead	lyse	madrepore	mail	mallemuck
lorn	lucid	lunula	lysigenic	madrigal	mailbag	malleolar
lorry	lucidity	lunular	lysimeter	madrona	mailbox	malleolus
lory	lucifee	lunulate	lysin	madrono	mailman	mallet
losable	lucifer	lunule	lysine	madstone	maim	malleus
lose	luciferin	luny	lysis	maduro	main	mallow
losel	luciform	lupin	lyssa	madwoman	mainland	malm
loss	lucivee	lupine	lyssae	madwort	mainmast	malmsey
lost	luck	lupulin	lytta	maelstrom	mainor	malodour
lot	luckless	lupus		maenad	mainour	malonic
lote	lucky	lurch	**M**	maenadic	mainsail	malt
loth	lucrative	lurdan		maestro	mainsheet	maltase
lotion	lucre	lurdane	ma	maffick	mainstay	maltha
loto	lucubrate	lure	macabre	magazine	maintain	maltose
lottery	lucule	lurid	macaco	mage	maintop	maltreat
lotto	luculent	lurk	macadam	magenta	maiolica	maltster
lotus	ludicrous	luscious	macaque	maggot	maize	malty
loud	lues	lush	macaroni	maggoty	majestic	malvasia
louden	luetic	lust		magic	majesty	malvasian
lough	luff	lustful		magical	majolica	malvoisie
louis	luffa	lustral		magician	major	mama

mamba	manifest	map	marron	matchlock	maybug	medjidie
mameluke	manifesto	maple	marrow	matchmark	mayfly	medlar
mamey	manifold	maquis	marrowfat	matchwood	mayhap	medley
mamma	manihot	mar	marry	mate	mayhappen	medulla
mammae	manikin	marabou	marsh	mateless	mayhem	medullae
mammal	manila	marabout	marshal	matelote	mayor	medullar
mammary	manilla	maranta	marshalcy	matelotte	mayoral	medullary
mammate	manioc	marasca	marshy	material	mayoralty	medusoid
mammilla	maniple	marasmic	marsupial	matériel	maypop	meech
mammillae	manipular	marasmus	marsupium	maternal	maze	meed
mammitis	manito	maraud	martello	maternity	mazily	meek
mammology	manitou	maravedi	marten	matey	mazourka	meet
mammon	manitu	marble	martial	math	mazurka	megalith
mammonish	mankind	marbelize	martin	matico	mazy	megaphone
mammonism	manlike	marbly	martinet	matin	me	megapod
mammonist	manna	marc	martingal(e)	matinal	mead	megascope
mammonite	mannequin	marcasite	martlet	matinée	meadow	megaspore
mammoth	manner	marcato	martonite	matrass	meagre	megass
mammy	mannered	marcel	martyr	matriarch	meal	megasse
man	mannerism	march	martyrdom	matrices	mealtime	megathere
manacle	mannerist	marchland	martyrize	matricide	mealworm	megatherm
manage	mannikin	marchpane	martyry	matrimony	mean	megilp
manakin	mannish	mare	marvel	matrix	meander	megrim
manatee	mannitol	margaric	marver	matron	meandrous	meiosis
mancipium	mannite	margarin	marzipan	matronal	meant	meiotic
manciple	mannitic	margarine	mascara	matronage	meantime	mel
mancus	mannose	margay	mascle	matronize	meanwhile	melamine
mandamus	manoeuvre	margent	mascot	matte	measle	melan(a)emi
mandarin	manometer	margin	masculine	matter	measled	melan(a)emi
mandatary	manor	marginal	mash	mattin	measles	melanian
mandate	manorial	marginate	mashie	mattock	measly	melanic
mandatory	manpower	margrave	mashy	mattoid	measure	melanin
mandelic	manrope	marigold	mask	mattrass	meat	melanism
mandible	mansard	marimba	masochism	mattress	meatless	melanite
mandola	manse	marimeter	masochist	maturate	meatus	melanoid
mandolin	mansion	marina	mason	mature	meatuses	melanoma
mandoline	manswear	marinade	masonry	maturity	meaty	melanosis
mandrake	manswore	matinate	masque	matutinal	mechanic	melanotic
mandrel	mansworn	marine	mass	matzoon	mechanism	melanous
mandril	manta	mariner	massacre	matzoth	mechanist	melaphyre
mandrill	manteau	marital	massage	maukin	mechanize	meld
manducate	manteaus	maritime	massagist	maul	medal	mélée
mane	manteaux	marjoram	masse	maulstick	medalist	mêlic
manège	mantel	mark	masseter	maunder	medallic	melilot
manful	mantelet	market	massicot	maundy	medallion	melinite
manganate	mantes	markka	massif	mausolean	medallist	meliorate
manganese	mantic	marksman	massive	mausoleum	meddle	meliorism
manganic	mantilla	marl	massy	mauve	media	meliorist
manganite	mantis	marlin	mast	mauvein	mediacy	meliority
manganous	mantises	marline	mastaba	mauveine	mediaeval	mellite
mange	mantissa	marlite	mastabah	mavis	medial	mellow
mangel	mantle	marly	master	mavournin	median	melodeon
manger	mantlet	marmalade	masterdom	maw	mediate	melodia
mangle	mantua	marmoreal	masterful	mawkish	mediative	melodic
mango	manual	marmorean	mastery	maxilla	mediatory	melodics
mangoes	manubria	marmoset	masthead	maxillae	mediation	melodious
mangonel	manubrial	marmot	mastic	maxillary	mediatize	melodist
mangos	manubrium	maroon	masticate	maxim	medic	melodize
mangrove	manumit	marplot	mastiff	maxima	medicable	melodrama
mangy	manure	marque	mastitis	maximal	medical	melody
manhandle	manus	marquee	mastodon	maximite	medicate	melomania
manhole	manward	marquess	mastoid	maximize	medicinal	melomaniac
manhood	manwards	marquetry	masurium	maximum	medicine	melon
mania	manwise	marquis	mat	maxixe	medieval	melonite
maniac	many	marquise	matador	maxwell	mediocre	melt
maniacal	manyplies	marram	match	may	meditate	meltage
manicure	manzanita	marriage	matchless	maybe	medium	melton

meltwater	mercuric	metabolic	metronym	middleman	milleped	minority
member	mercurous	metaboly	mettle	midge	millepede	minster
membrane	mercury	metage	mettled	midget	millipora	minstrel
memento	mercy	metal	mew	midgut	millepore	mint
mementoes	mere	metalist	mexcal	midland	millerite	mintage
mementos	merely	metalize	mezcaline	midmost	millet	minuend
memo	merganser	metallic	mezereon	midnight	millhand	minuet
memoir	merge	metalline	mezerum	midnoon	milliard	minus
memoirist	mergence	metallist	mezquit	midrib	milliary	minuscule
memorable	meridian	metallize	mezquite	midriff	millier	minute
memorably	meringue	metalloid	mezuzah	midship	milligram	minuteman
memoranda	merino	metalwork	mezuzoth	midships	milliner	minutia
memorial	meristem	metamer	mezza	midst	millinery	minutiae
memorize	meristic	metameral	mezzo	midstream	million	minx
memory	merit	metamere	mezzotint	midsummer	millionth	miocardia
men	merl	metameric	mho	midway	milliped	miosis
menace	merle	metameron	mi	midweek	millipede	miotic
menacme	merlin	metamery	miaou	midwife	millpond	miquelet
menad	merlon	metaphase	miaow	midwifery	millrace	mir
menadic	mermaid	metaphor	miasm	midwinter	millrun	miracle
ménage	mermaiden	metaplasm	miasma	mien	millstone	mirador
menagerie	merman	metapod	miasmal	might	millwheel	mirage
menarche	meroblast	metapode	miasmas	mighty	milo	mire
mend	merozoite	metasome	miasmata	mignon	milord	mirk
mendable	merriment	metaxylem	miasmatic	mignonne	milreis	mirmillon
mendacity	merry	metazoan	miasmic	migraine	milt	mirror
mendicant	mesa	metazoic	miaul	migrant	milter	mirth
mendicity	mescal	metazoon	mib	migrate	mime	mirthful
menhaden	mescaline	mete	mica	migration	mimesis	mirthless
menhir	mesdames	meteor	micaceous	migratory	mimetic	miry
menial	mesentery	meteoric	mice	mikado	mimetical	mirza
meningeal	mesh	meteorite	micell	mikron	mimic	misbecome
meninges	meshwork	meteoroid	micella	mil	mimical	misbrand
meninx	meshy	meter	micellae	miladi	mimicry	miscall
meniscus	mesial	meterage	micellar	milady	mimosa	miscarry
menology	mesian	metestrum	micelle	milage	mina	mischance
menopause	mesmeric	metestrus	micra	milch	minacious	mischief
mensa	mesmerism	methane	micraner	mild	minacity	miscible
mensal	mesmerize	methanol	micrify	milden	minae	miscolour
menses	mesnalty	metheglin	microbe	mildew	minah	miscreant
menstrua	mesnality	method	microbial	mildewy	minaret	miscue
menstrual	mesne	methodic	microbian	mile	minas	misdeed
menstruum	mesoblast	methodism	microbic	mileage	minatory	misdid
mensural	mesocarp	methodist	microbion	milestone	mince	misdo
mensurate	mesoderm	methodize	microcosm	milfoil	mincemeat	misdone
mental	mesologic	methyl	microcyte	miliaria	mind	mise
mentality	mesology	methylal	microdont	miliary	mindful	miser
menthane	meson	methylate	microfilm	militancy	mindless	miserere
menthene	mesophyl	methylene	microgram	militant	mine	misery
menthol	mesophyll	methylic	microgyne	military	mineral	misfeasor
mention	mesophyte	metochy	micrology	militate	mingle	misfire
mentor	mesoplast	metonym	micron	militia	miniature	misfit
mentum	mesotron	metonymic	micropia	milium	minify	misgive
menu	mesquit	metonymy	micropsia	milk	minikin	misguide
mephitic	mesquite	metralgia	microptic	milkfish	minim	mishap
mephitis	mess	metre	micropyle	milkmaid	minima	misinform
mephitism	message	metric	microsome	milkman	minimal	mislay
mercaptan	messaline	metrical	microtome	milksop	minimize	mislead
mercaptol	messenger	metrician	microtomy	milkvetch	minimum	mislike
mercenary	messuage	metricize	micrurgic	milkweed	minion	mismanage
mercer	messy	metrics	micrurgy	milkwort	minister	mismarry
mercerize	mestee	metrify	micturate	milky	ministry	misnomer
mercery	mesteso	metrist	mid	mill	minium	misogamy
merchant	mestino	metritic	midbrain	millboard	miniver	misogyny
merciful	mestiza	metritis	midday	millcake	mink	misology
merciless	mestizo	metrology	midden	milldam	minnow	misoneism
mercurial	met	metronome	middle	millenary	minor	misoneist

mispickel	mockery	molybdic	monody	moonwort	morpheme	moujik
misplace	modal	molybdous	monogamic	moony	morphia	moulage
misplay	modality	moment	monogamy	moor	morphic	mould
misplead	mode	momenta	monogenic	moorage	morphine	mouldwar
misprint	model	momental	monogeny	moorcock	morphosis	mouldy
misrule	moderate	momentary	monogram	moorfowl	morphotic	moulin
miss	modern	momentous	monograph	moorhen	morrice	mouline
missal	modernism	momentum	monogyny	moorland	morrion	moulinet
missay	modernist	monachal	monoicous	moorwort	morris	moult
misshape	modernity	monachism	monolater	moory	morrow	mound
misshapen	modernize	monacid	monolatry	moose	morsel	mount
missile	modest	monad	monolayer	moosebird	mort	mountain
mission	modesty	monadic	monolith	moosecall	mortal	mourn
missional	modica	monadical	monologic	moosewood	mortality	mournful
missive	modicum	monadism	monologue	moot	mortar	mouse
misspeak	modify	monadnock	monology	mop	morte	mouseban
misstep	modillion	monandry	monomania	mope	mortgage	mousebird
missy	modiolus	monarch	monomial	mopish	mortice	mousetail
mist	modish	monarchal	monoplane	mopoke	mortify	mousse
mistake	modiste	monarchic	monopode	moppet	mortise	moustache
mistaken	modular	monarchy	monopadia	moquette	mortmain	mousey
mistletoe	modulate	monas	monopoly	mora	morula	mousy
mistook	module	monastery	monorail	moraceous	morulae	mouth
mistral	moduli	monastic	monosome	morae	morular	mouthful
mistress	modulus	monatomic	monostich	morainal	mosaic	mouthy
mistrial	moellon	monaxial	monostome	moraine	mosaicist	move
mistrust	mofette	monazite	monotint	morainic	moscatel	mow
misty	moffette	monecian	monotone	moral	moschate	mown
misusage	mogul	monecious	monotony	morale	moschatel	moxa
misuse	mohair	monetary	monotreme	moralism	mosque	mozetta
mite	mohur	monetize	monotropic	moralist	mosquital	much
mitigable	moidore	money	monotype	morality	mosquito	mucic
mitigant	moiety	moneys	monotypic	moralize	moss	mucid
mitigate	moil	moneywort	monoxide	morass	mossback	mucilage
mitosis	moist	monger	monsignor	moratoria	mossboard	mucin
mitotic	moisten	mongoose	monsoon	moratory	mossy	mucinous
mitral	moisture	mongrel	monster	moray	most	much
mitre	mojarra	monism	monstrous	morbid	mot	muckrake
mitrewort	mol	monist	montage	morbidity	mote	muckworm
mitsvah	mola	monistic	montane	morbific	motet	mucky
mitt	molae	moniton	montanic	morbilli	motetto	mucoid
mitten	molal	monitive	monte	morceau	moth	mucosa
mittimus	molality	monitor	monteith	mordacity	mother	mucosal
mity	molar	monitory	montero	mordancy	mothery	mucose
mitzvah	molarity	monitress	month	mordant	mothy	mucosity
mitzvoth	molasses	monk	monument	mordent	motif	mucous
mix	mold	monkery	monzonite	mordente	motile	mucro
mixture	moldboard	monkey	moo	more	motility	mucronate
mizen	moldwarp	monkeyish	mood	moreen	motion	mucrones
mizzen	moldy	monkhood	moody	morel	motional	mucus
mizzle	mole	monkish	moolah	morelle	motivate	mud
mizzly	molecular	monkshood	mooley	morello	motive	mudcap
mneme	molecule	monoacid	moon	moreover	motivity	mudcat
mnemonic	molehill	monobasic	moonbeam	morganite	motley	muddle
moa	moleskin	monochord	moonblind	morgen	motmot	muddy
moan	molest	monocle	mooncalf	morgue	motor	mudfish
moat	molewarp	monocled	moonfish	moribund	motorboat	mudguard
mob	mollah	monocline	moonglade	morion	motorbus	mudpot
mobbish	mollient	monocot	moonish	morn	motorcar	mudpuppy
mobile	mollify	monocracy	moonlight	morning	motorist	mudsill
mobility	mollusc	monocular	moonlit	morocco	motorium	mudstone
mobilize	molluscan	monocycle	moonrise	moron	motorize	mueddin
mobocracy	molluscum	monocyte	moonseed	moronic	motorman	muezzin
mobocrat	moloch	monodic	moonset	moronism	motorship	muff
moccasin	molten	monodical	moonshine	moronity	mottle	muffin
mocha	moly	monodist	moonshiny	morose	motto	muffineer
mock	molybdate	monodrama	moonstone	morosity	moue	muffle

mufti	murex	mustard	myopathic	nameless	nativism	needfire
mug	murexes	mustee	myopathy	namesake	nativist	needful
muggar	murexide	musteline	myope	nankeen	nativity	needle
mugger	muriate	muster	myopia	nankin	natrium	needleful
muggur	muriatic	musty	myopic	naos	natrolite	needless
muggins	miricate	mutable	myops	nap	natron	needy
muggy	murices	mutably	myopy	nape	natural	nefarious
mugwort	muriform	mutant	myosin	napery	nature	negate
mugwump	murine	mutate	myosis	naphtha	naught	negation
mujik	murk	mutation	myosote	naphthene	naughty	negative
mulatto	murky	mutative	myosotis	naphthol	naumachia	negatory
mulberry	murmur	mute	myotic	naphtol	naumachy	neglect
mulch	murmurous	mutic	myriad	napiform	nauplius	negligé
mulct	murr	muticate	myriagram	napkin	nausea	negligee
mule	murrain	muticous	myriapod	napless	nauseate	negligent
muleteer	murre	mutilate	myrica	napoleon	nauseous	negotiant
muley	murrelet	mutineer	myrmidon	nappy	nautch	negotiate
mulish	murrey	mutinous	myrobalan	naprapath	nautic	negus
mull	murrhine	mutiny	myrrh	narceia	nautical	neigh
mulla	murrine	mutter	myrrhin	narcein	nautili	neighbour
mullah	musaceous	mutton	myrrhine	narceine	nautilus	neither
mullein	musca	mutual	myrtle	narcism	naval	nekton
mullen	muscadel	mutualism	myself	narcissus	nave	nelumbo
mullet	muscadine	mutuality	mystae	narcoma	navel	nematode
mulley	muscae	mutualize	mystagogy	narcose	navelseed	nemertean
mullion	muscarine	mutule	mystery	narcosis	navelwort	nemertian
mullock	muscat	muzhik	mystic	narcotic	navicert	nemertin(e)a
mullocky	muscatel	muzjik	mystical	narcotism	navicula	nemertine
mulse	muscavada	muzzle	mysticism	narcotize	navicular	nemesis
multifid	muscid	my	mystify	nard	navigate	nemoral
multifoil	muscle	myalgia	myth	nardine	navvy	nemorose
multifold	muscoid	myalgic	mythic	nares	navy	neodymium
multiform	muscovade	myasis	mythical	narghile	neap	neogenic
multipara	muscovado	mycele	mythicize	nargile	near	neolith
multiped	muscovite	mycelial	mythology	nargileh	nearby	neologism
multipede	muscovy	mycelian	mythop(o)eic	naris	neat	neologist
multiple	muscular	mycelium	myx(o)edema	narrate	neb	neology
multiplet	muse	myceloid	myx(o)edemic	narration	nebula	neomorph
multiplex	museful	mycetoma	myxoma	narrative	nebulae	neon
multiply	musette	mycologic	myxomata	naratory	nebular	neophyte
multitude	museum	mycology		narrow	nebulize	neoplasm
multure	mush	mycosis		narthex	nebulose	neoplasty
mum	mushroom	mycotic	**N**	narwal	nebulous	neostyle
mumble	mushy	mydriasis		narwhal	necessary	neoteric
mumm	music	mydriatic	nab	narwhale	necessity	neoterism
mummery	musical	myelin	nabob	nasal	neck	neoterist
mummiform	musicale	myeline	nacelle	nasality	neckband	neotype
mummify	musician	myeloid	nacre	nasalize	neckcloth	nep
mummy	musk	myiasis	nacreous	nascence	necklace	nepenthe
mump	muskeg	mylonite	nadir	nascency	neckwear	nepenthes
mumpish	musket	myna	naevoid	nascent	neckyoke	nepenthic
mumps	musketeer	mynah	naevus	naseberry	necraemia	neper
munch	musketry	myocardia	nag	nasial	necremia	nephelite
mundane	muskit	myogen	nagana	nasion	necrology	nephew
mungo	muskmelon	myogenic	naiad	nasology	necropsy	nephology
mungoose	muskrat	myogenous	naiant	nasoscope	necrose	nephric
municipal	muskroot	myogram	naif	nastic	necrosis	nephridia
muniment	musky	myograph	nail	nasty	necrotic	nephrism
munition	muslin	myography	nainsook	natal	necrotomy	nephrite
munity	musquash	myoid	naive	natality	nectar	nephritic
munnion	musquito	myologic	naiveté	natant	nectareal	nephritis
muraena	muss	myologist	naivety	natation	nectarean	nephroid
mural	mussel	myology	naked	natatory	nectarial	nephrosis
murder	mussy	myoma	namable	nates	nectarine	nephrotic
murderess	must	myomata	namaycush	nation	nectary	nepotic
murderous	mustachio	myomatous	name	national	née	nepotism
mure	mustang	myopathia		native	need	nepotist

neptunium	newsboy	nimbus	nodule	normality	nowise	nuraghe
nereis	newsman	nimbuses	nodulose	normalize	noxal	nurl
neritic	newspaper	nimiety	nodulous	north	noxious	nurse
neroli	newsprint	nimious	nodus	northeast	nozle	nurseling
nervate	newsreel	nine	noematic	northern	nozzle	nursemaid
nervation	newt	ninefold	noes	northland	nth	nursery
nervature	next	ninepin	noesis	northward	nuance	nursling
nerval	nexus	nineteen	noetic	northwest	nub	nurture
nerve	niacin	ninetieth	nog	nose	nubia	nut
nerveless	nib	ninety	noggin	noseband	nubile	nutant
nerviduct	nibble	ninny	noil	nosebleed	nubility	nutate
nervine	niblick	ninon	noise	nosedive	nubilose	nutation
nervosity	niccolite	ninth	noiseless	nosegay	nubilous	nutgall
nervous	nice	niobium	noisome	nosepiece	nucellar	nuthatch
nervule	nicety	nip	noisy	nosology	nucelli	nutlet
nervure	niche	nipa	noma	nostalgia	nucellus	nutmeg
nervy	nick	nipple	nomad	nostalgic	nucha	nutria
nescience	nickel	nippy	nomadic	nostoc	nuchae	nutrient
nescient	nickelic	nirvana	nomadical	nostology	nuchal	nutrimen
ness	nickelous	nisi	nomadism	nostril	nucleal	nutrition
nest	nicker	nit	nomarch	nostrum	nuclear	nutritive
nestle	nickernut	nite	nomarchy	not	nuclease	nutshell
net	nickname	nitid	nombril	notarial	nucleate	nutty
nether	nicol	niton	nome	notarize	nucleic	nuzzle
nettle	nicotin	nitrate	nominal	notary	nuclein	nyanza
neural	nicotine	nitre	nominate	notation	nuclei	nyctalopy
neuralgia	nicotinic	nitric	nominee	notch	nucleolar	nycterine
neuralgic	nictate	nitrid	nomism	note	nucleolus	nylghai
neuralist	nictation	nitride	nomistic	notebook	nucleus	nylghau
neuration	nictitate	nitrify	nomogram	nothing	nude	nymph
neuraxis	nide	nitrile	nomograph	notice	nudge	nympha
neuraxon	nidi	nitrite	nomology	notify	nudism	nymphae
neuremia	nidify	nitrogen	nomos	notion	nudist	nymphal
neuremic	nidus	nitrolic	nonage	notional	nudity	nymphalid
neuric	niece	nitrosyl	nonagon	notochord	nugatory	nymphean
neurilema	nielli	nitrous	nonan	notoriety	nugget	nymphic
neurine	niello	nitty	nonane	notorious	nuggety	nymphica
neuritic	niggard	nival	nonce	notornis	nuisance	nystagmic
neuritis	niggle	niveous	nonconcur	nougat	null	nystagmus
neurocyte	nigh	nix	none	nought	nullify	
neuroid	night	nixie	nonentity	noumenal	nullipara	
neurology	nightbird	nizam	nones	noumenon	nullipore	
neuroma	nightcap	nizamate	nonesuch	noun	nullity	O
neuromata	nightfall	no	nonfeasor	nounal	numb	
neuron	nightgown	nobble	nonillion	nourish	number	oaf
neurone	nighthawk	nobiliary	nonpareil	nous	numbles	oafish
neuronic	nightjar	nobility	nonplus	nova	numbskull	oak
neuropath	nightlong	noble	nonrigid	novae	numen	oaken
neurosal	nightmare	nobleman	nonsense	novas	numerable	oakum
neuroses	nightrobe	nobody	nonskid	novation	numeral	oar
neurosis	nighttide	nock	nonstop	novei	numerary	oarfish
neurotic	nighttime	noctiluca	nonsuit	novelist	numerate	oarlock
neurotomy	nigrify	noctuid	nonuple	novelize	numerical	oarsman
neuter	nigritude	noctule	noodle	novelty	numerous	oary
neutral	nigrosine	noctuoid	nook	novena	numina	oasis
neutron	nihil	nocturnal	noon	novenary	nummular	oast
never	nihilism	nocturne	noonday	novennial	nummulite	oat
nevermore	nihilist	nocuous	noontide	novercal	numskull	oatcake
nevi	hihility	nod	noontime	novice	nun	oaten
nevoid	nil	nodal	noose	noviciate	nunbird	oatgrass
nevus	nilgai	noddy	nopal	novitiate	nuncio	oath
new	nilgau	node	nor	now	nuncius	oatmeal
newcomer	nilghai	nodical	noraghe	nowadays	nunnation	obbligato
newel	nilghau	nodose	noria	noway	nunnery	obcordate
newish	nill	nodosity	norm	noways	nunnish	obduracy
newmarket	nimbi	nodous	normal	nowhere	nuptial	obdurate
news	nimble	nodular	normalcy	nowhither	nuragh	obe

obeah	obtund	octopi	ofttimes	omega	oophoric	optics
obedience	obtundent	octopod	ogam	omelet	oophyte	optime
obedient	obturate	octopoda	ogdoad	omelette	oophytic	optimism
obeisance	obtuse	octopus	ogee	omen	oosperm	optimist
obeisant	obverse	octopuses	ogham	omenta	oosphere	optimize
obeliscal	obversion	octoroon	ogival	omental	oospore	optimum
obelisk	obvert	octuple	ogive	omentum	oosporic	optima
obelize	obviate	octuply	ogle	omer	oosporous	option
obelus	obviation	octyl	ogre	omicron	ootheca	optional
oberek	obvious	ocular	ogreish	omikron	oothecae	optometer
obertas	obvolute	oculist	ogress	omissible	oothecal	optometry
obese	ocarina	od	ogrish	omission	ooze	optotype
obesity	occasion	odalisk	oh	omissive	oozy	opulence
obey	occident	odalisque	ohm	omit	opacity	opulency
obfuscate	occipital	odd	ohmage	ommatidia	opah	opulent
obi	occiput	oddity	ohmic	omnibus	opal	opuntia
obit	occlude	oddment	ohmmeter	omnific	opalesce	opus
obituary	occludent	odds	oii	omophagia	opalesque	opuscule
object	occult	ode	oil	omophagic	opaline	oquassa
objectify	occultism	odea	oilbird	omphalos	opaque	or
objection	occultist	odeon	oilcake	on	ope	ora
objective	occupancy	odeum	oilcloth	onager	open	orach
objurgate	occupant	odic	oilskin	onagri	opera	orache
oblate	occupy	odious	oilstone	once	operable	oracle
oblation	occur	odium	oilwell	oncology	operand	oracular
oblatory	occurrent	odograph	oily	ondogram	operate	oral
obligate	ocean	odometer	oinology	ondograph	operatic	orang
oblige	oceanad	odometry	oinomel	ondometer	operation	orange
obligee	oceanic	odonatous	ointment	one	operative	orangeade
oblique	ocellar	odontoid	oka	onerous	opercele	orangery
obliquity	ocellate	odorous	okapi	oneself	opercule	orate
oblivion	ocelli	odour	okay	onestep	operetta	oration
oblivious	ocellus	odourless	oke	onion	operose	oratorio
oblong	ocelot	odyl	okra	onionskin	ophidian	oratory
obloquy	ochlocrat	odyle	old	onlooker	ophidism	oratress
obnoxious	ochone	oedema	oldish	only	ophiology	orb
oboe	ochre	oenology	oldster	onomastic	ophite	orbicular
oboist	ochreish	oenomel	oldstyle	onomatopy	ophitic	orbit
obol	ochreous	oersted	oldwife	onrush	opthalmy	orbital
oboli	ochroid	oestrin	oleander	onset	opiate	orby
obolus	ochrous	oestrum	oleaster	onslaught	opine	orc
obovate	ocotillo	oestrus	oleate	onto	opinion	orchard
obovoid	ocrea	of	olecranal	ontogenic	opium	orcheitis
obscene	ocreae	off	olecranon	ontogeny	opiumism	orchestra
obscenity	ocreate	offal	olefiant	ontologic	opodeldoc	orchid
obscure	octachord	offcast	olefin	ontology	opossum	orchil
obscurity	octad	offence	olefine	onus	oppidan	orchis
obsecrate	octadic	offend	oleic	onward	oppilant	orchitic
obsequy	octagon	offensive	olein	onyx	oppilate	orchitis
observant	octagonal	offer	oleograph	oocyte	opponency	orcin
observe	octahedra	offertory	oleoresin	oogamy	opponent	orcinol
obsess	octameter	office	olfaction	oogenesis	opportune	ordain
obsession	octan	official	olfactory	oogenetic	opposable	ordeal
obsidian	octane	officiant	olibanum	oogeny	oppose	order
obsolete	octangle	officiary	oligarch	oogone	opposite	ordinal
obstacle	octant	officiate	oligarchy	oogonia	oppress	ordinance
obstetric	octantal	officinal	olio	oogonium	oppugn	ordinant
obstinacy	octarchy	officious	olivary	oolite	oppugnant	ordinary
obstinate	octaval	offing	olive	oologic	opsonic	ordinate
obstruct	octave	offish	olivine	oological	opsonify	ordnance
obstruent	octavo	offprint	olla	oologist	opsonin	ordure
obtain	octavos	offset	olycook	oology	opsonize	ore
obtect	octennial	offshoot	olykoek	oolong	opt	oread
obtected	octet	offshore	omasa	oomiak	optative	orectic
obtest	octette	offside	omasum	oomycete	optic	orective
obtrude	octillion	oft	omber	oophore	optical	oreide
obtrusion	octonary	often	ombre		optician	orexis

orfray	orthopter	otiose	outmoded	overblown	overskirt	oxidate
organ	orthoptic	otiosity	outmost	overboard	oversleep	oxidation
organdie	ortolan	otitis	outplay	overbuild	oversoul	oxidative
organdy	oryx	otocyst	outpoint	overbuilt	overspend	oxide
organic	os	otolith	outpost	overcast	overstate	oxidize
organical	osar	otologist	outpour	overcheck	overstay	oxim
organism	oscillate	otology	output	overcloud	overstep	oxime
organist	oscine	otoscope	outrage	overcoat	overt	oxlip
organize	oscitance	ottar	outrance	overcome	overtake	oxpecker
organon	oscitancy	otter	outrange	overcrop	overthrow	oxtail
organzine	oscitant	otto	outré	overdo	overtime	oxyacid
orgasm	oscula	ottoman	outreach	overdose	overtone	oxygen
orgastic	osculant	ouabain	outride	overdraft	overtop	oxygenate
orgeat	oscular	ouch	outrigger	overdraw	overtrade	oxygenic
orgiac	osculate	ought	outright	overdue	overtrick	oxygenize
orgiastic	oscule	ounce	outroot	overdye	overtrump	oxygenous
orgic	osculum	our	outrun	overfall	overture	oxygon
orgy	ose	ourebi	outsell	overflow	overturn	oxygonal
oribi	osier	ours	outsentry	overglaze	overwatch	oxymel
orichalc	osmic	ourself	outset	overgrow	overwear	oxymora
orichalch	osmious	ousel	outshine	overhand	overweary	oxymoron
oriel	osmium	oust	outshoot	overhang	overween	oxyntic
orient	osmose	out	outside	overhaul	overweigh	oxyphyte
oriental	osmosis	outbid	outsight	overhead	overwhelm	oxysalt
orientate	osmotic	outboard	outsize	overhear	overwind	oxytocic
orifice	osmund	outbound	outskirt	overissue	overword	oxytocin
oriflamme	osnaburg	outbrave	outsole	overjoy	overwork	oxytone
origan	osphresia	outbreak	outspan	overlade	overwrite	oyer
origin	osphresis	outbreed	outspeak	overland	ovibos	oyes
original	osphretic	outburst	outspent	overlap	oviduct	oyez
originate	osprey	outcast	outspoken	overlay	oviferous	oyster
orinasal	ossa	outclass	outspread	overleap	oviform	oysterman
oriole	ossature	outcome	outstand	overlie	ovine	ozaena
orle	ossein	outcrop	outstrip	overlive	ovipara	ozaenic
orlop	osseous	outcross	outstroke	overlook	oviparous	ozena
ormer	ossicle	outcry	outtell	overlord	oviposit	ozenic
ormolu	ossicular	outcurve	outturn	overly	ovisac	ozocerite
ornament	ossific	outdo	outward	overman	ovoid	ozonation
ornate	ossifrage	outdoor	outwards	overmatch	ovoidal	ozone
ornis	ossify	outer	outwash	overmight	ovoli	ozonic
ornithic	ossuary	outface	outwear	overmuch	ovolo	ozonide
ornithine	osteal	outfall	outweigh	overpart	ovotestis	ozonize
ornithoid	osteitis	outfield	outwit	overpass	ovulate	ozonous
orogenic	ostensive	outfit	outwork	overpay	ovulation	
orogeny	ostensory	outflow	ouzel	overplay	ovular	
orography	osteoid	outfoot	ova	overplus	ovulary	
oroide	osteology	outgo	oval	overpower	ovule	P
orologist	osteoma	outgone	ovaria	overprint	ovum	
orology	osteomata	outgrow	ovarial	overprize	owe	pa
orometer	osteopath	outgrowth	ovarian	overproof	owl	pabular
orometric	osteotome	outguard	ovaritis	overrate	owlet	pabulum
orotund	ostiary	outgush	ovarium	overreach	owlish	pac
orphan	ostiolar	outhaul	ovary	override	own	paca
orphanage	ostiole	outhouse	ovate	overrule	ownerless	pace
orphrey	ostler	outing	ovation	overrun	ownership	pacemaker
orpiment	ostosis	outland	ovational	oversea	ox	pacha
orpine	ostracism	outlast	oven	overseas	oxalate	pachalic
orrery	ostracize	outlaw	ovenbird	oversee	oxalic	pachisi
orrhology	ostrich	outlawry	over	oversell	oxalis	pachyderm
orris	otalgia	outlay	overact	overset	oxazin	pacific
orseille	otalgic	outleap	overage	oversew	oxazine	pacifical
ort	otalgy	outlet	overall	overshade	oxbow	pacifism
othodox	otarian	outlier	overalls	overshine	oxen	pacifist
orthodoxy	otary	outline	overbear	overshoe	oxeye	pacify
orthoepic	other	outlive	overbid	overshoot	oxid	pack
orthoepy	otherwise	outlook	overbite	oversight	oxidase	package
orthogamy	otic	outlying	overblow	oversize	oxidasic	packet

packwax	palish	panderism	pappus	pardon	part	pat
pact	pall	pandoor	pappy	pare	partake	patagium
pad	palladic	pandour	paprica	parecious	parterre	patch
paddle	palladium	pandowdy	paprika	paregoric	partial	patchwork
paddock	pallah	pandurate	papula	parent	partible	patchy
paddy	pallet	pandy	papulae	parentage	particle	pate
padlock	pallette	pane	papule	parental	partisan	patella
padre	pallia	panegyric	papyri	paresis	partite	patellae
padrone	palliasse	panel	papyrus	paretic	partition	patellar
padronism	palliate	panelwork	par	pareu	partitive	patellate
paduasoy	pallid	pang	para	parfait	partizan	paten
paean	pallium	pangamic	parablast	parfleche	partlet	patency
paederast	pallor	pangamous	parable	parget	partly	patent
paeon	palm	pangamy	parabola	pargo	partner	patentee
pagan	palmar	pangen	parabole	parhelic	partook	patera
paganism	palmate	pangolin	parabolic	parhelion	partridge	paterae
paganize	plamation	panhandle	parachor	parhelium	party	paternal
page	palmette	panic	parachute	pariah	parure	paternity
pageant	palmetto	panicky	paraclete	paries	parura	path
pageantry	palmettos	panicle	parade	parietal	parvenu	pathetic
paginal	palmiped	panmixia	paradigm	parietes	parvis	pathless
paginate	palmist	pannier	paradise	parillin	parvolin	pathogen
pagod	palmistry	pannikin	parados	parish	parvoline	pathogene
pagoda	palmitate	panocha	paradox	parity	pas	pathogeny
pagurian	palmitic	panoche	paraffin	park	pasch	pathology
pagurid	palmitin	panoply	paragoge	parka	pascha	pathos
pah	palmy	panoptic	paragogic	parkee	paschal	pathway
pahlavi	palmyra	panorama	paragon	parkway	pascual	patience
pahoehoe	palomino	pansophic	paragraph	parlance	pasha	patient
paid	palp	pansophy	parakeet	parley	pashalic	patina
paidology	palpable	pansy	paralalia	parlour	pashalik	patine
pail	palpably	pant	parallax	parlous	pasquil	patio
pailful	palpate	pantalets	parallel	parochial	pasquin	patios
paillasse	palpation	pantaloon	paralogy	parodic	pass	patriarch
paillette	palpebra	pantheism	paralysis	parodical	passage	patrician
pain	palpebrae	pantheist	paralytic	parodist	passant	patricide
painful	palpebral	pantheon	paralyze	parody	passbook	patrimony
painless	palpi	panther	paramatta	paroecism	passenger	patriot
paint	palpitate	pantile	paramecia	parol	passerine	patriotic
pair	palpus	pantology	parameter	parole	passible	patristic
pais	palsgrave	pantomime	paramount	paronym	passim	patrol
paktong	palsy	pantry	paramour	paronymic	passion	patrolman
palace	palter	panzer	parang	paroquet	passional	patron
paladin	paltry	pap	paranoea	paroral	passive	patronage
palankeen	paludal	papa	paranoeac	parotic	passivity	patronal
palanquin	paludism	papacy	paranoia	parotid	passkey	patroness
palatal	paly	papain	paranoic	parotitic	passover	patronize
palate	pam	papal	paranoid	parotitis	passport	patronym
palatial	pampas	papaw	paranymph	parotoid	passus	patroon
palatine	pampean	papaya	parapet	paroxysm	passuses	patten
palaver	pamper	paper	paraph	parquet	password	patter
palay	pamphlet	papery	paraplegy	parquetry	paste	pattern
pale	pan	papilla	parasang	parquette	pastel	patty
palea	panacea	papillae	parasceve	parr	pastern	patulous
paleae	panacean	papillary	parasite	parrakeet	pastiche	paucity
paleface	panache	papilloma	parasitic	parrel	pastil	pauldron
paleocene	panada	papillon	paratroop	parricide	pastille	paulin
paleolith	pancake	papillose	paravane	parroquet	pastime	paulownia
paleology	pancratic	papillous	parboil	parrot	pastor	paunch
palestra	pancreas	papist	parbuckle	parry	pastorage	paunchy
palet	panda	papistic	parcel	parse	pastoral	pauper
paletot	pandanus	papistry	parcenary	parsimony	pastorate	pauperism
palette	pandect	papoose	parcener	parsley	pastrami	pauperize
palfrey	pandemic	pappi	parch	parsnip	pastry	pause
palikar	pander	pappoose	parchment	parson	pasturage	pavan
palinode	panderage	pappose	parcimony	parsonage	pasture	pavane
palisade	panderess	pappous	pard	parsonic	pasty	pave

pavilion	peculium	pellet	penstemon	perfecto	permeate	petasus
pavior	pecuniary	pellicle	penstock	perfervid	permit	petcock
paviour	pedagogic	pellitory	pent	perfidy	permute	petechia
pavonine	pedagogue	pellmell	pentacle	perforate	peroneal	petechiae
paw	pedagogy	pellucid	pentagon	perforce	perorate	petechial
pawl	pedal	peloria	pentagram	perform	peroxid	peter
pawn	pedalier	peloriate	pentalpha	perfume	peroxide	petersham
pawnage	pedant	peloric	pentane	perfumery	perpend	petiolar
pawnee	pedantic	pelorism	pentarchy	perfuse	perpent	petiolate
pawnshop	pedantry	pelorus	penthouse	perfusion	perpetual	petiole
pawpaw	pedate	pelota	pentose	perfusive	perplex	petit
pax	pedatifid	pelt	penuchle	pergola	perplexity	petite
paxwax	peddle	peltast	penuckle	perhaps	perron	petition
pay	peddlery	peltate	penult	peri	perry	petitory
payee	pedes	peltry	penultima	perianth	persalt	petrel
paymaster	pedestal	pelvic	penumbra	periblem	perse	petrify
paynim	p(a)ediatric	pelvis	penumbrae	pericarp	persecute	petrol
payroll	pedicel	pemican	penumbral	pericline	persevere	petroleum
pea	pedicle	pemmican	penumbras	pericycle	persicary	petrolic
peabird	pedicellar	pemphigus	penurious	periderm	persienne	petrology
peace	pedicular	pemphix	penury	peridia	persimmon	petronel
peaceful	pedicure	pen	peon	peridial	persist	petrosal
peach	pediform	penal	peonage	peridium	person	petrous
peachy	pedigree	penalize	peony	peridot	persona	petticoat
peacock	pedigreed	penalty	people	peridotic	personae	pettish
peacocky	pediment	penance	pepla	perigeal	personage	pettitoes
peafowl	pedipalp	pence	peplos	perigean	personal	petty
peag	pedlar	pencel	peplum	perigee	personate	petulance
peahen	pedlary	penchant	peplus	perigonia	personify	petulancy
peajacket	pedler	pencil	pepo	perigyny	personnel	petulant
peak	pedograph	pend	peponida	peril	perspire	petunia
peal	pedology	pendant	pepper	perilous	persuade	pew
pean	pedometer	pendency	pepperbox	perimeter	pert	pewage
peanut	pedrail	pendent	pepperpot	perimetry	pertain	pewee
pear	pedro	pendragon	peppery	perimorph	pertinent	pewit
pearl	peduncle	pendulous	pepsin	perinaeal	perture	pewter
pearlite	pee	pendulum	pepsine	perinaeum	pertusis	pewterer
pearmain	peek	peneplain	pepsinate	perineal	pertussal	peyote
peasant	peel	penetrant	peptic	perineum	peruke	peyotl
peasantry	peen	penetrate	peptide	period	perusal	pfennig
peascod	peep	pengo	peptize	periodate	peruse	pfennige
pease	peephole	pengos	peptone	periodic	pervade	pfennigs
peasecod	peepshow	penguin	peptonic	periodid	pervasion	phaenogam
peat	peepul	penholder	peptonize	periodide	pervasive	phaeton
peatman	peer	peninsula	peracid	periotic	perverse	phagedena
peaty	peerage	penitence	perborate	periphery	pervert	phagocyte
peavey	peeress	penitent	peboric	peripter	pervious	phalange
peavy	peerless	penknife	percale	periptery	pes	phalangal
pebble	peeve	penman	percaline	perisarc	pesade	phalangeal
pebbly	peevish	penna	perceive	periscope	pesky	phalanger
pecan	peewee	pennae	percent	perish	pessimism	phalanges
peccable	peg	pennage	percept	perisperm	pessimist	phalangial
peccancy	pegmatite	pennant	perch	peristoma	pest	phalanx
peccant	pekan	pennate	perchance	peristome	pesthole	phalanxes
peccary	pekin	penniless	percoid	peristyle	pesthouse	phalarope
peck	pekoe	pennon	percolate	periwig	pestilent	phallic
pectase	pelage	pennoncel	percuss	periwinkle	pestle	phallical
pectate	pelagian	penny	perdition	perjure	pet	phallin
pecten	pelagic	pennywort	perdu	perjury	petal	phallism
pectic	pelerine	penology	perdue	perk	petaline	phallist
pectin	pelf	penoncel	perdure	perky	petalism	phallus
pectinate	pelican	penpoint	peregrin	perlite	petalodic	phaneric
pectines	pelisse	pensil	peregrine	permanent	petalody	phantasm
pectize	pelite	pensile	pereirine	permeable	petaloid	phantom
pectoral	pelitic	pensility	perennate	permeably	petalous	pharisaic
peculate	pellagra	pension	perennial	permeance	petard	pharmacal
peculiar	pellagrin	pensive	perfect	permeant	petasos	pharmacy

•haros	phonogram	pianist	pigskin	pinfish	pirouette	plain
•harynges	phonolite	piano	pigsty	pinfold	piscary	plainsman
•harynx	phonology	piasaba	pigtail	ping	piscina	plaint
•hase	phonotype	piasava	pigweed	pingrass	piscinae	plaintiff
•hasic	phonotypy	piassaba	pika	pinguid	piscinal	plaintive
•hasin	phoresis	piaster	pike	pinhead	piscine	plait
•hasine	phoresy	piastre	pikeman	pinhole	pish	plan
•hasis	phosgene	piazza	pikestaff	pinion	pisiform	planar
•hat	phosphate	pica	pilaf	pinite	pismire	planarian
•heasant	phosphene	pical	pilaff	pinitol	pisolite	planch
•hellogen	phosphid	picador	pilar	pink	pisolitic	planche
•henacite	phosphide	picaroon	pilaster	pinkeye	pistache	planchet
•henazin	phosphin	piccolo	pilau	pinkie	pistachio	plane
•henazine	phosphine	pice	pilaw	pinkish	pistareen	planet
•henetol	phosphite	piceous	pilchard	pinkroot	pistil	planetary
•henol	phosphor	pichurim	pilcher	pinky	pistol	planetoid
•henolate	phot	pick	pilcherd	pinna	pistole	plangency
•henolic	photic	pickaroon	pile	pinnace	pistoleer	plangent
•henology	photics	pickax	pileate	pinnacle	pistolier	planiform
•henomena	photocell	pickaxe	piles	pinnae	piston	planish
•henotype	photogen	pickerel	pileum	pinnal	pit	plank
•henyl	photogene	picket	pileus	pinnate	pita	plankton
•henylene	photon	pickle	pilewort	pinnation	pitch	plant
•hew	photoplay	picklock	pilfer	pinniped	pitchfork	plantain
•hial	photopsia	pickthank	pilgarlic	pinnula	pitchy	plantar
•hilander	photostat	pickup	pilgrim	pinnular	piteous	planter
•hilately	phototaxy	picnic	pili	pinnulate	pitfall	planula
•hilogyny	phototube	pircolin	pill	pinnule	pith	planulae
•hilologue	phototype	picoline	pillage	pinochle	pithless	planular
•hilology	phototypy	picot	pillar	pinocle	pithy	planulate
•hilomath	phrasal	picotee	pillbox	pinscher	pitiful	plaque
•hilomel	phrase	picquet	pillion	pint	pitiless	plash
•hilomela	phratric	picrate	pillory	pintado	pitman	plashy
•hilopena	phratry	picric	pillow	pintados	piton	plasma
•hilter	phreatic	picrite	pilose	pintail	pittance	plasmatic
•hiltre	phrenetic	picrol	pilosity	pintano	pituitary	plasmic
•hlebitic	phrenic	pictorial	pilot	pintle	pituitous	plastein
•hlebitis	phrenitis	picture	pilotage	pinto	pity	plaster
•hlegm	phrenosin	piddock	pilule	pinweed	pivot	plastic
•hlegmon	phthalein	pidgin	pilular	pinwheel	pivotal	plastid
•hlegmy	phthalic	pie	pilus	pinworm	pixilated	plastomer
•hloem	phthalin	piebald	pimelosis	piny	pixy	plastral
•hlogosed	phthisic	piece	pimelotic	pioneer	placable	plastron
•hlogosis	phthisis	piecemeal	pimento	pious	placably	plastrum
•hlogotic	phycology	piecework	pimola	pip	placard	plat
•hlorizin	phylae	piedmont	pimpernel	pipage	placate	platan
•hlox	phyle	pier	pimple	pipal	placation	platane
•hlyct(a)ena	phyletic	pierce	pin	pipe	placative	plate
•hobia	phylic	pieridine	pinaceous	piperazin	placatory	plateau
•hobic	phyllium	pierrot	pinafore	piperine	place	plateaus
•hoca	phyllode	piet	pinang	piperonal	placebo	plateaux
•hocae	phyllody	pietism	pinaster	pipestone	placeman	plateful
•hocine	phylloid	piety	pinball	pipet	placenta	platelet
•hocoid	phyllome	piffle	pincenez	pipette	placentae	platen
•hoebe	phyllopod	pig	pincers	pipit	placentas	platform
•hoebean	phylum	pigeon	pinch	pipkin	placental	platina
•hoenix	physic	piggery	pinchbar	pippin	placid	platinic
•honate	physical	piggie	pinchbeck	pipy	placidity	platinize
•honation	physician	piggin	pindling	piquant	plack	platinoid
•honeme	physics	piggish	pine	pique	placket	platinous
•honemics	physique	piggy	pineal	piquet	placoid	platinum
•honetic	phytin	pigment	pineapple	piracy	plagal	platitude
•honetics	phytoid	pigmy	pinedrops	piranha	plagiary	platoon
•honetist	pi	pignora	pinene	piraya	plague	platypus
•honic	piacular	pignus	pinery	pirate	plaguy	plaudit
•honics	piaffer	pignut	pinesap	piratic	plaice	plausible
•honodeik	pianism	pigpen	piney	piratical	plaid	plausive

play	plosion	pocoson	politics	pomelos	porgy	posture
playa	plosive	pod	polity	pommel	porism	postural
playbill	plot	podagra	polka	pomology	pork	posturist
playboy	plough	podagral	poll	pomp	porky	posturize
playday	ploughboy	podesta	pollack	pompadour	porkwood	postwar
playful	ploughman	podgy	pollard	pompano	poroscopy	posy
playgoer	plover	podia	pollen	pompanos	porosity	pot
dlayhouse	ploy	podiatry	pollenate	pompon	porous	potable
playmate	pluck	podium	pollex	pomposity	porphyry	potash
plaything	plucky	podsol	pollices	pompous	porpoise	potass
playtime	plug	podura	pollical	poncho	porridge	potassium
plaza	plum	poduran	pollinate	ponchos	porringer	potassic
plea	plumage	poduroid	pollinia	pond	port	potation
pleach	plumate	podzol	pollinium	ponder	portage	potato
plead	plumb	podzolic	polliwog	ponderous	portal	potatory
pleasance	plumbago	poem	pollock	pondlily	porte	potbelly
pleasant	plumbeous	poenology	pollute	pondweed	portend	potboy
please	plumbery	poesy	pollution	pone	portent	poteen
pleasure	plumbic	poet	polo	ponent	porter	potence
pleat	plumbism	poetaster	poloist	pongee	portfolio	potency
pleb	plumbous	poetess	polonaise	poniard	porthole	potent
plebian	plumbum	poetic	polonium	pontianak	portico	potentate
plebs	plume	poetical	poltroon	pontifex	porticoes	potential
plectron	plumelet	poetics	polyandry	pontiff	porticoed	pother
plectra	plumiped	poetize	polyarchy	pontific	porticos	pothole
plectrum	plumipede	poetry	polybasic	pontil	portière	pothook
pledge	plummet	pogonia	polydemic	ponton	portion	pothouse
pledgee	plummy	pogonip	polygala	pontonier	portly	pothunter
pledget	plumose	pogrom	polygamy	pontoon	portrait	potion
plenary	plumosity	pogy	polygenic	pony	portray	potlatch
plenism	plump	poh	polyglot	pood	portrayal	potlead
plenist	plumule	poignant	polygon	poodle	portress	potpie
plenitude	plumy	poinciana	polygonal	pooh	portulaca	potpourri
plenteous	plunder	point	polygonum	poohpooh	pose	potshard
plentiful	plunge	pointless	polygony	pool	posit	potsherd
plenty	plunk	pose	polygraph	poon	position	potstone
plenum	plural	poison	polygyny	poop	positive	pott
pleonasm	pluralism	poisonous	polyhedra	pooquaw	positron	pottage
pleopod	pluralist	poitrel	polymer	poor	posologic	potter
pleroma	plurality	poke	polymeric	poorhouse	posology	pottery
plerome	pluralize	pokeberry	polymorph	pop	posse	pottinger
plessor	plus	pokerface	polyose	popcorn	possess	pottle
plethora	plush	pokerish	polyp	pope	posset	potto
plethoric	plushy	pokeroot	polypary	popedom	possible	pottos
pleura	plutarchy	pokeweed	polyphase	popery	possibly	pouch
pleurae	plutocrat	pokey	polyphemus	popgun	possum	pouched
pleural	plutonic	poky	polyphonic	popinjay	possumhaw	pouchy
pleurisy	plutonium	polacca	polyphony	popish	post	poulaine
pleuritic	pluvial	polacre	polypi	poplar	postage	poulard
pleuron	pluviose	polar	polypidom	poplin	postal	poult
pleuston	pluvious	polarity	polyploid	popliteal	postcard	poulterer
plexiform	ply	polarize	polypod	poplitic	postdate	poultice
plexor	plywood	pole	polypody	popover	posterior	poultry
plexus	pneuma	polecat	polypous	poppet	posterity	pounce
plexuses	pneumatic	polemic	polypus	popple	postern	pound
pliable	pneumonia	polemical	polysperm	poppy	postfix	poundage
pliancy	pneumonic	polemics	polytonic	poppyhead	posthaste	poundal
pliant	poaceous	polestar	polytypic	populace	postil	pour
plica	poach	police	polyuria	popular	postilion	pourpoint
plicae	poachy	policeman	polyuric	populate	postlude	poussette
plicate	pochard	policy	polyzoic	populous	postman	pout
plication	pock	polish	pomace	porbeagle	postmark	pouter
plicature	pocket	polite	pomaceous	porcelain	postnatal	poverty
plight	pockety	politic	pomade	porch	postpone	powder
plinth	pockmark	political	pomander	porcine	postulant	powdery
plod	pocky	politician	pome	porcupine	postulata	power
plop	pocosin	politico	pomelo	pore	postulate	powerful

powerless	prefect	presswork	prior	profert	prophecy	protonema
powter	prefer	prester	priorate	profess	prophesy	protoneme
powther	prefigure	prestige	prioress	professor	prophet	prototype
pox	prefix	presto	priority	proffer	prophetic	protoxide
practical	prefixal	presume	priorship	profile	propionic	protozoan
practice	prefixion	pretence	priory	profit	propolis	protozoic
practicum	pregnable	pretend	prise	profiteer	propone	protozoon
practise	pregnancy	preterit	prism	profluent	proponent	protract
praenomen	pregnant	preterite	prismatic	profound	proposal	protrude
praetor	prejudge	pretermit	prismoid	profuse	propose	protyl
pragmatic	prejudice	pretext	prison	profusion	propositi	protyle
prahu	prelacy	pretor	pristine	prog	propound	proud
prairie	prelate	pretorian	privacy	progeny	propr(a)etor	prove
praise	prelatic	prettify	private	progestin	propriety	proven
praline	prelatism	pretty	privateer	prognosis	proptosis	proverb
prance	prelatist	pretzel	privation	program	propyl	provide
prandial	prelature	prevail	privative	programme	propyla	provident
prank	prelect	prevalent	privet	progress	propylaea	province
prankish	prelude	prevent	privilege	prohibit	propylene	provision
prase	preludial	preverb	privity	project	propylite	proviso
prate	prelusion	prevernal	privy	prolactin	propylon	provisory
pratique	prelusive	preview	prize	prolamin	prorate	provoke
prattle	prelusory	previous	pro	prolamine	proration	provost
pravity	premature	previse	proa	prolapse	prorogue	prow
prawn	premier	prevision	probable	prolapsus	prosaic	prowess
praxis	premise	prewar	probably	prolate	prosaical	prowl
pray	premium	prey	probands	proleg	prosaism	proximate
praya	premolar	price	probang	prolepsis	proscenia	proximity
prayer	premonish	priceless	probate	proleptic	proscribe	proximo
prayerful	premorse	pricelist	probation	proletary	proscript	proxy
preach	prenatal	prick	probative	prolicide	prose	prude
preadamic	prenomen	pricket	probatory	prolific	prosect	prudence
preamble	prenotion	prickle	probe	prolix	prosecute	prudent
preaxial	prentice	pride	probity	prolixity	proselyte	prudery
prebend	preoccupy	prideful	problem	prologize	proser	prudish
prebendal	preordain	priest	proboscis	prologue	prosodist	pruinose
precancel	prepare	priestess	procaine	prolong	prosodic	prune
precative	prepay	priestly	procarp	prolonge	prosodiac	prunella
precatory	prepense	prig	procedure	prolusion	prosodial	prunelle
precede	prepostor	priggish	proceed	promenade	prosody	prunello
precedent	prepotent	priggism	proceeds	prominent	prospect	prurience
precent	prepuce	prim	process	promise	prosper	pruriency
precept	preputial	primacy	prochain	promisee	prostate	prurient
precinct	presage	primage	prochein	promissory	prostatic	prurigo
precious	presbyopia	primal	proclaim	promote	prostrate	prussiate
precipe	presbyopic	primary	proclitic	promotion	prostyle	prussic
precipice	presbyter	primate	proconsul	promotive	prosy	pry
précis	prescient	primatial	procreant	prompt	protamin	psalm
precise	prescind	primavera	procreate	promulge	protamine	psalmist
precisian	prescribe	prime	proctor	pronate	protasis	psalmody
precision	prescript	primero	procuracy	pronation	protean	psalter
preclude	presence	primeval	procural	prone	protease	psaltery
precocial	present	primine	procure	prong	protect	psammite
preconize	presentee	primipara	procuress	pronghorn	protégé	psammitic
precursor	presentive	primp	prod	pronoun	protégée	psellism
predacity	preserve	primrose	prodigal	pronounce	protein	psephite
predate	preside	prince	prodigy	pronto	proteose	psephitic
predatory	presidency	princekin	prodromal	proof	protest	pseudaxes
predicant	president	princess	prodrome	prop	prothesis	pseudaxis
predicate	presidial	princesse	prodromi	propagate	prothetic	pseudonym
predict	presidio	principal	prodromus	propane	prothorax	pseudopod
predigest	presidium	principia	produce	propel	protist	pshaw
preempt	press	principle	product	propene	protistan	psilosis
preen	pressgang	prink	proem	propense	protistic	psilotic
preexilic	pressman	print	proemial	proper	protocol	psoas
preface	pressmark	printery	profane	property	protogram	psora
prefatory	pressure	printless	profanity	prophase	proton	psoric

psoriasis	pulex	pupil	putrid	pyrometer	quandary	quietus
psoriatic	pulicene	pupilage	putridity	pyrometry	quandong	quill
psyche	pulkha	pupilary	putrify	pyrone	quanta	quillai
psychic	pull	puppet	putt	pyrope	quantic	quillaia
psychical	pullback	puppy	puttee	pyrophore	quantify	quillback
psychics	pullet	puppyfish	puttier	pyrosis	quantity	quilt
psychopath	pulley	pur	putty	pyrostat	quantum	quinary
psychosis	pullulate	purblind	puttyroot	pyrotic	quarrel	quinate
psychotic	pulmonary	purchase	puy	pyrotoxin	quarry	quince
psyllium	pulmonate	pure	puzzle	pyroxene	quart	quincunx
ptarmigan	pulmonic	pureblood	puaemia	pyroxenic	quartan	quinic
pteropod	pulp	purebred	pyaemic	pyroxylin	quarte	quinidine
pterygoid	pulpit	purée	pycnidia	pyrrhic	quarter	quinin
ptisan	pulpiteer	purfle	pycnidial	pyrrol	quartern	quinine
ptomain	pulpless	purgative	pycnidium	pyrrole	quartet	quinnat
ptomaine	pulpwood	purgatory	pye	python	quartette	quinoid
ptosis	pulpy	purge	pyeletic	pythoness	quartile	quinoidin
ptotic	pulque	purify	pyeletis	pythonic	quarto	quinolin
ptyalin	pulsate	purin	pyelogram	pyuria	quartz	quinoline
ptyalism	pulsatile	purine	pyemia	pyx	quartzite	quinone
puberty	pulsation	purism	pyemic	pyxides	quash	quinonoid
pubes	pulsative	purist	pygidia	pyxidium	quassia	quinsy
pubescent	pulsatory	puristic	pygidium	pyxie	quassiin	quint
pubic	pulse	purity	pygmaean	pyxis	quassin	quintal
pubis	pulseless	purl	pygmean		quatorze	quintan
public	pulverize	purlieu	pygmy		quaver	quintet
publican	pulvillus	purlin	pyic		quavery	quintette
publicist	pulvinar	purline	pyin	**Q**	quay	quintile
publicity	pulvinate	purloin	pyjamas		quayage	quintuple
publish	puma	purple	pylon	qua	quean	quip
puccoon	pumice	purplish	pyloric	quack	queasy	quippish
puce	pummel	purport	pylorus	quackery	quebracho	quipster
pucelle	pump	purpose	pyogenic	quackhood	queen	quipu
puck	pumpkin	purpura	pyoid	quackism	queenpost	quire
pucker	pun	purpure	pyorrhea	quad	queer	quirk
puckery	puna	purpuric	pyorrhoea	quadrant	quell	quirky
puckish	punch	purr	pyorrheal	quadrat	quench	quirl
pudding	puncheon	purse	pyosis	quadrate	quercetic	quirt
puddle	punctate	purser	pyralid	quadratic	quercetin	quish
puddlebar	punctilio	pursiness	pyralidan	quadric	quercine	quislin
puddly	punctual	purslane	pyralidid	quadrifid	querist	quit
pudency	punctuate	pursuance	pyramid	quadriga	querl	quite
pudenda	puncture	pursuant	pyramidal	quadrigae	quern	quittance
pudendal	pundit	pursue	pyramidic	quadrille	querulous	quiver
pudendum	pungence	pursuit	pyran	quadrivia	query	quixotic
pudgy	pungency	pursy	pyre	quadroon	quest	quixotism
pudic	pungent	purulent	pyrene	quadruped	question	quiz
pueblo	punish	purulence	pyrenoid	quadruple	quetzal	quizzical
pueblos	punitive	purulency	pyrethrum	quaere	quetzales	quod
purile	punitory	purvey	pyretic	quaestor	queue	quohog
puerility	punk	purview	pyrexia	quaff	quezal	quoin
puff	punka	pus	pyrexial	quag	quibble	quoit
puffball	punkah	push	pyrexic	quagga	quick	quondam
puffery	punkey	pushball	pyridic	quaggy	quicken	quorum
puffin	punkie	pushcart	pyridine	quagmire	quicklime	quota
puffy	punky	puss	pyriform	quagmiry	quicksand	quotation
pug	punster	pussy	pyrite	quahaug	quickset	quote
pugh	punt	pussyfoot	pyrites	quahog	quickstep	quotidian
pugilism	punto	pustulant	pyritic	quail	quid	quotient
pugilist	punty	pustular	pyritical	quaint	quiddity	
pugnacity	puny	pustulate	pyrogenic	quake	quiddle	
puisne	pup	pustule	pyrograph	qualify	quidnunc	**R**
puissance	pupa	put	pyrology	quality	quiescent	
puissant	pupae	putamen	pyrolysis	qualm	quiet	rab
puke	pupal	putamina	pyrolitic	qualmish	quietism	rabat
pulay	pupate	putative	pyromancy	qualmy	quietist	rabato
pule	pupation	putlog	pyromania	quamash	quietude	

rabbet	radiology	ramble	rapine	raw	recall	recusant
rabbi	radish	rambutan	rapparee	rawhide	recant	recusancy
rabbin	radium	ramee	rappee	rawish	recap	recuse
rabbinic	radius	ramekin	rappel	ray	recapture	red
rabbinism	radix	ramenta	rapport	raya	recast	redact
rabbinist	radixes	ramentum	rapt	rayah	recede	redaction
rabbit	radon	ramequin	raptorial	raygrass	receipt	redan
rabbitry	radula	ramet	rapture	rayless	receive	redbird
rabble	radulae	rami	rapturous	rayon	recension	redbreast
rabboni	raff	ramie	rare	raze	recent	redbud
rabic	raffia	ramiform	rarebit	razee	recency	redbug
rabid	raffinose	ramify	rarefy	razor	recept	redcap
rabies	raffish	ramilie	rareripe	razorback	receptacle	redcoat
raca	raffle	ramillie	rarity	razorbill	reception	redd
raccoon	rafflesia	rammish	rascal	razzia	receptive	redden
race	raft	rammy	rascality	re	receptor	reddenda
raceme	rafter	ramose	rase	reach	recess	reddendum
racemic	raftsman	ramous	rash	react	recession	reddish
racemism	rag	ramp	rasher	reactance	recessive	reddle
racemize	rage	rampage	rasorial	reaction	recipe	reddleman
racemoid	ragee	rampancy	rasp	reactive	recipient	redeem
racemose	ragged	rampant	raspberry	read	recision	redeliver
racemous	raggee	rampart	raspy	readjust	recital	redemand
racetrack	raggstone	rampion	rasure	readmit	recite	redevelop
raceway	raggy	ramrod	rat	ready	reckless	redfin
rachial	ragi	ramson	ratafee	reagent	reckon	redhead
rachides	raglan	ramtil	ratafia	real	reclaim	redingote
rachis	ragman	ramulose	ratal	reales	recline	redirect
rachises	ragout	ramus	ratan	realgar	recluse	redolence
rachitic	ragpicker	rance	ratany	realism	reclusive	redolent
rachitis	ragstone	ranch	rataplan	realist	reclusion	redolency
racial	ragtime	rancher	ratch	realistic	recognize	redouble
racialism	ragweed	rancheria	ratchet	reality	recoil	redoubt
racialist	ragwort	ranchero	rate	realize	recollect	redound
racism	raia	ranchman	ratel	realm	recommend	redowa
racist	raid	rancho	rather	reals	recommit	redpoll
rack	rail	ranchos	ratify	realty	recompose	redraft
racket	railbird	rancid	ratio	ream	reconcile	redress
rackety	railhead	rancidity	ration	reanimate	recondite	redroot
racketeer	raillery	rancorous	rational	reap	reconsign	redshank
rackwork	railroad	rancour	rationale	rear	reconvey	redskin
racon	railway	rand	ratite	rearhorse	record	redstart
raconteur	raiment	randan	ratlin	rearm	recount	redtop
racoon	rain	randem	ratline	rearmost	recoup	reduce
racquet	rainband	random	ratling	rearmouse	recourse	reductase
racy	rainbow	rang	ratoon	rearrange	recover	reduction
radar	raincoat	range	ratsbane	rearward	recovery	reductive
raddle	raindrop	rangy	rattan	rearwards	recreant	redundant
raddleman	rainfall	rank	ratteen	reason	recreate	redware
radial	rainproof	rankle	ratten	reassure	recrement	redwing
radian	rainstorm	ransack	rattish	rebat	recruit	redwood
radiance	rainy	ransom	rattle	rebate	rectal	ree
radiancy	raise	rant	rattlebox	rebec	rectangle	reed
radiant	raisin	ranunculi	rattrap	rebeck	recti	reedling
radiate	raisonné	rap	ratty	rebel	rectify	reedmace
radiative	raj	rapacious	raucous	rebeldom	rectitude	reedy
radiation	raja	rapacity	raucity	rebellion	recto	reef
radiator	rajah	rape	ravage	rebill	rector	reefy
radiatory	rake	rapist	rave	rebirth	rectorate	reek
radical	rakehell	rapeseed	ravel	reboant	rectorial	reeky
radicel	rakehelly	raphe	ravelin	reborn	rectory	reel
radices	rakish	raphia	raven	rebound	rectus	reenforce
radicle	rale	raphide	ravenous	rebuff	recumbent	reenter
radii	ralliform	raphis	ravin	rebuke	recur	reentrant
radio	ralline	rapid	ravine	rebus	recurrent	reentry
radiode	rally	rapidity	ravioli	rebut	recurvate	reeve
radiogram	ram	rapier	ravish	rebuttal	recurve	refection

refective	regular	remarry	repertory	reserve	retable	revenant
refectory	regulate	remedial	repetend	reservist	retail	revenge
refer	reguli	remedy	repine	reservoir	retain	revenue
referee	reguline	remember	replace	reset	retake	reverb
reference	regulus	remex	repleader	resh	retaliate	revere
refill	rehash	remiges	replenish	reship	retard	reverence
refine	rehearsal	remigial	replete	reside	retardant	reverend
refinery	rehearse	remind	repletion	residence	retch	reverent
refit	reheat	remindful	replevin	residency	rete	reverie
reflate	reify	reminisce	replevy	resident	retia	revers
reflect	reign	remise	replica	residual	retell	reversal
reflex	reimburse	remiss	replicate	residuary	retene	reverse
reflexive	rein	remission	reply	residue	retent	reversion
refluence	reindeer	remit	report	residuua	retention	reverso
refluency	reinforce	remittal	reposal	residuum	retentive	revert
refluent	reins	remittent	repose	resign	retiarii	revertive
reflux	reinstall	remnant	reposeful	resile	retiarius	revery
reforest	reinstate	remodel	reposit	resilient	retiary	revest
reform	reinsure	remontant	repossess	resin	reticence	revet
reformist	reinvest	remontoir	repoussé	resinate	reticency	review
refract	reis	remora	reprehend	resinoid	reticent	reviewal
refractor	reissue	remorse	represent	resinous	reticle	revile
refrain	reitbok	remote	repress	resiny	reticula	revisal
refresh	reiterate	remotion	reprieve	resist	reticular	revise
reft	reject	remount	reprimand	resistant	reticule	revision
refuge	rejection	removal	reprint	restistive	reticulum	revisit
refugee	rejoice	remove	reprisal	resole	retiform	revisory
refulgent	rejoin	renal	reprise	resoluble	retina	revival
refund	rejoinder	renascent	reproach	resolute	retinae	revive
refusal	relapse	rend	reprobate	resolve	retinal	revivify
refuse	relate	render	reprocess	resolvent	retinas	revocable
refutal	relation	rendition	reproduce	resonance	retinene	revocably
refute	relative	renegade	reproof	resonant	retinite	revoice
regain	relax	renegado	reproval	resonate	retinitis	revoke
regal	relay	renege	reprove	resonator	retinol	revolt
regale	release	renew	reptant	resorb	retinue	revolute
regalia	relegate	renewal	reptile	resorcin	retiracy	revolve
regality	relent	reniform	reptilian	resort	retire	revolving
regard	relevance	renig	republic	resound	retort	revue
regardant	relevancy	renin	republish	resource	retorsion	revulsion
regardful	relevant	renitence	repudiate	respect	retortion	revulsive
regatta	reliance	renitency	repugnant	respell	retouch	reward
regelate	reliant	renitent	repulse	respire	retrace	rewind
regency	relic	rennet	repulsion	respite	retract	rewire
regent	relict	rennin	repulsive	respond	retral	reword
regicidal	relief	renounce	repute	response	retread	rewrite
regicide	relieve	renovate	reputed	rest	retreat	reynard
régime	religion	renown	request	rester	retrench	rhaphe
regimen	religious	renowned	requiem	restful	retrieval	rhapsodic
regiment	reliquary	rent	require	restiform	retrieve	rhapsody
reginal	relique	rental	requisite	restive	retroact	rhatany
region	relish	reopen	requital	restless	retrocede	rhea
regional	relocate	reorient	requite	restock	retroflex	rhein
register	relucent	repair	reredos	restore	retrorse	rhematic
registrar	reluct	repand	rerun	restrain	retrospect	rhenium
registry	reluctant	reparable	rescind	restraint	retroussé	rheology
reglet	relume	reparably	rescript	restrict	retrovert	rheometer
regma	relumine	repartee	rescue	result	return	rheoscope
regnal	rely	repast	research	resultant	retuse	rheostat
regnant	remain	repay	reseat	resumable	reunion	rheotaxis
regorge	remainder	repeal	resect	resume	reunite	rheotron
regrade	reman	repeat	resection	resupine	revamp	rheotrope
regrate	remand	repel	reseda	resurface	reveal	rhesus
regress	remanence	repellent	resell	resurge	reveille	rhetor
regret	remanent	repent	resemble	resurgent	revel	rhetoric
regula	remark	repentant	resent	resurrect	revelator	rheum
regulae	remarque	repeople	resentful	ret	revelry	rheumatic

rheumy	riddle	risible	rogue	rosiny	royal	rum
rhigolene	ride	risky	roguery	rosinweed	royalism	rumba
rhinal	rident	risqué	roguish	rosolio	royalist	rumble
rhinitis	riderless	rissole	roil	roster	royalmast	rumen
rhino	ridge	risus	roily	rostra	royalty	rumina
rhinology	ridgy	rite	roister	rostral	rub	ruminant
rhizobium	ridicule	ritual	rokelay	rostrate	rubace	ruminate
rhizoid	ridotto	ritualism	role	rostrum	rubasse	rummage
rhizoidal	rietbok	ritualist	roll	rostrums	rubato	rummer
rhizoma	rife	rival	rollic	rosy	rubber	rummy
rhizome	riffle	rivalry	rollicky	rot	rubbery	rumour
rhizopod	rifle	rive	rollway	rota	rubberize	rump
rhizotomy	rifleman	riven	rolypoly	rotary	rubbish	rumple
rhodamin	rift	river	romaine	rotate	rubbishy	run
rhodamine	rig	riverine	roman	rotation	rubble	runagate
rhodic	rigadoon	riverside	romance	rotative	rubella	runcinate
rhodium	right	riverweed	romantic	rotatores	rubellite	rundle
rhodolite	righteous	rivet	romaunt	rotatory	rubeola	rundlet
rhodonite	rightful	rivulet	romp	rotch	rubeolar	rune
rhodopsin	rightist	roach	rompish	rotche	rubescent	runic
rhodora	rigid	road	rondeau	rote	rubicund	rung
rhomb	rigidity	roadbed	rondel	rotenone	rubidium	runlet
rhombic	rigmarole	roadblock	rondelet	rotifer	rubigo	runnel
rhombical	rigor	roadstead	rondo	rotiferal	rubious	runt
rhomboid	rigorism	roadster	rondure	rotiform	ruble	runty
rhombus	rigorist	roadway	ronquil	rotl	rubric	runway
rhonchal	rigorous	roam	rood	rotograph	rubrical	rupee
rhonchi	rigour	roan	roof	rotor	rubricate	rupture
rhonchial	rile	roar	roofage	rotten	rubrician	rural
rhonchus	riled	roast	roofless	rotund	ruby	ruralism
rhubarb	rill	rob	rooftree	rotunda	rucervine	ruralist
rhumb	rille	robalo	rook	rotundity	ruche	rurality
rhumba	rillet	roband	rookery	rouble	ruching	ruralize
rhyme	rim	robbin	rookie	rouche	ruck	ruse
rhymeless	rime	robber	rooky	roué	rucksack	rush
rhymester	rimester	robbery	room	rouge	ructation	rushlight
rhyolite	rimose	robe	roomful	rough	rudbeckia	rushy
rhythm	rimosity	robin	roommate	roughage	rudd	rusine
rhythmic	rimous	roble	roomy	roughen	rudder	rusk
rhythmics	rimple	roborant	roorback	roughneck	ruddle	russet
rhythmist	rimy	robot	roost	rouleau	ruddleman	russety
rial	rind	roburite	root	roulette	ruddock	rust
rialto	ring	robust	rootless	round	ruddy	rustic
riant	ringbone	roc	rootlet	roundel	rude	rustical
riata	ringent	rocambole	rootstalk	roundelay	rudiment	rusticate
rib	ringhals	rochet	rootstock	roundhand	rue	rusticity
ribald	ringlet	rock	rooty	roundish	rueful	rustle
ribaldry	ringneck	rockaway	rope	roundlet	rufescent	rusty
riband	ringshake	rocket	ropery	roundworm	ruff	rut
ribband	ringworm	rocketeer	ropewalk	roup	ruffe	rutabaga
ribbon	rink	rockfish	ropy	roupy	ruffed	rutaceous
ribwort	rinse	rockrose	roque	rouse	ruffian	ruth
rice	riot	rockweed	roquet	roust	ruffle	ruthenic
ricebird	riotous	rockwork	rorqual	rout	rufous	ruthenium
ricer	rip	rocky	rosaceous	route	rug	ruthful
rich	riparian	rococo	rosary	routine	ruga	ruthless
richweed	riparious	rod	rose	routinism	rugae	rutilant
ricin	ripcord	rodent	roseate	routinist	rugate	rutilated
rick	ripe	rodential	rosebay	rove	rugged	rutile
rickets	ripen	rodeo	rosebud	rowan	rugose	rutting
rickety	ripost	rodman	rosefish	rowboat	rugosity	ruttish
ricochet	riposte	rodsman	rosemary	rowdy	rugous	rutty
rictal	ripple	roe	roseola	rowdyish	ruin	rye
rictus	ripplet	roebuck	rosette	rowdyism	ruinate	rynd
rid	ripply	roentgen	rosewater	rowel	ruination	ryot
riddance	ripsaw	rogation	rosewood	rowen	ruinous	
ridden	rise	rogatory	rosin	rowlock	rule	

S

	saggar	saltation	sandpaper	sard	sausage	scammony
	saggard	saltatory	sandpeep	sardine	sauterne	scamp
sabadilla	sagger	saltern	sandpiper	sardius	sautoir	scamper
sabbat	sagittal	saltier	sandstone	sardonic	savage	scampish
sabicu	sagittate	saltire	sandstorm	sardonyx	savagedom	scampy
sabine	sago	saltish	sandwich	sargasso	savagery	scan
sable	saguaro	saltlick	sandwort	sargassum	savagism	scandal
sabotage	saguaros	saltpan	sandy	sarment	savanna	scandent
saboteur	sagum	saltpetre	sane	sarmenta	savannah	scandia
sabre	sagy	saltworks	sangaree	sarmentum	savant	scandic
sabulose	said	saltwort	sanguine	sarsar	save	scandium
sabulous	saiga	salty	sanicle	sarsenet	savin	scansion
sac	sail	salubrity	sanies	sartor	savine	scant
sacaton	sailboat	saluki	sanious	sartorial	saviour	scantling
saccate	sailcloth	salutary	sanitaria	sartorius	savory	scanty
saccaton	sailfish	salute	sanitary	sash	savour	scape
saccharic	sainfoin	salvable	sanitate	sashay	savoury	scapegoat
saccharin	saint	salvage	sanity	saskatoon	savoy	scaphoid
sacculate	sainthood	salvation	sannup	sass	saw	scapolite
saccule	saith	salve	sans	sassaby	sawn	scapose
sacculi	sajou	salver	sansar	sasafras	sawbuck	scapula
sacculus	sake	salvia	santonica	satang	sawdust	scapulae
sachem	saker	salvo	santonin	satanic	sawfish	scapular
sachet	salaam	salvos	santonine	satanical	sawfly	scapulary
sack	salacious	salvoes	sap	satchel	sawgrass	scar
sackbut	salacity	salvor	sapadillo	sate	sawhorse	scarab
sackcloth	salad	samara	sapajou	sateen	sawmill	scarabee
sackful	salary	samarium	sapanwood	satellite	sawpit	scarabaei
sacque	sale	sambar	saphead	satiable	sawyer	scarab(a)eu
sacra	saleratus	sambuca	saphena	satiably	sax	scaraboid
sacral	salesman	sambuke	saphenae	satiate	saxatile	scarce
sacrament	salicin	sambur	saphenous	satiation	saxhorn	scarcity
sacraria	salicine	same	sapid	satiety	saxifrage	scare
sacrarium	salicylic	samech	sapidity	satin	saxophone	scarecrow
sacred	salience	samek	sapience	satinet	saxtuba	scarehead
sacrifice	saliency	samekh	sapiency	satinette	say	scarf
sacrilege	salient	samisen	sapient	satinpod	says	scarfskin
sacrist	salify	samite	sapless	satinwood	scab	scarify
sacristan	salimeter	samlet	sapling	satiny	scabby	scariose
sacristy	salina	samp	sapodilla	satire	scabbard	scarious
sacrum	saline	sampan	saponify	satiric	scabbling	scarlet
sad	salinity	samphire	saponin	satirical	scabies	scarp
sadden	saliva	sample	saponine	satirist	scabietic	scarves
saddle	salivary	sanative	saponite	satirize	scabiosa	scat
saddlebow	salivate	sanatoria	sapor	satisfy	scabious	scathe
saddlery	sallet	sanatory	saporific	satrap	scabrous	scathless
sadism	sallow	sanbenito	saporous	satrapy	scaffold	scatology
sadist	sallowfish	sanctify	sapota	satrapate	scaglia	scatter
sadistic	sallowy	sanction	sapour	saturant	scagliola	scaup
safari	sally	sanctity	sapphire	saturate	scalade	scaur
safe	salmi	sanctuary	sappy	saturable	scalado	scavenge
safeguard	salmis	sanctum	sapraemia	saturnid	scalage	scenario
safety	salmon	sand	sapremia	saturnine	scalar	scenarios
safflower	salmonoid	sandal	sapr(a)emic	saturnism	scald	scenarist
saffron	salol	sandaled	saprolite	satyr	scaldic	scend
safranin	salon	sandarac	sapsago	satyric	scale	scene
safranine	saloon	sandarach	sapsucker	satyrical	scalene	scenery
safrol	salpa	sandbag	sapwood	sauce	scalenous	scenic
safrole	salpian	sandbar	saraband	saucepan	scalenus	scenical
sag	salpid	sandblast	sarabande	saucer	scall	scent
saga	salpiform	sandblind	sarcasm	saucy	scalled	scentless
sagacious	salpinges	sandbox	sarcastic	sauger	scallion	sceptic
sagacity	salpinx	sandbur	sarcenet	saunter	scallop	sceptical
sagaman	salsify	sandburr	sarcocarp	saurel	scalp	sceptre
sagamore	salsilla	sandcrack	sarcoma	saurian	scalpel	schappe
sage	salt	sandeel	sarcomata	sauropod	scaly	schatchen
sagebrush	saltant	sandman	sarcous	saury	scamble	schedule

scheelite	scission	scramble	scurf	secondine	seignior	semivowel
scheik	scissor	scrap	scurfy	secrecy	seigniory	semolina
schema	scissors	scrapbook	scurril	secret	seine	senary
schemata	scissure	scrape	scurrile	secretary	seise	senate
scheme	sciurine	scrapple	scurry	secrete	seisin	senator
schematic	sciuroid	scrappy	scurvy	secretin	seismal	send
scherzi	sclera	scratch	scuta	secretion	seismic	sendal
scherzo	sclerite	scratchy	scutage	secretive	seismical	sendaline
scherzos	scleritic	scrawl	scutate	secretory	seismism	senega
schilling	scleritis	scrawny	scutch	sect	seismotic	seneka
schism	scleroid	screak	scutcheon	sectarian	seize	senescent
schist	scleroma	scream	scutella	sectarist	seizin	seneschal
schistic	sclerosal	scree	scutellar	sectary	seizor	senile
schistose	sclerosed	screech	scutiform	sectile	seizure	senility
schistous	sclerosis	screechy	scutter	sectility	sejant	senior
schizont	sclerotic	screed	scuttle	section	sejeant	seniority
schizopod	sclerous	screen	scutum	sectional	selachian	senna
schliere	scoff	screw	scythe	sector	selachoid	sennet
schlieren	scold	screwbean	sea	secular	selah	sennit
schlieric	scoleces	scribal	seaboard	secund	selamik	señor
schnapper	scolecite	scribble	seafarer	secundine	seldom	señora
schnapps	scolex	scribe	seafaring	secure	select	señorita
schnaps	scolices	scrim	seal	security	selectee	sensate
schnauzer	scolioma	scrimmage	sealery	sedan	selection	sensated
scholar	scoliosis	scrimp	seam	sedate	selective	sensation
scholarch	scoliotic	scrimpy	seaman	sedative	selectman	sense
scholia	scollop	scrimshaw	seamless	sedentary	selenate	senseless
scholiast	scombroid	scrip	seamster	sedge	selenic	sensitive
scholium	sconce	script	seamy	sedged	selenious	sensitize
scholiums	scone	scripture	séance	sedgy	selenite	sensor
school	scoop	scrive	seaplane	sedile	selenium	sensoria
schoolboy	scoopful	scrivello	seaport	sedilia	self	sensorial
schooling	scoot	scrivener	seaquake	sedilium	selfheal	sensorium
schoolman	scope	scrod	sear	sediment	selfhood	sensory
schooner	scopoline	scrofula	search	sedition	selfish	sensual
schorl	scopulate	scroll	seascape	seditious	selfless	sensuous
schuit	scorbutic	scroop	seashore	seduce	sell	sent
schuyt	scorbutus	scrota	seasick	seduction	selvage	sentence
schwa	scorch	scrotal	seaside	seductive	semanteme	sentience
sciaenid	scordato	scrotum	season	sedulity	semantic	sentiency
sciaenoid	score	scrub	seasonal	sedulous	semantics	sentient
sciagraph	scoria	scrubby	seasoning	sedum	semaphore	sentiment
sciamachy	scoriae	scrubland	seat	see	sematic	sentinel
sciascope	scorify	scruff	seawan	seecatch	semblable	sentry
sciascopy	scoriform	scrum	seawant	seed	semblably	sepal
sciatic	scorn	scrummage	seaward	seedcake	semblance	sepaline
sciatica	scornful	scrunch	seawards	seedcase	semble	sepalous
science	scorpioid	scruple	seaware	seedless	semeiotic	separable
sciential	scorpion	scrutiny	seaway	seedling	semen	separata
scientism	scotch	scud	seaweed	seedman	semester	separate
scientist	scoter	scudi	seaworthy	seedsman	semestral	separatum
scilicet	scotfree	scudo	sebaceous	seedy	semibreve	sepia
scimetar	scotia	scuff	sebacic	seek	semicolon	sepiolite
scimitar	scotoma	scuffle	seborrh(o)ea	seel	semidome	sepoy
scincoid	scotomata	scull	sebum	seem	semifinal	sepsis
scintilla	scoundrel	scullery	secant	seep	semifluid	sept
sciolism	scour	scullion	secede	seepage	semilunar	septa
sciolist	scourge	sculpin	secern	seer	semimute	septal
sciolous	scourings	sculptor	secession	seeress	seminal	septangle
sciomachy	scouse	sculpture	seck	seethe	seminar	septaria
scion	scout	scum	seckel	segment	seminary	septarian
sciophyte	scow	scumble	seclude	segmental	semiology	septarium
scirrhi	scowl	scummer	seclusion	segno	semiotic	septate
scirrhoid	scowler	scummy	seclusive	segregate	semirigid	septemia
scirrhous	SCRABBLE	scup	second	seicento	semiround	septaemia
scirrhus	scrag	scuppaug	secondary	seiche	semitone	septemvir
scissile	scraggy	scupper	seconde	seigneur	semitonic	septenary

septenate	serpent	sexfid	shape	shift	short	si
septet	serpigo	sexifid	shapeless	shiftless	shortage	sialid
septette	serranid	sexless	shard	shifty	shortcake	sialidan
septic	serranoid	sext	share	shikaree	shorten	sialogogue
septicide	serrate	sextan	shark	shikari	shorthand	sialoid
septicity	serrated	sextant	sharkskin	shill	shorthorn	sib
septime	serration	sextarius	sharp	shillala	shortia	sibb
septa	serrature	sextet	sharpen	shillalah	shorting	sibilant
septal	serried	sextette	sharpie	shillaly	shortish	sibilance
septum	serriform	sextile	shatter	shillelah	shot	sibilancy
septuple	serrulate	sexton	shave	shilling	shote	sibilate
sepulchre	serry	sextuple	shaveling	shily	shotgun	sibling
sepulture	serta	sextuplet	shawl	shim	shotten	sibyl
sequacity	serum	sexual	shawm	shimmer	should	sibyllic
sequel	serums	sexuality	shay	shimmery	shoulder	sibylline
sequela	serval	shabbily	she	shimmy	shout	sic
sequelae	servant	shabby	shea	shin	shove	siccate
sequence	serve	shack	sheaf	shine	shovel	siccation
sequency	service	shackle	shear	shingle	show	siccative
sequent	serviette	shacko	shears	shinleaf	showbill	sice
sequester	servile	shad	sheatfish	shinney	showboat	sick
sequestra	servility	shadberry	sheath	shinny	showbread	sickbay
sequin	servitor	shadblow	sheathe	shiny	showcase	sickbed
sequoia	servitude	shadbush	sheave	ship	showdown	sicken
ser	sesame	shaddock	sheaves	shipboard	shower	sickish
sera	sesamoid	shade	shed	shipload	showery	sickle
sérac	sessile	shadeless	sheen	shipman	shown	sicklist
seraglio	sessility	shadfly	sheeny	shipmate	showy	sid
serai	session	shadoof	sheep	shipment	shrank	siddur
serail	sessional	shadow	sheepcote	shippable	shrapnel	side
serape	sesterce	shadowy	sheepfold	shipshape	shred	sideband
seraph	sestet	shadrach	sheepfold	shipway	shrew	sideboard
seraphim	sestina	shaduf	sheepish	shipworm	shrewd	sidecar
seraphina	set	shady	sheepskin	shipwreck	shrewish	sidelight
seraphine	seta	shaft	sheer	shipyard	shriek	sideline
seraphs	setaceous	shag	sheet	shire	shrieval	sideling
serenade	setae	shagbark	sheeting	shirk	shrift	sidelong
serene	setback	shaggy	sheik(h)	shirr	shrike	sidepiece
serenity	setiform	shagreen	shekel	shirt	shrill	siderite
serf	seton	shah	sheldrake	shirting	shrimp	sideritic
serfdom	setose	shaik(h)	shelf	shiv	shrine	siderosis
serf'hood	setscrew	shake	shell	shivaree	shrink	sidesman
serge	settee	shako	shellac	shive	shrinkage	sidetrack
sergeancy	settle	shaky	shellack	shiver	shrivel	sidewalk
sergeant	seven	shale	shellback	shivery	shroud	sideward
serjeancy	sevenfold	shall	shellbark	shivey	shrove	sidewards
serjeant	seventeen	shalloon	shellfire	shivvy	shrub	sideway
serial	seventh	shallop	shellfish	shoal	shrubbery	sideways
seriate	seventhly	shallot	shellheap	shoat	shrubby	sidewise
seriatim	seventy	shallow	shellhole	shock	shrug	siding
seriation	sever	shaly	shelly	shod	shrunk	sidle
sericeous	several	sham	shelter	shoddy	shrunken	siege
seriema	severance	shaman	shelve	shoe	shuck	sienna
series	severe	shamanic	shelvy	shoebill	shudder	sierra
serif	severity	shamble	shend	shoeblack	shuffle	siesta
serin	sew	shame	shepherd	shoehorn	shun	sieur
serine	sewage	shameful	sherbet	shoemaker	shunpike	sieve
serious	sewan	shameless	shereef	shogun	shunt	sifaka
sermon	sewellel	shammer	sherif	shogunate	shut	siffle
sermonic	sewen	shammy	sheriff	shone	shutdown	sift
sermonize	sewer	shamois	sherry	shoo	shutoff	sigh
serology	sewerage	shampoo	shew	shook	shutout	sight
seroon	sewn	shamrock	shewbread	shoot	shuttle	sightless
serosity	sex	shanghai	shewer	shop	shy	sightseer
serotinal	sexangle	shank	sheyk	shore	shyer	sigil
serotine	sexangled	shanty	shield	shoreless	shyly	sigillary
serous	sexennial	shantyman	shier	shorl	shyster	sigma

sigmate	simmer	siskiwit	skillet	sleep	sluice	smut
sigmatism	simnel	siskowet	skilling	sleepless	sluiceway	smutch
sigmoid	simoinac	siskowit	skim	sleepy	slum	smutchy
sign	simony	siskin	skimpy	sleet	slumber	smutty
signal	simoom	siss	skin	sleety	slumbery	snack
signalize	simoon	sister	skinflint	sleeve	slumbrous	snaffle
signalman	simper	sistroid	skink	sleigh	slump	snag
signatory	simple	sistra	skinless	sleight	slung	snaggy
signature	simpleton	sistrum	skinny	slender	slungshot	snail
signboard	simplex	sistrums	skip	sleuth	slunk	snake
signet	simplify	sit	skipjack	slew	slur	snakebird
signify	simply	site	skippet	slice	slurry	snakehead
signior	simulacra	sitfast	skirmish	slick	slush	snakeroot
signor	simulant	situate	skirr	slidden	slut	snakeweed
sinory	simular	situation	skirret	slide	sluttish	snaky
signpost	simulate	six	skirt	slideknot	sly	snap
silage	simurg	sixfold	skit	slight	slyboots	snappish
silence	sin	sixpence	skittish	slily	smack	snappy
silent	sinalbin	sixpenny	skittle	slim	small	snapshot
silesia	sinapin	sixscore	skive	slime	smallage	snapweed
silex	sinapine	sixteen	skoal	slimily	smallish	snare
silica	sinapism	sixteenmo	skua	slimy	smallpox	snarl
silicate	since	sixteenth	skulk	sling	smalt	snatch
siliceous	sincere	sixth	skull	slingshot	smaltine	snatchily
silicic	sincerity	sixtieth	skullcap	slink	smaltite	snatchy
silcide	sinciput	sixty	skunk	slip	smart	snath
silicify	sine	sizable	skunkweed	slipknot	smarten	snathe
silicle	sinecure	sizar	sky	slippage	smartweed	sneak
silicon	sinew	sizarship	skyey	slipper	smash	sneaky
silicosis	sinewless	size	skylark	slippery	smatter	sneck
siliqua	sinewy	sizy	skylight	slipshod	smear	snecket
siliquae	sing	sizz	skyrocket	slipslop	smearcase	sneer
silique	singe	sizzle	skysail	slit	smeary	sneeze
siliquose	single	sjambok	skyward	lither	smeath	snell
siliquous	singlet	skald	slab	slithery	smee	snicker
silk	singleton	skat	slabby	sliver	smell	sniff
silkalene	singsong	skate	slack	slob	smelt	sniffle
silkaline	singular	skatol	slacken	slobber	smeltery	snifter
silken	sinigrin	skatole	slag	slobbery	smew	snigger
silkman	sinister	skean	slaggy	sloe	smilax	snip
silkweed	sinistrad	skee	slain	slogan	smile	snipe
silkworm	sinistral	skeen	slake	sloid	smirch	snippet
silky	sink	skeet	slalom	slojd	smirk	snippy
sill	sinkhole	skeg	slam	sloop	smite	snivel
sillabub	sinless	skein	slander	slop	smith	snob
silly	sinter	skeletal	slang	slope	smithers	snobbery
silo	sinuate	skeleton	slant	sloppy	smithery	snobbish
silos	sinuosity	skelp	slantwise	slopwork	smithy	snood
silt	sinuous	skep	slap	slosh	smitten	snore
silty	sinus	skeptic	slapdash	sloshy	smock	snort
silurid	sinusitis	skeptical	slapstick	slot	smog	snout
siluroid	sip	sketch	slash	sloth	smoke	snow
silva	siphon	sketchy	slat	slothbear	smokeless	snowball
silvae	siphonage	skew	slate	slothful	smokepot	snowberry
silvan	sippet	skewbald	slattern	slough	smoky	snowbird
silver	sir	skewer	slaty	sloughy	smolt	snowbroth
silvern	sirdar	ski	slaughter	sloven	smooch	snowbush
silvery	sire	skiagraph	slave	slow	smooth	snowdrift
simar	siren	skiascope	slavery	slowworm	smoothen	snowdrop
simarouba	sirenia	skiascopy	slavish	sloyd	smote	snowfall
simaruba	sirenian	skid	slavocrat	slub	smother	snowflake
simian	siriasis	skidway	slaw	sludge	smothery	snowshed
similar	sirloin	skiff	slay	sludgy	smoulder	snowshoe
simile	sirocco	skijoring	sleave	slue	smudge	snowstorm
simioid	sirrah	skilful	sled	slug	smudgy	snowwhite
simious	sisal	skill	sledge	sluggard	smug	snowy
simlin	siscowet	skilless	sleek	sluggish	smuggle	snub

snuff	solarium	something	soritical	spagiric	spectra	spicular
snuffbox	solarize	sometime	sorority	spagyric	spectral	spiculate
snuffle	solatia	sometimes	sorosis	spahee	spectre	spicule
snuffy	solatium	someway	sorption	spahi	spectrum	spiculum
snug	sold	somewhat	sorrel	spait	specula	spicy
snuggery	solder	somewhen	sorrow	spall	specular	spider
snuggle	soldier	somewhere	sorrowful	spalpeen	speculate	spidery
soak	soldiery	somital	sorry	span	speculum	spiegel
soakage	soldo	somite	sort	spandrel	speculums	spigelia
soaky	soldi	somitic	sortie	spanaemia	speech	spigot
soap	sole	somnific	sorus	spanaemic	speechify	spike
soapbark	solecism	somnolent	sot	spanemia	speed	spikelet
soapberry	solecist	son	sotol	spanemic	speedster	spikenard
soapbox	solecistic	sonance	sottish	spangle	speedway	spiky
soapstone	solecize	sonant	sou	spaniel	speedwell	spile
soapsuds	solemn	sonar	souari	spank	speedy	spill
soapwort	solemnity	sonata	soubrette	spanless	speise	spillage
soapy	solemnize	sonatina	souchong	spar	speiss	spillikin
soar	solenoid	sonatine	soufflé	spare	spelaean	spillway
sob	soleret	sonder	sough	sparerib	spelean	spilosite
sober	solfatara	song	sought	sparge	spell	spilth
sobriety	solfeggi	songbird	soul	spark	spellbind	spin
sobriquet	solfeggio	songful	souled	sparkish	spelt	spinach
socage	solferino	songster	soulful	sparkle	spelter	spinal
sociable	soli	sonic	soulless	sparkling	spencer	spinate
sociably	solicit	sonnet	sound	sparling	spend	spindle
social	solid	sonneteer	soundbox	sparoid	spent	spindrift
socialism	solidago	sonority	soup	sparrow	sperm	spine
socialist	solidary	sonorous	soupçon	sparry	spermary	spinel
socialite	solideme	sonship	sour	sparse	spermatia	spineless
sociality	solidi	soochong	source	sparsity	spermatic	spinet
socialize	solidify	soon	sourdine	sparteine	spermatid	spinifex
society	solidity	soot	sourgum	spasm	spermic	spinnaker
sociologic	solidus	soothe	souse	spasmodic	spermine	spinner
sociology	soliloquy	soothfast	south	spastic	spermism	spinnery
socket	solipsism	soothsay	southeast	spate	spew	spinney
socle	solipsist	sooty	souther	spathal	sphagnous	spinny
socman	solitaire	sop	southerly	spathe	sphagnum	spinose
sockman	solitary	sophism	southern	spathic	sphene	spinosity
sod	solitude	sophist	southing	spathose	sphenic	spinous
soda	solleret	sophister	southron	spatial	sphenodon	spinster
sodalite	solmizate	sophistic	southward	spatter	sphenoid	spinula
sodality	solo	sophistry	southwest	spatula	spheral	spinule
sodden	solos	sophomore	souvenir	spatular	sphere	spinulose
sodium	solstice	sopor	sovereign	spatulate	spheric	spiny
soever	soluble	soporific	soviet	spavin	spherical	spiracle
sofa	solubly	soppy	sovietdom	spawn	spherics	spiraea
soffit	solum	soprani	sovietism	spay	spheroid	spiral
soft	solute	soprano	sovietist	speak	spherular	spirant
soften	solution	sopranos	sovietize	spear	spherule	spire
soggy	solutive	sora	sow	spearfish	sphery	spirea
soil	solvation	sorbitol	sowther	spearhead	sphincter	spirem
soilage	solve	sorbose	soy	spearman	sphinges	spireme
soilure	solvency	sorcerer	soya	spearmint	sphinx	spirilla
soja	solvent	sorceress	soybean	spearsman	sphinxes	spirillum
sojourn	soma	sorcerous	sozin	spearwort	sphygmic	spirit
soke	somatic	sorcery	sozine	special	sphygmoid	spiritism
sokeman	somatics	sordid	spa	specie	sphygmus	spiritist
sol	somatism	sore	space	species	spica	spiritous
solace	somatist	sorede	spacial	specific	spicae	spiritual
solan	sombre	soredia	spacious	specify	spical	spirituel
soland	sombrero	soredium	spade	specimen	spicate	spiritus
solano	some	sorel	spadeful	specious	spice	spirogyra
solanum	somebody	sorghum	spadefish	speck	spicebush	spiroid
solar	somehow	sori	spadices	speckle	spicery	spirula
solaria	someone	soricine	spadix	spectacle	spicewood	spiry
solarism	somerset	sorites	spaghetti	spectator	spicula	spissate

spit	sporocyte	squad	staghound	startle	stele	stilbene
spite	sporogony	squadron	stagnancy	starve	stelene	stilbite
spittle	sporophyl	squail	stagnant	starwort	steles	stile
spittoon	sporozoan	squalid	stagnate	stasis	stelic	stilet
spitz	sporran	squall	stagy	state	stellar	stilette
splash	sport	squalor	staid	statement	stellate	stiletto
splashy	sportful	squalus	stain	stateroom	stellular	stilettos
splatter	sportive	squama	stainless	statesman	stem	still
splay	sportsman	squamae	stair	static	stemless	stillborn
splayfoot	sporty	squamate	staircase	statical	stemson	stilt
spleen	sporulate	squamose	stairway	statics	stench	stilted
spleenful	sporule	squamosal	stake	station	stencil	stimulant
spleenish	spot	squamous	stale	stationer	stenosis	stimulate
spleeny	spotless	squander	stalemate	statism	stenotype	stimuli
splendent	spotlight	squantum	stalk	statist	stenotypy	stimulus
splendid	spotty	square	stalkless	statistic	stentor	stimy
splendour	spousal	squarrose	stalky	stator	step	sting
splenetic	spouse	squarrous	stall	statuary	steppe	stingaree
splenia	spout	squash	stallion	statue	steradian	stingy
splenial	sprag	squashy	stalwart	statuette	stere	stink
splenic	sprain	squat	stamen	stature	stereome	stinkard
splenii	sprang	squatty	stamina	status	steric	stinkball
splenium	sprat	squaw	staminal	statute	sterical	stinkbomb
splenius	sprawl	squawbush	staminate	statutory	sterile	stinkbug
splice	spray	squawfish	stamineal	staunch	sterility	stinkhorn
spline	spread	squawk	staminode	stave	sterilize	stinkpot
splint	spree	squawroot	staminody	stay	sterlet	stinkweed
splinter	sprig	squeak	stammel	staysail	sterling	stinkwood
splintery	spriggy	squeaky	stammer	stead	stern	stint
split	spright	squeal	stamp	steadfast	sterna	stipe
splotch	spring	squeamish	stampede	steady	sternal	stipel
splotchy	springal	squeegee	stanch	steak	sternmost	stipend
splutter	springald	squeeze	stanchion	steal	sternpost	stipes
spodumene	springbok	squelch	stand	stealth	sternson	stipiform
spoil	springe	squib	standard	stealthy	sternum	stipitate
spoilage	springy	squid	standish	steam	sternums	stipple
spoilsman	sprinkle	squilgee	standpipe	steamer	sternward	stipular
spoke	sprint	squill	stanhope	steamship	sternway	stipulate
spoken	sprit	squilla	staniel	steamy	steroid	stipule
spokesman	sprite	squinch	stannary	steapsin	sterol	stir
spoliator	spritsail	squint	stannel	stearate	stertor	stirabout
spondaic	sprocket	squire	stannic	stearic	sterule	stirk
spondee	sprout	squirelet	stannous	stearin	stet	stirps
sponge	spruce	squirm	stannum	stearine	stevedore	stirrup
spongin	sprue	squirmy	stanza	stearrh(o)ea	stew	stitch
spongy	spry	squirrel	stanzaic	steatite	steward	stithy
sponsal	spud	squirt	stapedial	stedfast	sthenia	stiver
sponsion	spume	stab	stapelia	steed	sthenic	stoa
sponson	spumous	stabile	stapes	steel	stibial	stoae
sponsor	spumy	stability	staple	steelhead	stibium	stoas
spook	spunk	stabilize	star	steely	stibnite	stoat
spookily	spur	stable	starboard	steelyard	stich	stob
spookish	spurge	stableman	starch	steenbok	stichic	stock
spooky	spurious	stably	starchy	steep	stichwort	stockade
spool	spurn	staccato	stare	steepen	stick	stockinet
spoon	spurrey	stack	starfish	steeple	stickle	stockish
spoonbill	spurry	stacte	stargrass	steer	stickseed	stockman
spoonful	spurt	stadia	stark	steerage	stickweed	stockpot
spoor	sputa	stadium	starless	steersman	sticky	stockwork
sporadial	sputter	stadiums	starlight	steeve	stiff	stocky
sporadic	sputum	staff	starlike	stegomyia	stiffen	stockyard
sporangia	spy	stag	starling	stein	stifle	stodge
spore	spyglass	stage	starlit	steinbok	stigma	stodgy
sporidia	squab	stagey	starnose	stela	stigmas	stogies
sporidium	squabbish	staggard	starry	stelae	stigmata	stogy
sporocarp	squabble	staggart	starshell	stelai	stigmatic	stoic
sporocyst	squabby	stagger	start	stelar	stilb	stoical

stoicism	strain	strive	stutter	sublation	subvert	suitcase
stoke	strait	strobic	sty	sublease	subway	suite
stokehold	straiten	strobil	stylar	sublet	succeed	suitor
stokehole	strake	strobile	style	sublethal	succentor	sukiyaki
stole	stramony	stroke	stylet	sublimate	success	sulcate
stoled	strand	stroll	styliform	sublime	successor	sulcated
stolid	strange	stroma	stylish	sublimity	succi	sulci
stolidity	strangle	stromatic	stylist	sublunar	succinate	sulcus
stolon	strangury	strong	stylistic	sublunary	succinct	sulfonyl
stoma	strap	strongyl	stylite	submarine	succinic	sulk
stomach	strapless	strongyle	stylize	submental	succory	sulky
stomachal	strappado	strontia	stylobate	submentum	succotash	sullage
stomacher	strass	strontian	styloid	submerge	succour	sullen
stomachic	strata	strontic	stylolite	submicron	succubi	sully
stomachy	stratagem	strontium	stylus	submine	succubus	sulphate
stomata	stratal	strop	stymie	submission	succulent	sulphid
stomatal	stategic	strophe	stypsis	submissive	succumb	sulphide
stomate	strategy	strophic	styptic	submit	succus	sulphite
stomatic	stratify	stroud	styptical	submittal	succuss	sulphonal
stomod(a)ea	stratum	structure	styrene	submontane	such	sulphone
stomod(a)eal	stratums	struggle	styrolene	subnormal	suck	sulphonic
stomod(a)eum	stratus	strum	stythe	suboceanic	suckfish	sulphur
stone	straw	struma	suability	suborder	suckle	sulpheret
stonechat	strawy	strumae	suable	subordinal	sucre	sulphuric
stonecrop	stray	strumatic	suasion	suborn	sucrose	sulphury
stonewall	streak	strumose	suasive	suboxide	suction	sulphryl
stoneware	streaky	strumous	suasory	subphylum	suctorial	sultan
stonework	stream	strumpet	suave	subplinth	sudan	sultana
stonewort	streamlet	strut	suavity	subpoena	sudaria	sultanate
stonish	street	strychnia	subacid	subramose	sudarium	sultaness
stony	strength	strychnin(e)	subacute	subregion	sudary	sultry
stood	strenuous	stub	subaerial	subrogate	sudation	sum
stook	stress	stubble	subalpine	subscribe	sudatory	sumac
stool	stretch	stubborn	subaltern	subscript	sudd	sumless
stoop	stretta	stubby	subarctic	subserve	sudden	summarist
stop	strettas	stucco	subarea	subside	sudor	summarize
stopcock	strette	stuccoes	subarid	subsidize	sudorific	summary
stope	stretti	stuccos	subatom	subsidy	suds	summation
stopgap	stretto	stud	subatomic	subsist	sudsy	summer
stoppage	strettos	studding	subcellar	subsistent	sue	summit
stopple	strew	student	subclimax	subsoil	suède	summital
stopwatch	stria	studfish	subdeacon	subsolar	suet	summon
storage	striae	studio	subdean	subsonic	suety	summons
storax	striate	studwork	subdepot	substance	suffari	sump
store	striation	study	subdivide	substrata	suffer	sumpter
storeroom	striature	stuff	subdual	substrate	suffice	sumptuary
storey	stricken	stuffy	subdue	subsume	suffix	sumptuous
storiette	strickle	stull	suber	subtenant	suffixal	sumpweed
stork	strict	stultify	subereous	subtend	suffixion	sun
storksbill	striction	stum	suberic	subtense	suffocate	sunbeam
storm	stricture	stumble	suberin	subtile	suffragan	sunbird
stormbelt	stride	stump	suberine	subtility	suffrage	sunbonnet
stormy	stridence	stumpage	suberize	subtilism	suffrutex	sunbow
story	stridency	stumpy	suberose	subtilize	suffuse	sunburn
stoss	strident	stun	suberous	subtility	suffusion	sunburnt
stotinka	strife	stunsail	subfamily	subtitle	suffusive	sunburned
stotinki	strigil	stunt	subgenus	subtle	sufism	sunburst
stoup	strigose	stupa	subgroup	subtlety	sugar	sundae
stout	strike	stupe	subhead	subtly	sugarbird	sunder
stove	string	stupefy	subhumid	subtonic	sugarcane	sundew
stow	stringent	stupid	subindex	subtorrid	sugarplum	sundial
stowage	stringhalt	stupidity	subinfeud	subtract	sugary	sundrops
stowp	stringy	stupor	subjacent	subtropic	suggest	sundry
strabism	strip	stuporous	subject	subulate	suicidal	sunfish
straddle	stripe	stupp	subjoin	suburban	suicide	sunflower
straggle	stripling	sturdy	subjugate	subvene	suint	sunglass
straight	stripy	sturgeon	sublate	subversal	suit	sunglow

sunken	surfbird	swampy	swipple	symbiosis	synodical	tabouret
sunless	surfboard	swamy	swirl	symbiotic	synodic	tabourine
sunlight	surfboat	swan	swirly	symbol	synonym	tabu
sunny	surfeit	swanherd	swish	symbolic	synonyme	tabular
sunrise	surficial	swannery	switch	symbolics	synonymic	tabulate
sunset	surge	swanskin	switchman	symbolism	synonymy	tacamahac
sunshade	surgeon	swap	swivel	symbolist	synopses	tace
sunshine	surgeoncy	swaraj	swizzle	symbolize	synopsis	tachinid
sunshiny	surgery	swarajism	swob	symbology	synoptic	tachiol
sunspot	surgical	swarajist	swollen	symmetric	synovia	tachylyte
sunstone	surgy	sward	swoon	symmetry	synovial	tacit
sunstroke	suricate	swarm	swoop	sympathin	synovitis	taciturn
sunstruck	surloin	swart	sword	sympathy	syntactic	tack
sunward	surly	swarth	swordbill	symphonic	syntax	tackle
sunwards	surmise	swarthy	swordfish	symphony	syntheses	tacky
sunwise	surmount	swarty	swordknot	symphyses	synthesis	tact
sup	surmullet	swash	swordman	symphysis	synthetic	tactful
super	surname	swastica	swordplay	sympodia	syntonic	tactic
superable	surpass	swastika	swordsman	sympodial	syntonize	tactical
superadd	surplice	swat	swot	sympodium	syntony	tactician
superb	surplus	swatch	swounds	symposia	synura	tactile
supercool	surprint	swath	swouns	symposiac	synurae	tactility
superego	surprisal	swathe	sybarite	symposial	sypher	taction
superfine	surprise	sway	sybo	symposion	syphon	tactless
superfuse	surrender	swayback	syboes	symposium	syren	tactual
superheat	surrey	sweal	sycamine	symptom	syringa	tad
superior	surrogate	swear	sycamore	synagogal	syringe	tadpole
supermale	surround	sweat	syce	synagogue	syrinx	tael
superman	surtax	sweatband	sycee	synal(o)epha	syringeal	taenia
supernal	surtout	sweatshop	sycon	synalgia	syrphian	taeniasis
superpose	survey	sweaty	syconia	synalgic	syrphid	tafferel
supersede	survival	sweep	syconium	synapse	syrphus	taffeta
supersex	survive	sweepback	sycophant	synapsis	syrup	taffrail
supertax	suslik	sweepy	sycosis	synaptic	syrupy	taffy
supervene	suspect	sweet	syenite	synaxis	systalic	tag
supervise	suspend	sweeten	syenitic	syncarp	system	tahsildar
supinate	suspense	sweetflag	syllabary	syncarpia	systemic	tail
supine	suspensor	sweetgale	syllabi	synclinal	systole	tailboard
supper	suspicion	sweetgum	syllabic	syncline	systolic	tailfirst
supplant	suspire	sweeting	syllabify	syncopal	syzygial	tailor
supple	sustain	sweetish	syllabism	syncopate	syzygy	tailpiece
suppliant	susurrant	sweetmeat	syllabist	syncope		tailskid
supply	susurrate	sweetshop	syllabize	syncopic		tailspin
support	susurrus	sweetsop	syllable	syncrasy	**T**	tailstock
supposal	sutler	swell	syllabub	syncrisis		tain
suppose	sutta	swellbox	syllabus	syndactyl	tab	taint
suppress	suttee	swellfish	syllepses	syndesis	tabanid	take
suppurate	sutteeism	swelter	syllepsis	syndetic	tabard	talapoin
supremacy	suttle	sweltry	sylleptic	syndic	tabby	talar
supreme	sutural	sweptback	syllogism	syndical	tabes	talbot
sura	suture	swerve	syllogize	syndicate	tabescent	talc
surah	suzerain	swift	sylph	syndrome	tabetic	talcose
sural	svelte	swifter	sylphid	syndromic	tablature	talcum
surbase	swab	swig	sylphish	synecious	table	tale
surbased	swaddle	swill	sylpblike	syneresis	tableau	talent
surcease	swag	swim	sylphy	synergia	tableaus	talented
surcharge	swagbelly	swimmeret	sylva	synergic	tableaux	taler
surcingle	swage	swindle	sylvae	synergism	tableland	talesman
surcoat	swagger	swine	sylvan	synergist	tablet	tali
surculose	swagman	swineherd	sylvanite	synergy	tableware	talion
surd	swain	swinepox	sylvas	synesis	tabloid	taliped
sure	swainish	swing	sylvin	syngamic	taboo	talipes
sureness	swale	swinge	sylvine	syngamous	tabor	talipot
surety	swallow	swingle	sylvinite	syngamy	taboret	talisman
surf	swami	swinish	sylvite	synizesis	taborin	talk
surfy	swamp	swipe	symbion	synod	taborine	talkative
surface	swampish	swiple	symbiont	synodal	tabour	tall

tallage	tantivy	tasteless	technical	tellurite	tension	terpino
tallish	tap	tasty	technique	tellurium	tensional	terrace
tallith	tapa	tat	technism	tellurize	tensity	terrain
tallol	tapadera	tatouay	techy	tellurous	tensive	terrane
tallow	tapadero	tattle	tectonic	teloblast	tensor	terrapin
tallowy	tape	tattoo	tectonics	telophase	tent	terraria
tally	tapeline	tau	tectrices	telpher	tentless	terrarium
tallyho	taper	taught	tectrix	telpheric	tentacle	terreen
tallyman	tapestry	taunt	ted	telson	tentage	terrene
talon	tapeta	taupe	tedious	temerity	tentation	terret
taluk	tapetum	taurine	tedium	temper	tentative	terrible
talus	tapeworm	taut	tee	tempera	tenth	terrier
tam	tapioca	tauten	teem	temperate	tenues	terrific
tamal	tapir	tautaug	teens	tempest	tenuis	terrify
tamale	tapis	tautog	teepee	templar	tenuity	terrigene
tamandu	tappet	tautology	teeter	template	tenuous	terrine
tamandua	taproom	tautonym	teeth	temple	tenure	territ
tamarack	taproot	tautonymy	teethe	tempo	tenurial	territory
tamarin	tapster	tavern	teetotal	temporal	teocalli	terror
tamarind	tar	taw	teetotum	temporary	teosinte	terrorism
tamarisk	tarantas	tawdry	tegmen	temporize	tepee	terrorist
tamasha	tarantass	tawny	tegmina	tempt	tepefy	terrorize
tambour	tarantism	tax	tegminal	temptress	tephrite	terry
tambourin	tarantula	taxaceous	tegula	ten	tephritic	terse
tame	taraxacum	taxation	tegulae	tenable	tepid	tertial
tameless	tarboosh	taxi	tegular	tenably	tepidity	tertian
tamis	tarbush	taxiarch	tegulated	tenace	tepidaria	tertiary
tamp	tardy	taxicab	tegumen	tenacious	teraph	tervalent
tampala	tare	taxidermy	tegument	tenacity	teraphim	terzarima
tampan	targ	taximeter	teil	tenacula	teratism	terzerime
tampion	targe	taxin	tela	tenaculum	teratoid	tessera
tampon	target	taxine	telae	tenail	terbia	tesserae
tan	targeteer	taxis	telamon	tenaille	terbic	test
tanager	tariff	taxite	telamones	tenancy	terbium	testa
tanbark	tarlatan	taxitic	telegonic	tenant	tercel	testae
tandem	tarn	taxonomer	telegony	tenantry	tercelet	testacean
tang	tarnish	taxonomic	telegram	tench	tercet	testacy
tangelo	taro	taxonomy	telegraph	tend	terebene	testament
tangence	taros	taxpayer	telemark	tendency	terebic	testate
tangency	tarot	taxy	telemater	tendinous	terebinth	testatrix
tangent	tarpaulin	tchick	telemetry	tendon	teredo	testes
tangental	tarpon	tea	telemotor	tendril	terek	testify
tangerine	tarragon	teaball	teleology	tenebrae	terete	testimony
tangible	tarry	teaberry	teleost	tenebrous	terfa	testis
tangle	tarsal	teach	telepathy	tenement	tergal	testudo
tangly	tarsi	teacup	telephone	tenendum	tergum	testy
tango	tarsier	teacupful	telephony	tenesmic	term	tetanic
tangos	tarsus	teak	telephote	tenesmus	termagant	tetanical
tangram	tart	teakettle	telephoto	tenet	termer	tetanize
tanist	tartan	teal	telescope	tenfold	terminal	tetanus
tanistry	tartar	team	telescopy	t(a)enia	terminate	tetany
tank	tartaric	teamster	telestich	t(a)eniacide	terminer	tetchy
tankage	tartarize	teamwork	teletype	t(a)eniafuge	termini	tether
tankard	tartarous	teapot	televise	t(a)eniasis	terminism	tetotum
tannage	tartlet	teapoy	telford	tennis	terminus	tetracid
tannate	tartrate	tear	telial	tenon	termite	terad
tannery	tartufe	teardrop	telic	tenonitis	termless	tetragram
tannic	tartuffe	tearful	telically	tenor	termor	tetrapod
tannin	tasimeter	tearless	telium	tenorite	tern	tetrapody
tanrec	tasimetry	teary	tell	tenotomy	ternary	tetrarch
tansy	task	tease	telltale	tenpenny	ternate	tetrarchy
tantalate	tass	teasel	tellurate	tenpins	terne	tetraseme
tantalic	tasse	teaspoon	telluret	tenrec	ternion	tetrode
tantalite	tassel	teat	tellurian	tense	terpene	tetroxid
tantalize	tasset	teazel	telluric	tensible	terpin	tetroxide
tantalum	taste	teazle	tellurid	tensile	terpine	tetryl
tantara	tasteful	technic	telluride	tensility	terpineol	tetter

text	theology	thievery	threnode	thyself	timpanist	titmouse
textile	theomachy	thievish	threnodic	ti	timpano	titrate
textual	theopathy	thigh	threnody	tiara	tin	titration
textuary	theophany	thill	thresh	tibia	tinamou	titre
texture	theorbo	thimble	threshold	tibiae	tincal	titter
textural	theorem	thin	threw	tibial	tinct	tittle
thalami	theoremic	thine	thrice	tibias	tincture	titular
thalamic	theoretic	thing	thrift	tic	tinder	titulary
thalamus	theorist	think	thrifty	tical	tinderbox	tittup
thalassic	theorize	thinnish	thrill	tick	tindery	tivy
thaler	theory	thiogen	thrips	ticket	tine	tmesis
thalli	theosophy	thiol	thrive	tickle	tinea	to
thallic	therapist	thionic	thriven	ticklish	tineid	toad
thallin	therapy	thionin	throat	tickseed	tinfoil	toadfish
thalline	there	thionine	throaty	tidal	ting	toadflax
thallium	thereat	thionyl	throb	tidbit	tinge	toadstone
thalloid	thereby	thiophen	throe	tide	tingle	toadstool
thallous	therefor	thiophene	thrombin	tideland	tink	toady
thallus	therefore	thiourea	thrombus	tideless	tinker	toadyish
thalluses	therefrom	third	throne	tiderip	tinkle	toadyism
than	therein	thirl	throng	tidewater	tinnitus	toast
thanage	thereinto	thirlage	throttle	tideway	tinny	tobacco
thanatoid	thereof	thirst	through	tidings	tinsel	tobaccoes
thane	thereon	thirsty	throve	tidy	tinsmith	tobaccos
thank	thereto	thirteen	throw	tidytips	tinstone	toboggan
thankful	thereunto	thirtieth	throwster	tie	tint	toby
thankless	thereupon	thirty	thru	tier	tintype	toccata
that	therewith	this	thrum	tierce	tinware	tocolog
those	theriac	thistle	thrummy	tiff	tinwork	tocsin
thatch	theriaca	thither	thrush	tiffany	tiny	tod
thatchy	theriacal	thitherto	thrust	tiger	tip	today
thaw	therm	tho	thud	tigerish	tipcart	toddle
the	thermae	thole	thug	tight	tipcat	toddy
theaceous	thermal	thong	thuggee	tighten	tipi	tody
thearchy	thermic	thoraces	thuggery	tightrope	tippet	toe
theatre	thermion	thoracic	thuggish	tights	tipple	toehold
theatric	thermite	thorax	thuja	tiglic	tipstaff	toenail
theatrics	theroid	thoraxes	thulia	tiglinic	tipstaffs	toffee
thebain	theropod	thoria	thulium	tigrish	tipstaves	toffy
thebaine	thesauri	thoric	thumb	tike	tipsy	toga
theca	thesaurus	thorite	thumbkin	til	tiptoe	togae
thecae	these	thorium	thumbling	tilbury	tirade	togas
thecal	theses	thorn	thumbnail	tilde	tire	togated
thecate	thesis	thornback	thumbnut	tile	tireless	together
thee	theta	thornbill	thumbtack	tilefish	tiresome	toggle
theft	thetic	thornless	thump	till	tiro	toil
thegn	thetical	thorny	thunder	tillage	tisane	toile
thein	theurgic	thoro	thundrous	tilt	tissue	toilet
theine	theurgist	thoron	thurible	tilth	tit	toiletry
their	theurgy	thorough	thurifer	tiltyard	titan	toilette
theirs	thew	those	thus	timarau	titaness	toilful
theism	they	thou	thuya	timbal	titanate	toilsome
thelitis	thiamin	though	thwack	timbale	titanic	token
them	thiamine	thought	thwart	timber	titanite	tokology
theme	thiazin	thousand	thy	timbre	titanium	tolane
thematic	thiazine	thraldom	thylacine	timbrel	titanous	told
then	thiazole	thrall	thyme	time	titbit	tole
thenal	thick	thralldom	thymy	timeless	titer	toledo
thenar	thicken	thrash	thymic	timema	tithable	tolerable
thence	thicket	thread	thymol	timepiece	tithe	tolerably
theocracy	thickhead	threadfin	thymus	timid	tither	tolerance
theocrasy	thickish	thready	thyreoid	timidity	titi	tolerant
theodicy	thickleaf	threat	thyroid	timing	titian	tolerate
theogonic	thickness	threaten	thyroxin	timocracy	titillant	tolidin
theogony	thickskin	three	thyrse	timorous	titillate	tolidine
theologic	thief	threefold	thyrsoid	timothy	titlark	toll
theologue	thieve	threesome	thyrsus	timpan	title	tollage

toilgate	tooth	torrid	townsman	traitor	tread	tribunary
tollhouse	toothache	torridity	towpath	traitress	treadle	tribunate
tolu	toothless	torrify	towrope	traject	treadmill	tribune
toluate	toothpick	torsade	towy	tram	treadway	tributary
toluene	toothsome	torsi	toxaemia	tramcar	treason	tribute
toluic	toothwort	torsion	toxaemic	trame	treasure	trice
toluid	tootle	torsional	toxemia	tramel	treasury	triceps
toluide	top	torso	toxemic	trammel	treat	trichina
toluidine	topaz	torsos	toxic	tramp	treatise	trichinae
toluol	topboot	tort	toxical	trample	treaty	trichite
toluole	tope	tortile	toxicant	tramroad	treble	trichitic
toluyl	topek	tortility	toxicity	tramway	trebuchet	trichoid
tolyl	toph	tortilla	toxicoses	trance	treddle	trichoma
tom	tophamper	tortious	toxicosis	tranquil	tree	trichome
tomahawk	topheavy	tortoise	toxin	transact	trefoil	trichomic
tomalley	tophi	tortricid	toxine	transcend	trehala	trichosis
tomally	tophus	tortuous	toxophil	transect	trehalose	trichroic
toman	topiary	torture	toxophile	transept	treillage	trichrome
tomato	topic	torulose	toy	transeunt	trek	trick
tomb	topical	torulous	toyish	transfer	trellis	trickery
tombac	topknot	torus	toyon	transflux	trematode	trickish
tomback	topmast	tory	trabeate	transform	trematoid	trickle
tombak	topmost	toss	trabeated	transfuse	tremble	tricklet
tomboy	topology	tosspot	trabecula	tranship	tremetol	trickster
tomboyish	toponym	total	trace	transient	tremolite	tricksy
tombstone	toponymic	totality	tracery	transit	tremor	tricky
tomcat	toponymy	totalize	trachea	translate	tremulant	triclinia
tomcod	topotype	totaquina	tracheae	translunar	tremulent	triclinic
tome	topple	totem	tracheal	transmit	tremulous	tricolor
tomenta	topsail	totemic	tracheid	transom	trench	tricolour
tomentose	topside	totemism	trachoma	transpire	trenchant	tricorn
tomentous	topsoil	totemist	trachyte	transport	trend	tricot
tomentum	topstone	totter	trachytic	transpose	trepan	tricrotic
tomfool	toque	tottery	track	transude	trepang	tricuspid
tomorrow	toquet	toucan	trackage	trap	trepanize	tricycle
tompion	tora	touch	trackless	trapes	trephine	tricyclic
tomtit	torah	touchback	trackman	trapeze	treponeme	tridactyl
ton	torc	touchdown	trackway	trapezia	trespass	trident
tonal	torch	touchhole	tract	trapezium	tress	triennial
tonality	torchwood	touchwood	tractate	trapezoid	tressour	trierarch
tone	tore	touchy	tractile	trapfall	tressure	trieteric
toneless	toreador	tough	traction	trappean	trestle	trifacial
tong	toreutic	toughen	tractive	trappist	tret	trifid
tongue	toreutics	toupee	tractor	trappose	trevet	trifle
tonic	tori	tour	tractus	trappous	trevis	trifold
tonicity	toric	touraco	trade	trash	trey	trifolium
tonight	torment	tourist	tradesfolk	trashy	triable	triforia
tonite	tormentil	touristic	tradesman	trashily	triacid	triforial
tonnage	torn	tourmalin(e)	tradition	trasko	triad	triforium
tonneau	tornadic	tourney	traditor	trass	triadic	triform
tonneaus	tornado	tournure	traduce	trauma	triagonal	trig
tonneaux	tornadoes	tousle	traffic	traumata	trial	trigemini
tonograph	tornados	touzle	tragedian	traumatic	triamorph	trigger
tonometer	toroid	tow	tragedy	travail	triangle	triglyph
tonometry	toroidal	towage	tragi	travel	triarchy	trigon
tonoscope	torose	toward	tragic	traversal	triatic	trigonal
tonsil	torosity	towards	tragical	traverse	triatomic	trigonous
tonsilar	torous	towboat	tragopan	travertin(e)	triaxial	trigraph
tonsillar	torpedo	towel	tragus	travesty	triazine	trithedral
tonsorial	torpid	tower	trail	travois	triazoic	trihedron
tonsure	torpidity	towery	train	travoise	triazole	trihybrid
tontine	torpor	towhead	trainless	travoises	tribal	trihydric
tonus	torquate	towhee	trainband	trawl	tribasic	trijugate
too	torque	towline	trainee	tray	tribe	trijugous
tool	torreador	town	trainman	treachery	tribesman	trilby
toon	torrefy	townfolk	traipse	treacle	tribrach	trilinear
toot	torrent	township	trait	treacly	tribunal	trill

trillion	tritheist	tropology	tuatara	tunicated	tusk	twist
trillium	trithing	trot	tuatera	tunicle	tusked	twit
trilobal	triton	troth	tub	tunnel	tusker	twitch
trilobate	tritone	trotyl	tuba	tunny	tussah	two
trilobed	triturate	trouble	tubae	tup	tussar	twofold
trilobite	triumph	troublous	tubal	tupelo	tusseh	twopence
trilogy	triumphal	trough	tubas	tupelos	tusser	twopenny
trim	triumvir	trounce	tubate	tuque	tussore	twyblade
trimerous	triumviri	troupe	tubby	turacou	tussur	twyer
trimester	triumvirs	troupial	tube	turban	tussle	twyere
trimeter	triune	trousers	tuber	turbaned	tussock	tycoon
trimetric	triunity	trousse	tubercle	turbary	tussocky	tyke
trimorph	trivalent	trousseau	tuberoid	turbeth	tussuck	tymbal
trinal	trivalve	trout	tuberose	turbith	tut	tympan
trinary	trivet	trouvère	tubiform	turbid	tutelage	tympana
trindle	trivia	trouveur	tubular	turbidity	tutelar	tympani
trine	trivial	trover	tubulate	turbinal	tutelary	tympanic
trinity	trivium	trow	tubule	turbinate	tutenag	tympanist
trinket	triweekly	trowel	tubulose	turbine	tutenague	tympano
trinodal	trocar	troy	tubulous	turbit	tutor	tympanum
trinomial	trocha	truancy	tubulure	turbot	tutorage	tympany
trintle	trochaic	truant	tuck	turbulent	tutorial	typal
trio	trochal	truantry	tuckahoe	turdiform	tutorship	type
triode	trochar	truce	tucket	turdine	tutti	typha
trioicous	troche	truck	tufa	tureen	tutty	typhlitic
triolet	trochee	truckage	tufaceous	turf	tuxedo	typhlitis
trionym	trochil	truckhead	tuff	turfs	tuyère	typhlosis
trionymal	trochili	truckle	tuft	turves	twaddle	typhoid
trios	trochilic	truckman	tufty	turfman	twain	typhoidal
trioxid	trochilos	truculent	tug	turfy	twang	typhoidin
trioxide	trochilus	trudge	tugboat	turgent	twangy	typhoon
trip	trochlea	trudgen	tuille	turgid	twangle	typhose
tripe	trochlear	true	tuition	turgidity	twank	typhous
tripedal	trochoid	trueblue	tuitional	turgite	twanky	typhus
triphase	trod	truelove	tular(a)emia	turgor	twattle	typic
triplane	trodden	truffle	tule	turkey	twayblade	typical
triple	trogon	truism	tulip	turkois	tweak	typify
triplet	trold	trull	tuliptree	turmaline	tweaky	typist
triplex	troll	truly	tulipwood	turmeric	tweed	typology
triplite	trolley	trump	tulle	turmoil	tweedle	tyrannic
triploid	trollop	trumpery	tumble	turn	tweese	tyrannize
triploidy	trollopy	trumpet	tumblebug	turncoat	tweet	tyrannous
tripod	trolly	truncate	tumbrel	turnery	tweeze	tyranny
tripodal	trombone	truncheon	tumbril	turnip	tweezers	tyrant
tripodial	trommel	trundle	tumefy	turnix	twelfth	tyre
tripodic	tromp	trunk	tumescent	turnkey	twelve	tyro
tripody	trompe	trunkfish	tumid	turnout	twelvemo	tyrosin
tripoli	troop	trunnel	tumidity	turnover	twentieth	tyrosine
tripos	troopial	trunnion	tumour	turnpike	twenty	tzar
trippet	troopship	truss	tumular	turnsole	twibil	tzarina
triptote	troostite	trust	tumuli	turnspit	twibill	tzetze
triptyca	tropaeum	trustee	tumulose	turnstile	twice	
triptych	tropaion	trustful	tumulous	turnstone	twicer	
triradial	troparia	trusty	tumult	turntable	twiddle	U
trireme	troparion	truth	tumulus	turnup	twier	
triscele	trope	truthful	tun	turpeth	twig	ubiquity
trisect	trophic	truthless	tuna	turpitude	twigless	udder
triseme	trophical	try	tundra	turquoise	twiggen	udometer
trisemic	trophied	tryma	tune	turrel	twiggy	udometric
triserial	trophy	trypsin	tuneful	turret	twilight	udometry
triskele	tropic	tryptic	tungsten	turreted	twill	ugh
trismic	tropical	tryst	tungstic	turrical	twilled	uglify
trismus	tropin	tryster	tungstite	turrilite	twin	ugly
trisporic	tropine	tsar	tunic	turtle	twinberry	uhlan
tristich	tropism	tsarina	tunica	turtlepeg	twine	uintahite
trite	tropist	tsetse	tunicae	tush	twinge	uintaite
tritheism	tropistic	tsunami	tunicate	tushed	twinkle	ukase

ukulele	unbelt	undecagon	unduly	unify	unnerve	unstable
ulan	unbend	undeceive	undying	unijugate	unpack	unstate
ulcer	unbiased	undecided	unearned	union	unpaid	unsteel
ulcerate	unbiassed	undecked	unearth	unionism	unpaired	unstep
ulcerous	unbid	undecuple	uneasy	unionist	unpeg	unstopped
ulema	unbidden	undée	unequal	unionize	unpeople	unstowed
ullage	unbind	under	unerring	uniparous	unpick	unstrap
ulmaceous	unbitted	underbid	uneven	uniplanar	unpin	unstring
ulna	unblessed	underbred	uneventful	unipolar	unplumbed	unstriped
ulnar	unbloody	underbush	unfailing	unique	unpoised	unstrung
ulster	unbodied	underbuy	unfair	unisexual	unpolitic	unstudied
ulterior	unbolt	underclay	unfasten	unison	unpolled	unsung
ultima	unboned	undercool	unfeeling	unisonal	unpopular	unswathe
ultimata	unbonnet	undercut	unfeigned	unisonant	unpriced	unswear
ultimate	unborn	underdo	unfit	unisonous	unprizable	untangle
ultimatum	unbosom	underdone	unfix	unit	unquiet	untaught
ultra	unbounded	underdose	unfledged	unitary	unravel	unteach
ultraism	unbowed	underfeed	unfleshy	unite	unread	untenable
ultraist	unbrace	underfoot	unfold	unitive	unready	untented
ululant	unbred	underfur	unformed	unity	unreal	unthanked
ululate	unbridle	undergird	unfounded	univalent	unreality	unthink
ululation	unbroke	undergo	unfrock	univalvate	unreason	unthread
umbel	unbroken	underhand	unfumed	univalve	unreel	untidy
umbellar	unbuckle	underhung	unfunded	universal	unreeved	untie
umbellate	unbuild	underlaid	unfurl	universe	unreserve	until
umbellet	unburden	underlay	ungainly	univocal	unrest	untimely
umbellule	unbutton	underlet	ungifted	unjust	unriddle	untitled
umber	uncage	underlie	ungodly	unkempt	unrifled	unto
umbery	uncalled	underline	ungotten	unkennel	unrig	untold
umbilical	uncanny	underling	ungual	unkind	unrip	untoward
umbilici	uncap	undermine	unguard	unknown	unripe	untread
umbilicus	uncaused	undermost	unguent	unlace	unroll	untried
umbles	uncertain	underpass	ungues	unlade	unroot	untrimmed
umbo	unchain	underpay	unguiform	unlaid	unruffled	untrod
umbonal	uncharged	underpin	unguinous	unlatch	unrove	untrodden
umbonate	unchurch	underplot	unguis	unlawful	unruly	untrue
umbonated	uncial	underprop	ungula	unlay	unsaddle	untruly
umbones	unciform	underrate	ungulae	unlead	unsaid	untruss
umbonic	uncinal	underrun	ungular	unlearn	unsavoury	untruth
umbos	uncinate	undersea	ungulate	unleash	unsay	untutored
umbra	uncivil	undersell	unhair	unless	unscathed	untwine
umbrae	unclad	underset	unhallow	unlike	unscrew	untwist
umbrage	unclasp	undershot	unhand	unlimber	unseal	unused
umbrella	uncle	underside	unhandy	unlimited	unseam	unusual
umbrette	unclean	undersign	unhappy	unlisted	unseat	unvalued
umlaut	unclench	undersoil	unharness	unlive	unseemly	unveil
umpirage	unclew	undersong	unhat	unload	unseen	unvoiced
umpire	unclinch	underspin	unhealthy	unlock	unsettle	unwary
unable	uncloak	undertake	unheard	unlooked	unsex	unwearied
unadvised	unclose	undertint	unhelm	unloose	unshackle	unwelcome
unalloyed	uncock	undertone	unhinge	unloosen	unshaped	unwell
unanimity	uncoil	undertook	unhitch	unlovely	unshapen	unwept
unanimous	uncoined	undertow	unholy	unlucky	unsheathe	unwieldy
unapt	uncommon	undervest	unhook	unmake	unship	unwilled
unargued	unconcern	underwear	unhoped	unman	unsighted	unwilling
unarm	uncork	underwent	unhorse	unmarked	unsightly	unwind
unau	uncounted	underwing	unhurried	unmask	unskilful	unwise
unaware	uncouple	underwood	unhusk	unmeaning	unskilled	unwish
unawares	uncouth	underwork	uniaxial	unmeet	unsling	unwitting
unbacked	uncover	undine	unicolour	unmew	unsnap	unwonted
unbaked	uncreate	undo	unicorn	unmindful	unsnarl	unwordly
unbalance	unction	undraw	unicycle	unmitre	unsolder	unworthy
unbar	unctuous	undress	unideaed	unmoor	unsound	unwrap
unbarbed	uncut	undue	unifiable	unmoral	unsparing	unwrinkle
unbear	undamped	undulant	unific	unmortise	unspeak	unwritten
unbeknown	undaunted	undulate	unifilar	unmuffle	unsphere	unyoke
unbelief	undé	undulous	uniform	unnatural	unspotted	unyoked

up	ureal	utmost	valiancy	vaqueros	vegetate	venosity
upas	urease	utopia	valiant	var	vegetive	venous
upbraid	uredo	utopian	valid	vara	vehemence	vent
upcast	ureide	utricle	validate	varan	vehemency	ventage
upgrade	uremia	utricular	validity	varanid	vehement	ventail
upgrowth	uremic	utriculi	valise	varanidae	vehicle	ventiduct
upheaval	ureter	utriculus	valkyr	varanus	vehicular	ventilate
upheave	ureteral	utter	valkyria	variance	veil	ventrad
uphill	ureteric	uttermost	valkyrian	variant	vein	ventral
uphold	urethan	uva	valkyrie	variation	veinless	ventricle
upholster	urethane	uvarovite	vallation	varicella	veinlet	venture
uphroe	urethra	uvea	vallatory	varices	veinstone	venturous
upkeep	urethral	uveal	vallecula	varicose	veiny	venue
upland	uretic	uveous	valley	varicosis	vela	venular
uplift	urge	uvula	valonia	variegate	velamen	venule
upmost	urgency	uvular	valorous	varietal	velamenta	venulose
upon	urgent	uvulitis	valour	variety	velamina	venulous
upper	urn	uxorial	valuation	variform	velar	venus
uppercut	urochord	uxoricide	value	variola	velarize	veracious
uppermost	urochrome	uxorious	valueless	variolar	velate	veracity
upraise	urochs		valval	variolate	velation	veranda
uprear	urogenous		valvar	variole	velite	verandah
upright	urolith		valvate	variolite	velites	verano
uprise	urolithic	**V**	valve	varioloid	velleity	veratria
uprising	urologic		valveless	variolous	vellicate	veratric
uproar	urologist	vacancy	valvelet	variorum	vellum	veratrin
uproot	urology	vacant	valvula	various	velocity	veratrina
uprouse	uropod	vacate	valvular	varix	velodrome	veratrine
upset	uropodal	vacation	valvule	varlet	velour	veratrize
upshot	uropodous	vaccina	vambrace	varletry	velours	veratrum
upside	uropygial	vaccinal	vamp	varmint	velum	verb
upsilon	uropygium	vaccinate	vampire	varmintry	velure	verbal
upspring	uroscopic	vaccine	vampiric	varnish	velvet	verbalism
upstage	uroscopy	vaccinia	vampirish	varus	velveteen	verbalist
upstairs	ursiform	vacillate	vampirism	varve	velvety	verbalize
upstart	ursine	vacillant	van	vary	vena	verbatim
upstroke	urticaria	vacua	vanadate	vascula	venae	verbena
upsweep	urticate	vacuity	vanadiate	vascular	venal	verbiage
upswing	urus	vacuole	vanadic	vasculose	venality	verbify
uptake	urushi	vacuous	vanadious	vasculous	venatic	verbose
upthrow	urushiol	vacuum	vanadium	vasculum	venatical	verbosity
upthrust	us	vagabond	vanadous	vase	venation	verdancy
upturn	usable	vagary	vandal	vasomotor	vend	verdant
upward	usage	vagi	vandalic	vassal	vendace	verderer
uraemia	usance	vaginate	vandalism	vassalage	vendee	verderor
uraemic	usaunce	vaginitis	vane	vassalize	vendetta	verdict
uraeus	use	vagitus	vang	vast	vendettas	verdigris
uralite	useable	vagotonia	vanguard	vastation	vendible	verdin
uralitic	useful	vagotonic	vanilla	vasty	vendibly	verditer
uranic	useless	vagrancy	vanillic	vat	vendis	verdure
uraninite	usher	vagrant	vanillin	vatic	vendition	verdurous
uranite	ustion	vague	vanilline	vatical	vendue	verecund
uranitic	ustulate	vagus	vanish	vaticide	veneer	verge
uranium	usual	vain	vanity	vaticinal	venerable	veridic
uranology	usufruct	vainglory	vanquish	vault	venerate	veridical
uranous	usurer	vair	vantage	vaunt	venereal	verify
uranyl	usurious	valance	vantbrace	veal	venery	verily
urare	usurp	valanced	vanward	vection	vengeance	veritable
urari	usury	vale	vapid	vector	vengeful	veritism
urate	ut	valence	vapidity	vectorial	venial	veritist
urban	utensil	valency	vaporific	vedette	veniality	verity
urbane	uterine	valencia	vaporize	vee	venially	verjuice
urbanity	uteritis	valentine	vaporous	veer	venire	vermeil
urbanize	uterus	valerian	vapour	veery	venison	vermicide
urceolate	utile	valeric	vapourish	vegetable	venom	vermiform
urchin	utility	valet	vapoury	vegetal	venomous	vermifuge
urea	utilize	valiance	vaquero	vegetant	venose	vermilion

vermin	vestryman	vicugna	violation	visional	vocative	votress
verminate	vesture	vicuna	violative	visionary	vodka	vouch
verminous	vesuvian	vide	violence	visit	vogue	vouchee
vermouth	vetch	videlicet	violent	visitant	voice	vouchsafe
vermuth	vetchling	vidette	violet	visor	voiceful	voussoir
vernal	veteran	viduage	violin	vista	voiceless	vow
vernalize	vetiver	vie	violinist	visual	void	vowel
vernation	veto	view	violist	visualism	voidance	vowelize
vernicose	vetoes	viewless	violone	visualist	voile	vox
vernier	vex	viewpoint	viosterol	visuality	volant	voyage
veronica	vexation	vigesimal	viper	visualize	volar	vug
verruca	vexatious	vigil	viperine	vitaceous	volatile	vugg
verrucae	vexil	vigilance	viperish	vital	volcanic	vuggy
verrucano	vexilla	vigilant	viperous	vitalism	volcanism	vugh
verrucose	vexillar	vigilante	virago	vitalist	volcanist	vulcanian
verrucous	vexillary	vignette	viragoes	vitality	volcanize	vulcanic
versant	vexillate	vignettist	viragos	vitalize	volcano	vulcanite
versatile	vexillum	vigorous	virelai	vitals	volcanoes	vulcanize
verse	via	vigour	virelay	vitamin	volcanos	vulgar
versicle	viable	viking	vireo	vitamine	vole	vulgarian
versify	viability	vilayet	vireonine	vitaminic	volery	vulgarism
version	viaduct	vile	virescent	vitascope	volitant	vulgarity
verso	viagraph	vilify	virga	vitellin	volitient	vulgarize
verst	vial	vilipend	virgate	vitelline	volition	vulgate
versus	viand	vill	virgin	vitellus	volitive	vulnerary
vert	viatic	villa	virginal	vitiable	volley	vulpicide
vertebra	viatical	villadom	virginity	vitiate	volplane	vulpine
vertebrae	viaticum	village	virginium	vitiation	volt	vulpinite
vertebral	viator	villager	virgulate	vitiligo	voltage	vulture
vertebras	viatores	villain	virgule	vitreous	voltaic	vulturine
vertex	vibrancy	villainy	viridian	vitric	voltaism	vulturous
vertexes	vibrant	villanage	viridity	vitriform	voltigeur	vulva
vertical	vibrate	villatic	virile	vitrify	voltmeter	vulvae
vertices	vibratile	villein	virilism	vitriol	voluble	
verticil	vibration	villenage	virility	vitriolic	volume	
verticity	vibrative	villiform	virology	vitta	volumed	
vertigo	vibrator	villosity	virosis	vittae	volumeter	**W**
vertigoes	vibratory	villous	virtu	vittate	volumetry	
vervain	vibrio	villus	virtual	vituline	voluntary	wabble
verve	vibrioid	vim	virtue	viva	volunteer	wabbly
vervet	vibrissa	vimen	virtuosi	vivace	volute	wacke
very	vibrissae	viminal	virtuoso	vivacious	volution	wad
vesica	viburnum	vimineous	virtuosos	vivacity	volva	waddle
vesicae	vicar	vina	virtuous	vivaria	volvuli	waddy
vesical	vicarage	vinaceous	virulence	vivarium	volvulus	wade
vesicant	vicarial	vincible	virulent	vivariums	vomer	wadi
vesicate	vicariate	vincula	virus	vivary	vomerine	wadset
vesicle	vicarious	vinculum	vis	viverrine	vomica	wady
vesicula	vicarship	vindicate	visa	vives	vomicae	wafer
vesiculae	vice	vine	visaed	vivid	vomit	waffle
vesicular	vicegeral	vinegar	visage	vivify	vomitive	waft
vesiculate	vicenary	vinegary	visard	vivisect	vomito	waftage
vesper	vicennial	vinery	viscacha	vixen	vomitory	wafture
vesperal	viceregal	vineyard	viscera	vizard	voodoo	wag
vespiary	viceroy	vinic	visceral	vizier	voodooism	wage
vespid	viceroyal	vinometer	viscid	vizierate	voracious	waggery
vessel	vicinage	vinosity	viscidity	vizir	voracity	waggish
vest	vicinal	vinous	viscoidal	vizirate	vortex	waggle
vesta	vicinism	vintage	viscose	vizi(e)rship	vortexes	waggly
vestal	vicinity	vintner	viscosity	vizor	vortical	wagon
vestee	vicious	viny	viscount	vocable	vortices	wagonage
vestibule	victim	vinyl	viscounty	vocal	vorticose	wagonet
vestige	victimize	viol	viscous	vocalic	votaress	wagonette
vestigia	victor	viola	viscus	vocalism	votarist	wagsome
vestigium	victoria	violable	visé	vocalist	votary	wagtail
vestment	victory	violably	visible	vocalize	vote	wahconda
vestry	victual	violate	vision	vocation	votive	wahoo

waif	warhead	wattage	ween	wheelbug	whipworm	widowhood
wail	warison	wattle	weep	wheelman	whir	width
wailful	warlike	wattless	weet	wheelsman	whirl	widthway
wain	warlock	wattmeter	weever	wheelwork	whirligig	widthwise
wainscot	warm	waul	weevil	wheeze	whirlpool	wield
waist	warmish	wave	weft	wheezy	whirlwind	wieldable
waistband	warmth	waveless	weigela	whelk	whish	wieldy
waistcoat	warn	wavelet	weigh	whelky	whisht	wife
waister	warp	wavellite	weight	whelm	whisk	wifedom
waisting	warpath	wavemeter	weighty	whelp	whisker	wifehood
waistline	warplane	waver	weir	when	whiskery	wifeless
wait	warragal	wavey	weird	whence	whiskey	wig
waitress	warrant	wavy	wejack	whenever	whisky	wigan
waive	warrantee	wawl	weka	where	whisper	wigeon
waiver	warranty	wax	welcome	whereas	whispery	wiggery
wakanda	warren	waxberry	weld	whereases	whist	wiggle
wake	warrigal	waxbill	welfare	whereat	whistle	wiggly
wakeful	warrior	waxen	welkin	whereby	whit	wight
wakeless	warsaw	waxmyrtle	well	wherefore	white	wigwag
waken	warship	waxpalm	wellsite	wherefrom	whitebait	wigwam
wakerobin	wart	waxweed	welsh	wherein	whitecap	wikiup
waldgrave	warthog	waxwing	welt	whereinto	whitefish	wild
wale	warty	waxwork	welter	whereof	whitegum	wildcat
walk	wary	waxworker	wen	whereon	whiten	wildfire
walkway	was	waxy	wend	whereto	whitetail	wildfowl
wall	wash	way	wennish	whereupon	whitewash	wilding
wallabies	washboard	waybill	wenny	wherever	whiteweed	wildling
wallaby	washcloth	wayfarer	were	wherewith	whitewood	wildwood
wallet	washerman	wayfaring	weregeld	wherry	whither	wile
wallop	washrag	waylay	weregelt	wherve	whiting	wilful
wallow	washstand	wayside	weregild	whet	whitish	will
walnut	washwoman	wayward	werewolf	whether	whitlow	willemite
walrus	washy	wayworm	wergeld	whetslate	whittle	willet
waltz	wasp	we	wergelt	whetstone	whiz	willful
wampum	waspish	weak	wergild	whew	whizz	williwaw
wan	waspy	weaken	wernerite	whey	whoa	willow
wand	wassail	weakfish	werwolf	wheyey	whoever	willower
wander	wastage	weakling	west	which	whole	willowish
wanderoo	waste	weakly	wester	whichever	wholesale	willowy
wane	wasteful	weal	western	whicker	wholesome	willpower
waney	wastrel	weald	westerner	whidah	wholly	willy
wangle	wat	wealth	westing	whiff	whom	wilt
wangan	watap	wealthy	westward	whiffle	whomever	wily
wangun	watape	wean	wet	whifflery	whomso	wimble
wanigan	watch	weanling	wether	while	whoop	wimple
wanion	watchcase	weapon	whack	whiles	whoopee	win
wannigan	watchdog	wear	whale	whilom	whopping	wince
want	watchful	weariful	whaleback	whilst	whorl	winch
wantage	watchman	weariless	whaleboat	whim	whorled	wind
wanton	watchword	wearisome	whalebone	whimbrel	whose	windage
wany	water	weary	whaleman	whimper	whoso	windbreak
wapentake	waterback	weasand	whang	whimsical	whosoever	windcone
wapiti	waterbuck	weasel	whangee	whimsey	why	windfall
war	waterfall	weather	wharf	whimsy	whydah	windflaw
warble	waterflea	weave	wharfage	whin	wich	windgall
warblefly	watergum	web	wharfs	whinchat	wick	windgalled
ward	waterish	webby	wharve	whine	wicking	windigo
warden	waterless	webworm	wharves	whiny	wicked	windlass
wardenry	waterlily	wed	what	whinny	wicker	windle
wardress	watermark	wedge	whatever	whip	wicket	windless
wardrobe	waternut	wedgy	wheal	whipcord	wickiup	windmill
wardroom	watershed	wedlock	wheat	whipgraft	wicopy	window
wardship	waterside	wee	wheaten	whiphand	wide	windpipe
ware	waterway	weed	wheatworm	whippet	widen	windrow
warehouse	waterweed	weedy	wheedle	whipsaw	widgeon	windsock
wareroom	watery	week	wheel	whipstall	widow	windstorm
warfare	watt	weekly	wheelbase	whipstock	widower	windward

windy	wizen	woof	wrathy	xyloid	yes	zamindar
wine	woad	wool	wreak	xylol	yeses	zanana
wineglass	woadwaxen	woolfell	wreath	xylophage	yesterday	zany
winery	woald	woollen	wreathe	xylophone	yestereve	zapote
wing	wobble	woolly	wreathy	xylose	yestreen	zaptiah
wingback	wobbly	woolpack	wreck	xylotomy	yet	zaptieh
wingbow	wobegone	woolsack	wreckage	xylyl	yew	zarape
wingless	wocas	woorali	wreckful	xylylene	yield	zaratite
winglet	woe	woorari	wren	xyst	yip	zareba
wingy	woebegone	word	wrench	xyster	yodel	zareeba
wink	woeful	wordage	wrest		yodle	zarf
winkle	woesome	wordbook	wrestle		yoga	zax
winnow	woful	wordily	wretch	**Y**	yogee	zeal
winsome	wokas	wording	wriggle		yogh	zealot
winter	wold	wordless	wriggly		yogi	zealotry
winterish	wolf	wordy	wright	yacht	yogin	zealous
winterly	wolfbane	work	wring	yachtman	yoghourt	zebec
wintery	wolfberry	workaday	wrinkle	yachtsman	yoghurt	zebeck
wintry	wolfhound	workbag	wrinkly	yah	yogurt	zebra
winy	wolfish	workbench	wrist	yahoo	yoicks	zebras
winze	wolfram	workbox	wristband	yak	yoke	zebrass
wipe	wolver	workday	wristlet	yam	yokefellow	zebrawood
wire	wolverene	workfolk	writ	yank	yokel	zebrine
wiredraw	wolverine	workfolks	write	yanking	yokemate	zebrula
wireless	wolves	workhouse	writhe	yapon	yolk	zebrule
wireman	woman	workless	wrong	yard	yolky	zebu
wirework	womanhood	workman	wrongful	yardage	yon	zebub
wireworm	womanize	workroom	wroth	yardarm	yond	zecchin
wirra	womankind	workshop	wrought	yardgrass	yonder	zecchini
wiry	womb	worktable	wrung	yardstick	yonker	zecchino
wisdom	wombat	workweek	wry	yarn	yore	zechin
wise	womby	world	wryneck	yarrow	you	zed
wiseacre	women	worldling	wulfenite	yarrup	young	zedoary
wish	womenfolk	worm	wych	yashmac	youngish	zein
wishbone	won	wormhole	wye	yashmak	youngling	zemindar
wishful	wonder	wormholed	wyvern	yasmak	youngster	zemstvo
wisp	wonderful	wormil		yatagan	younker	zenana
wispy	wondrous	wormroot		yataghan	youpon	zendik
wist	wont	wormseed	**X**	yaup	your	zenith
wistaria	woo	wormwood		yaupon	yours	zeolite
wistful	wood	wormy		yaw	yourself	zephyr
wit	woodbin	worry	xanthate	yawl	youth	zero
witan	woodbine	worse	xanthein	yawmeter	youthful	zeroes
witch	woodblock	worsen	xanthic	yawn	yow	zeros
witchery	woodborer	worship	xanthin	yawp	yowe	zest
with	woodchat	worshipful	xanthous	ycleped	yowie	zestful
withal	woodchuck	worst	xebec	yclept	yowl	zeta
withdraw	woodcock	worsted	xenia	ye	ytterbia	zeugma
withe	woodcraft	wort	xenogamy	yea	ytterbic	zibeline
wither	woodcut	worth	xenogenic	yean	ytterbium	zibelline
witherite	wooden	worthies	xenogeny	yeanling	ytria	zibet
withers	woodhen	worthless	xenolith	year	ytric	zibeth
withhold	woodland	worthy	xenon	yearbook	ytrium	ziggurat
within	woodlark	wot	xeroderma	yearling	yuan	zigzag
without	woodman	would	xerophyte	yearlong	yucca	zikkurat
withstand	woodnote	wound	xerosis	yearn	yupon	zinc
withy	woodpile	wove	xerotic	yeast		zincate
witless	woodprint	woven	xerotropic	yeasty		zinced
witling	woodruff	wow	xerus	yell	**Z**	zincic
witness	woods	wrack	xiphoid	yellow		zincid
witticism	woodshed	wraith	xylan	yellowish	zacaton	zincide
witty	woodsia	wrangle	xylem	yellowy	zaffar	zincify
wive	woodwaxen	wrap	xylene	yelp	zaffer	zincing
wivern	woodwind	wrapt	xylic	yen	zaffir	zincite
wives	woodwork	wrasse	xylidin	yeoman	zaffre	zincked
wizard	woodworm	wrath	xylidine	yeomanly	zaibatsu	zinckic
wizardry	woody	wrathful	xylograph	yeomanry	zamia	zincking

zincky	zirconate	zombi	zoography	zoons	zoril	zymase
zincode	zirconia	zombie	zooid	zoophile	zorilla	zyme
zincoid	zirconic	zombiism	zooidal	zoophobia	zoster	zymic
zincotype	zirconium	zonal	zoolater	zoophobic	zounds	zymogen
zincous	zither	zonary	zoolatry	zoophyte	zucchetta	zymogene
zincy	zittern	zonate	zoologic	zoophytic	zucchetto	zymogenic
zinfandel	zloty	zonation	zoologist	zooplasty	zwieback	zymologic
zinkenite	zlotys	zone	zoology	zoosperm	zygoma	zymologist
zinkify	zodiac	zoneless	zoom	zoospore	zygomatic	zymology
zinkite	zodiacal	zonula	zoometric	zoosporic	zygophyte	zymolysis
zinky	zoea	zonule	zoometry	zoosporous	zygosis	zymolytic
zinnia	zoetrope	zoo	zoomorph	zoosterol	zygosperm	zymometer
zip	zoetropic	zoochore	zoomorphy	zootomic	zygospore	zymosis
zipper	zoic	zoogloea	zoon	zootomy	zygote	zymotic
zircon	zoisite	zoogloeae	zoonomy	zootoxin	zygotic	zymurgy